THE BOLD

AND BEAUTIFUL

THE

THE BOLD AND THE BEAUTIFUL

A TENTH ANNIVERSARY CELEBRATION

Robert Waldron

HarperCollins*Publishers*

THE BOLD AND THE BEAUTIFUL. Copyright © 1996 by Bell-Phillip Television Productions, Inc. All rights reserved. Printed in the United States of America. No part of this book may be used or reproduced in any manner whatsoever without written permission except in the case of brief quotations embodied in critical articles and reviews. For information address HarperCollins Publishers, Inc., 10 East 53rd Street, New York, NY 10022.

HarperCollins books may be purchased for educational, business, or sales promotional use. For information please write: Special Markets Department, HarperCollins Publishers, Inc., 10 East 53rd Street, New York, NY 10022.

FIRST EDITION

Designed by Barbara Gold/Logo Studios

ISBN 0-06-018688-7

96 97 98 99 00 ❖/RRD 10 9 8 7 6 5 4 3 2 1

ACKNOWLEDGMENTS

This book was made possible by the participation of several people who graciously offered their time, insight, experience, and knowledge of *The Bold and the Beautiful*'s ten-year history. They include executive producer and head writer Bradley Bell; creators William J. Bell and Lee Phillip Bell; supervising producer John C. Zak, who was instrumental in launching the project; coordinating producer Ron Weaver, who patiently lent his expertise and guidance; associate producer Rhonda Friedman, whose commitment to accuracy and her good-natured temperament were extremely appreciated; former producer Hope Smith, who generously provided significant insights and fascinating anecdotes—even in the midst of a heavy schedule that included editing several episodes from a location shoot in Barbados; current and former cast members of *The Bold and the Beautiful;* publicists Frank Tobin and David Sperber, who made themselves available at every opportunity to coordinate interviews, arrange photographs, and supply key background information, and their associates at Frank Tobin Public Relations, Charles Sherman, Nicole Millett, and Todd Lieberman; David Vigliano, my literary agent; director Michael Stich; production designer Sy Tomashoff; art director Jack Forrestel; set decorators Lee Moore Jr. and Joseph A. Armetta; costume designer Lori Robinson; former costume designer Sandra Bojin-Sedlik; production personnel Shannon Bradley, Jennifer Hodill, Rita D. Russell, Mimi Kersey, and Erin E. Stewart; and transcribers Deidra Kelzin and Grace Rutledge.

Michael J. Maloney, West Coast editor of *Soap Opera Digest*, whose invaluable contribution as research consultant on this project far surpassed my expectations.

I'd also like to extend a special thank you to Roberta Caploe, Paulette Cohn, Rick Copp, Janet Di Lauro, Brenda Feldman, Eddie Garcia, David Giella, David Goodman and Wendy Felsom, David Johnson, Russell Latham, Rachelle Marmet, Thom McMorris, Griffin Meyer, Josef Patric, John Paschal, David Rieken, Rosemary Sneeringer, Mindy Staley, Jess Walton, Jim Warren, Marilyn Webber, Jonathan Zaleski, and Lorraine Zenka, for their encouragement and support, as well as to the editors of *Soap Opera Update* and *Soap Opera Magazine*, for their patience and cooperation.

Finally, my editor at HarperCollins, Eamon Dolan, for his enthusiasm and vision, and Sarah Polen, who put in long hours to keep this book on track and always kept her cool.

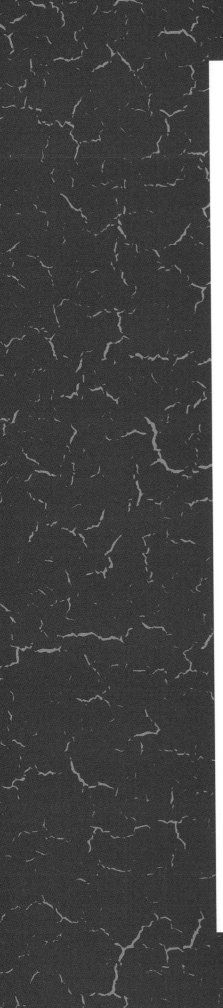

Part IV:
Bold and Beautiful People

Part V:
Behind the Scenes

APPENDICES

THE BOLD AND THE BEAUTIFUL

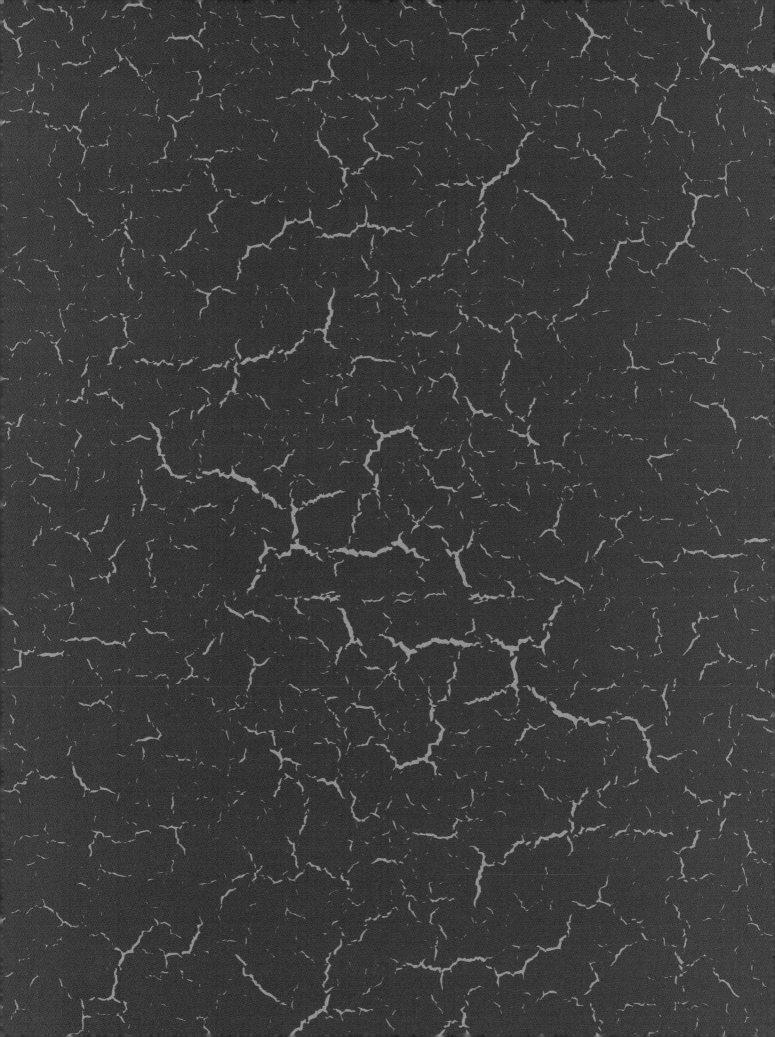

Part 1

A History of
The Bold and the Beautiful

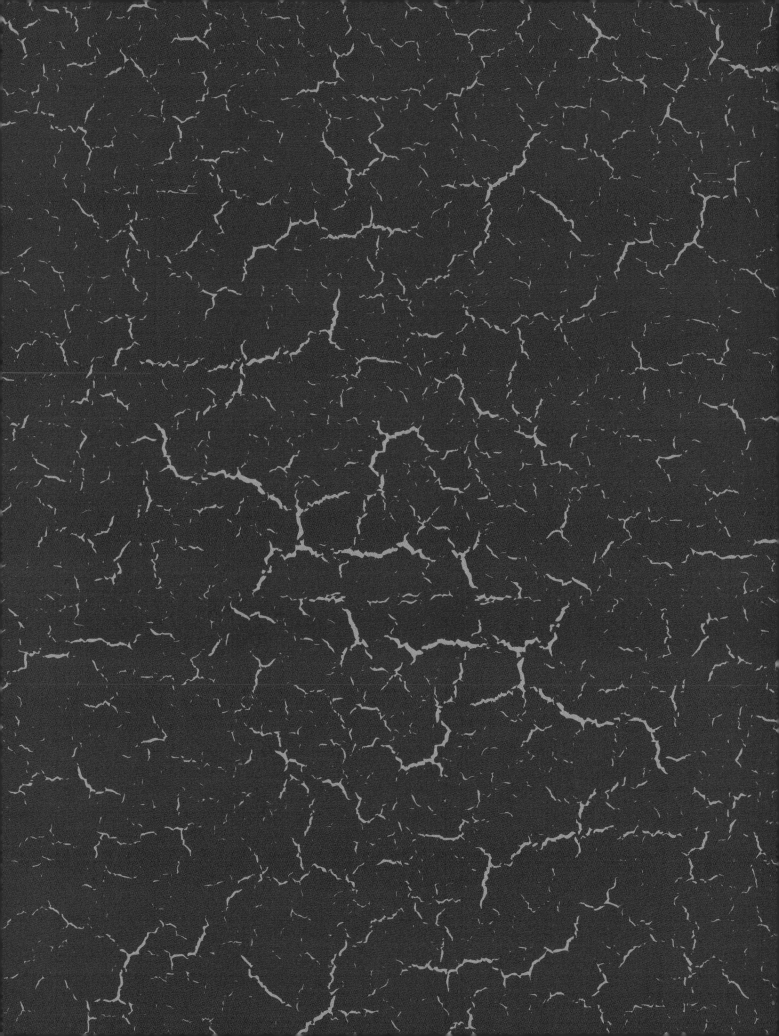

Creating *The Bold and the Beautiful*

William J. Bell and Lee Phillip Bell created The Bold and the Beautiful *so that their sons, Bill Jr. and Bradley, could learn how a soap develops from its inception.*

William J. Bell and his wife, Lee Phillip Bell, had admirable motivation for creating *The Bold and the Beautiful*. Quite simply, they wanted to work with their sons, Bill Jr. and Bradley, in putting together a new daytime drama. Based on the immense success of the Bells' first creation, *The Young and the Restless*, which premiered in 1973 on CBS and has been daytime TV's top-rated program since 1988, television executives from the network had approached the talented couple several times over the years about doing another show. Bill graciously declined their solicitations because he enjoyed focusing his attention exclusively on producing and headwriting *The Young and the Restless*.

At the time, Bill Bell did the bulk of his work on *The Young and the Restless* from the Bells' Chicago apartment, while Lee hosted, and later produced, her long-running television talk show on WBBM, a CBS-TV affiliate. Bill Jr. had a seat on the Chicago Board of Trade, and Bradley was a student at UCLA. He also wrote scripts for *The Young and the Restless*, which was shot in Los Angeles. Meanwhile, the Bells' daughter, Lauralee, was a popular cast member of *The Young and the Restless*, playing Cricket Blair.

Since Bill spent most of his work time at their Chicago home in front of the typewriter writing scripts for *The Young and the Restless* or talking on the phone with the show's writing staff, producers, and network executives, the Bells thought it would be nice for the children to see the other factors that went into bringing the show to life. During school breaks, Bill Jr., Bradley, and Lauralee each had the chance to join their father on his business trips to Los Angeles for story conferences and production meetings.

Recalling Bill Jr.'s and Bradley's first visits to *The Young and the Restless*, Lee told *Soap Opera People*'s West Coast editor, Lillian Smith, "Bill brought each boy out when they were ten or eleven years old. They came out with him when they were on vacation. They sat in through all the meetings, sat in the control room, in the studio for a day or two, and he put them in tiny parts." But thanks to the short attention span of a ten- or eleven-year-old boy, the initial set visits to *The Young and the Restless* paled in comparison to other activities, such as spending the day at Disneyland.

Lauralee's first visit to *The Young and the Restless*, however, fueled her desire to become an actress. As she grew older, Lauralee was appearing on the series in day roles, such as a volunteer hospital candy striper. By the summer of 1984, Lauralee, who displayed a natural talent for acting, was cast in the short-term role of Cricket, the niece of Joe Blair, a photographer at Jabot Cosmetics. Lauralee's interest in acting continued to grow, and as her talent blossomed, her role as Cricket was expanded. By the following summer she was a regular cast member of *The Young and the Restless.*

It wasn't until Bradley's late teens that he found himself intrigued by the myriad creative challenges inherent in creating a daily television drama. Like Lauralee, Bradley also started making more visits to the *Young and the Restless* set. No longer a restless boy, he sat in rapt silence in the control booth and listened attentively as *The Young and the Restless*'s producers and directors gave acting notes to the actors. On other days, he watched in fascination as Bill and his writing staff developed surprising twists in their storylines. After two years of observing, Bradley wrote his first script for *The Young and the Restless* and eventually became a member of the writing staff. Bill says, "We really wanted Bradley to capture the form, and feel secure with it, before we got him into day-by-day script development."

Meanwhile, Bill Jr. told his parents he wanted to shift his focus from stock trading and contribute his well-honed talents to participating in the business end of Bill and Lee's television ventures. With Bill and Lee's television work literally developing into a family venture, the seeds were sown for the creation of a second series. Bradley says, "What my dad had in mind was using the new series as a learning tool for all of us, so that we could understand what it took to put a show on the air."

Over the 1985 Christmas holidays, Bill and Lee arranged to spend ten creatively charged days holed up in a hotel room, brainstorming ideas for their proposed new series. Early on, Bill and Lee resolved that they didn't want the series to be a spinoff of *The Young and the Restless*. Instead, they decided that the new show would have its own separate personality and identity. The first two characters they created were a middle-aged married couple whose relationship was in serious trouble. Next, they focused on the couple's children. "You know you're going to have kids," explains Bill. "The younger people give you a chance to tell a younger story. So you think of the kinds of characters that you want. If you have a rich family, then you also want to have a family of much lesser economic advantage." By the end of the Bells' hotel stay, they had created two families, the wealthy Forresters and the lower-middle-class Logans, headed by a strong mother, the sole provider, who struggled to make ends meet for her four children. The thirty-six-page draft the Bells wrote also contained descriptions of characters connected to the two families. Upon their return to Chicago, the Bells submitted their draft to CBS. In rapid time, Bill and Lee heard from CBS executives, who were eager to snap up the series.

CBS wanted the serial ready for broadcast in roughly a year's time, so the Bells geared themselves up to begin work. It was decided that, like *The Young and the Restless*, the new series would be shot in Los Angeles. Unlike *The Young and the Restless*, however, which was jointly produced by the Bells and Columbia Television, the second series would be entirely produced by a new production company created by the Bells. Bill Jr. left his seat at the Chicago Board of Trade, was appointed director of business affairs for the newly created production company, and moved to Los Angeles, where he applied his astute business skills to forming the production company, Bell-Phillip Television Productions, Incorporated.

Since their children were already in Los Angeles and Bill and Lee would be involved in the day-to-day operations of their new series, they also made plans to relocate. Bill and Lee purchased a three-acre Beverly Hills estate previously owned by Howard Hughes. Besides a main house, the estate also includes two guest houses. Lauralee, who was still a teenager, would live in the main house with her parents, while Bill Jr. and Bradley each resided in one of the guest houses.

After packing their belongings and shipping them to Los Angeles, the Bells made the trip west to their new home, accompanied by Bill Jr. It turned out to be a very fortuitous trip for the new series. En route to Los Angeles, Bill Jr. suggested to Bill the possibility of using the fashion industry as a backdrop for the new show. "I filed it in the back of my head," says Bill.

The new house, meanwhile, served as an appropriate metaphor for the Bells' upcoming second series. Bradley explains, "The house was still under construction. My dad was actually living in one room, because they were still trying to get the rest of the house ready. He wrote the bible in the guest room." It was while writing the bible, which included the new series' premise, character histories, descriptions of the various relationships between the characters, and projected storylines, that Bill realized the fashion industry, with its inherent cachet of glamour and mystique, was a fantastic idea to develop and enhance.

Although it was six months before *The Bold and the Beautiful*'s scheduled premiere, behind-the-scenes production was moving at a swift pace. Bill, who had accumulated twenty-eight years' experience in daytime television, including the launching of *The Young and the Restless* and *Another World,* which he co-created with Irna Phillips, understood that building a top-notch band of talented people behind the camera was as important as assembling a compelling cast of actors.

The production office was opened in the fall of 1986 with the hiring of producer Gail Kobe. Gail had extensive experience in daytime drama. As executive producer of *The Guiding Light,* she had revitalized that long-running serial. Now the Bells picked her to put together a first-rate production staff and gear up for the season premiere in March 1987.

During the first week of October, Ron Weaver, a *Sesame Street* pioneer who had recently shifted into the daytime genre as associate producer for a syndicated serial, *Rituals,* was hired as the first of two associate producers, and Cindy Popp, then a member of the CBS Television Operations Department, was hired as office manager.

Ron had not worked with either the Bells or Gail Kobe. He had made a "cold" job inquiry about the new Bell series to the *Y&R* office about three months before Gail was hired, and in a long phone conversation, he hit it off with Tom Langan, who was at that time on the producing staff at *Y&R*. Both had a strong interest in computerizing all aspects of a production office and Tom was eager to do so with the *Y&R* office, which was still handling many of its operations manually. Ron had used computers extensively in his most recent job at *Rituals*. Tom suggested that Ron might be useful on the new show after they hired a producer in a few months. He asked Ron to send him a résumé to be passed on to the new producer and said that if Ron hadn't heard from anyone in three months to call him again. Ron recalls that one morning about three months later he awakened "with a little voice in my head saying, 'Call Tom Langan, call Tom Langan.'" The timing was right. Tom told him the new show had just hired a producer and gave him Gail Kobe's number. Ron remembers that after a "great interview" with Gail and Bill Bell Jr., he was told that the business and financially oriented associate producer job he'd be great for had already been offered to someone else from CBS, and they suggested that Ron might come on as a consultant to help get the production office on its feet. "But I left that interview," says Ron, "knowing that somehow the job was mine." His instinct was right. A couple of weeks later they called again to tell him that the person who had been offered the job had decided not to take it.

Next began an intensive process of selecting the rest of the staff, cast, and crew. Ron recalls that during the first three months of the preproduction phase, "Gail, Bill Bell Jr., and I must have interviewed several hundred people for the handful of staff and crew positions. I guess we did it right because most of those people are still with the show and many have risen through the ranks to more serious senior spots."

Directors are a key creative element in any production. Bill Bell had previously worked with Bill Glenn, a director of many early episodes of *The Young and the Restless*. The producers invited Bill Glenn to take part in many of the creative meetings during the preproduction phase. Michael Stich, who had been a staff director on *Capitol*, was added to the directing staff just prior to production.

It was imperative to begin the arduous process of choosing the actors, so the producers searched urgently for a casting director. The search ended with longtime Hollywood casting director John Conwell and associate casting director Jill Newton, from the casting department at *The Young and the Restless*. Starting in mid-October, John and Jill auditioned hundreds of actors before narrowing the field down to the fifteen contract roles.

The producers' next focus was the look of the show. They hired Sy Tomashoff, who was finishing up as production designer on the last season of *Capitol*. He was brought on just before the Christmas holidays as production designer to begin creating the many new sets, including the Forrester home and the Forrester Creations offices as well as the Logan house. Sy had extensive experience designing sets for such New York–based shows as *One Life to Live*, *Ryan's Hope*, and *Dark Shadows*.

Sy needed someone he could count on to decorate the beautiful sets he was creating. Sy had worked with Jay Garvin, who was the set decorator on *Capitol*, and was impressed with Jay's impeccably good taste and the speed with which he could take a concept from the designer, find furniture and decorative elements, and bring it to life on stage—a vital talent in the fast-moving world of daytime drama.

Meanwhile, Bill Bell was seeking scriptwriters he could count on to execute his vision of *The Bold and the Beautiful*—writers who could get inside Bill's head and the heads of those new characters he was creating. John F. (Jack) Smith, who had been a longtime writer on *The Young and the Restless*, and Meg Bennett, an actress and writer on *Y&R,* were brought on to fill out the writing staff. Jack's contribution to the series has been substantial. He continues to write two to three scripts a week for *B&B* and he also still writes outlines for *Y&R* episodes as well.

Gail Kobe had worked with two people on *The Guiding Light* whom she wanted to bring to Los Angeles. David Dangle had been costume designer for that series and was eager to relocate to Los Angeles to create the brand-new look for each of the new characters of *The Bold and the Beautiful*.

Gail was also eager to hire her former associate producer from *The Guiding Light,* Hope Harmel Smith. Over a long holiday weekend, Hope flew out to Los Angeles from Manhattan to interview for a similar position and was subsequently hired. "I had always wanted to work with Bill Bell because he was the quintessential soap creator and soap writer," she says. It was an ironic job switch for Hope, who was coming from the oldest soap on the air to the newest.

Ron Weaver tracked down Rhonda Friedman, who had been the production coordinator a couple of years earlier on *Rituals*. Ron wanted someone who knew well how to break down and schedule a soap script, while ensuring that a smooth sense of continuity was maintained from one episode to the next. He brought Rhonda in to interview with Gail for the production coordinator post. "One of the things Gail was adamant about in putting together the staff," Ron remembers, "is that people not only have to be experienced and superb at what they do, but they also have to be good people. In daytime, we work together, intensely, fifty-two weeks a year, and you need to create a family. Rhonda is not only great at what she does, but she is also very upbeat and enthusiastic. She hit it off with Gail immediately." Rhonda was ending a self-imposed six-month rest from television production and "was literally getting ready to update my résumé when the call from Ron came," she says. "It was as if the skies opened up and this job fell from heaven," she enthuses.

As production continued, Bill decided the new show's working title, *Rags,* was too irreverent. By October, Bill came up with a new title, *The Bold and the Beautiful*. Bill told *Soap Opera Now,* "I wasn't sure how much I liked it or not, so I started trying it out on people and got not just favorable responses but very, very positive responses. So I thought, well, why not. My one negative was 'The Young and the Restless,' 'The Bold and the Beautiful'; it was sort of a repetition of rhyme."

Bill had also created names for his new characters. Two of them, Ridge and Thorne, were particularly unusual. Bradley reveals that Ridge was named after a friend of his, who lived a couple of doors down from the Bells' summer home in Lake Geneva, Wisconsin. "He used to come over and play tennis," says Bradley. "I remember my dad telling him, 'Ridge, someday I'm going to name a character after you because I love that name. But I'm going to wait and make sure that it's a very special character.' Ridge wasn't sure it was true. But now he travels all over the country telling people, 'I'm the real Ridge!'"

"Names aren't something that are easy to come by," Bill told *Soap Opera Now.* "And not only that, you don't want to get too cutesy with names, and yet you like to have a few different-sounding names that represent strength. In this case, I wanted the names to suggest wealth and power because certainly the rich Forresters of this world represent youth, power, strength, arrogance, and captivation. Eric, the father, is like Bill Blass—he has Forrester Creations, his family is in the couture business manufacturing and licensing beautiful gowns, dresses, and suits, essentially fashions for women."

Originally, *The Bold and the Beautiful* was supposed to be set in Chicago. But the locale was soon changed to Los Angeles. Bill told *Soap Opera Now,* "The switch was pure and simply this—when we go on location it just makes more sense to be able to remain here in Television City and go four or five miles to get some of the most spectacular footage ever than go to the expense of going all the way back to Chicago—not that there isn't beautiful footage to be gotten there. I lived there all my life and know the place, but it just made more sense for us to do it in Los Angeles in terms of the money and the expediency."

By December 1986, a buzz was circulating throughout the industry about the new Bell show, which eventually reached John McCook's ears. "I heard Bill Bell had a new show from somebody who was a writer at my daughter Becky's preschool," recounts John, who previously starred as Lance Prentiss on *The Young and the Restless.*

Bill also had a dynamic leading lady for his new series, Susan Flannery, who won an Emmy as Outstanding Actress for her riveting performance as Dr. Laura Horton on *Days of Our Lives,* which was also written by Bill. Susan was the first actor cast.

Susan Flannery and John McCook were the first two actors brought on board as Stephanie and Eric Forrester. Susan worked with Bill on Days of Our Lives *as Dr. Laura Horton and John McCook played Lance Prentiss on Bill's* The Young and the Restless.

She would play Stephanie Forrester, the formidable matriarch of the wealthy Forrester family.

For his second role, the patriarch, Eric Forrester, Bill set his sights on John. Bradley says, "My dad really loves Susan Flannery and he wanted her to be Stephanie. He really had his eye on her, as he did with John McCook. These are two people that he enjoyed working with, and my dad knew that he wanted them."

Since leaving *The Young and the Restless* in 1980, John had turned down three different offers from various producers to return to daytime drama. Instead, he preferred guest-starring in episodic television and theater. But would John turn down a role specifically created for him in a new series by Bill Bell? John says, "Shortly after I heard about the new show, my agent got a call asking if I would be interested in coming in on this. I respectfully declined." After a few more phone calls from executives at CBS, John's agent told him it might be a good idea to meet with Bill Bell, just to see what he had in mind.

"We met at the production offices at CBS, right before the Christmas holidays," recalls John. "I hadn't seen Bill in seven years and he said, 'Oh, I thought you would look older.' I said, 'Bill, it's only been seven years!' We sat down and Bill was very excited about the show." Bill described the role of Eric Forrester to John. Since Eric was the father of several grown children, John was surprised that Bill was interested in him for the part. "At the time, I was forty-three years old," says John, "and I thought, I'm not really old enough to play the father of all these people. Bill was thinking that when he saw me, too. But he told me that after the first three or four episodes, nobody was going to care." To illustrate his point, Bill told John about a New York soap he had written for that featured two actresses playing a mother and daughter who were only four years apart in age. Bill proceeded to reveal more details about Eric Forrester, including his troubled marriage to Stephanie Forrester and his success as a clothing designer. "I found it fascinating that this character wasn't just the patriarch of the show and a successful businessman," offers John. "He was also a creative artist in his chosen field, the fashion industry."

Finally, Bill told John that Susan Flannery would be on the show, playing Eric's wife. "That was a big plus in my mind," says John, who first met Flannery when he was guest-starring on *Harper Valley, PTA*, which aired on NBC in the early eighties, starring Barbara Eden and Fannie Flagg. "I played Fannie's old boyfriend from high school," says John. During a dinner break, Susan Flannery, a friend of Fannie's, visited the set and was introduced to John. "Of course, I knew who Susan was," says John, "but it wasn't so much because she was on *Days of Our Lives*. Susan was one of the few people to step directly out of soap opera and into a major motion picture, *The Towering Inferno,* which starred Paul Newman and Steve McQueen. I was very impressed with her reputation, and her history in daytime television. I thought it was a coup that Bill had her."

John's meeting with Bill ended on a cordial note. He agreed to think about joining the show. At home, John discussed the new role with his wife, Laurette, and found himself becoming more excited by the prospects. "I thought about how much fun it would be starting a new show," said John.

"Bill Glenn had worked with me on *The Young and the Restless*. Bill told me about Gail Kobe, and that Hope Smith would be coming with her from *Guiding Light*. So this was a creative team that knew what they were doing. They weren't just flying by the seat of their pants." Finally, John decided he wanted the role and contacted Bill to break the news.

With his two leading players in place, Bill Bell and his company focused their attention on casting the rest of the show. Bradley says, "I was in on all of the casting sessions with my parents. It was a long and difficult process. Aside from Susan and John, we really went with a lot of people who had very little acting experience. So it was a real gamble, and a lot of the actors really grew on the show. Sometimes we went in different directions, but it was fun starting the show that way because so often in soaps, you see producers trying to get actors who are known quantities in daytime. It's like you're putting on a play. You're getting people who haven't been through the circuit. It's risky, but it can also be very rewarding."

Bradley Bell vividly recalls the day Ronn Moss arrived at the studio to read for the role of Ridge, the Forresters' oldest son. Bradley recounts, "We were casting Ridge and Ronn Moss came in. There was something about him. My dad calls it the 'x' factor. It's a mystery. We looked at several wonderful actors, but Ronn had something that you couldn't quite figure out. It's something that's hard to find, and is really valuable, especially in the way that my dad tells a story."

Hope Smith, who was also present at the casting sessions, says, "Ronn had a 'Peck's bad boy' quality about him and a great sense of humor. He was also devastatingly good-looking."

"We knew Ronn was our Ridge," states Bradley.

After Ronn was cast, the search was on for the two actresses who would play Brooke Logan and Caroline Spencer, the women romantically linked to Ridge.

Casting Brooke proved to be easier than finding an actress to play Caroline. Katherine Kelly Lang, who guest-starred on several prime-time series and

Ronn Moss was a newcomer to soaps, playing Ridge Forrester, but Lauren Koslow, who played Margo Lynley, already had a daytime soap on her résumé. She played Lindsey Wells on The Young and the Restless.

also had a short-term role on *The Young and the Restless*, was a standout during her audition for Brooke. "Katherine was the quintessential 'California girl,'" observes Hope. "Her hair could be wind-tossed, and she could be sunburned, wearing no makeup, and she still looked gorgeous."

Katherine says, "I used to model, and did all the surfing magazine shoots. Every year I'd go to Hawaii and shoot the swimwear. I was also the girl in The Beach Boys' 'Little Surfer Girl' video. I grew up in California. So I guess I did fit the image of the 'California girl.'"

Katherine performed her screen test with John McCook. Although John read lines that were written for Ridge, the producers felt they'd get a clearer impression of the actresses testing if they read opposite someone who already had experience working in soaps. "John really made me feel so comfortable and at ease," says Katherine. "I really got into doing the scene and doing the test."

Katherine's commitment to fully playing the role in her screen test helped to sway everyone in her favor. Bradley says, "Katherine is a unique and wonderful actress. She gives it her all."

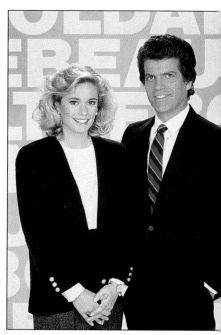

Meanwhile, two other roles on *The Bold and the Beautiful* were cast with actors who also had worked with Bill Bell on *The Young and the Restless*. Lauren Koslow, who had played Lindsey Wells, says, "When my role ended on *The Young and the Restless* I wasn't planning on going back to daytime. I had been cast as a regular on *The A-Team*. But it turned out to be the series' last season. It went off the air, and the part on *The Bold and the Beautiful* came up." Lauren screen-tested with Ronn Moss for the role of Margo Lynley, Eric Forrester's personal assistant. Jim Storm, who played Neil Fenmore on *The Young and the Restless*, was cast as Bill Spencer, Caroline's father. "Bill had a good relationship with them and he knew he could count on them," says Hope. "We felt good about having core veterans who knew the genre and what was expected of them in this medium."

RIGHT: *When William J. Bell and Lee Phillip Bell wrote the outline for* The Bold and the Beautiful, *Caroline (Joanna Johnson) was originally a short-term character. But as Bill worked on the story, he found himself fascinated by Caroline. His revised plans extended Caroline's stay, and also included the addition of her father, Bill Spencer (Jim Storm), a publisher.*

BELOW: *Ethan Wayne and Carrie Mitchum, who played brother and sister Storm and Donna Logan, came from an impressive Hollywood genealogy. John Wayne is Ethan's father and Robert Mitchum is Carrie's grandfather.*

Carrie Mitchum, Robert Mitchum's granddaughter, and Ethan Wayne, John Wayne's son, two newcomers, were cast as brother and sister Donna and Storm Logan.

The casting process also netted a few surprise switches. "Some people were testing for some roles and they were cast in others," says Hope. "We were trying to determine chemistry and establish the look of the show."

Bryan Genessee, who was raised in Canada but lived in Harlem for a while, originally auditioned for the role of Storm, but was eventually cast as Rocco. "They didn't have Rocco at first," Bryan told *The Daily Bruin.* "When we were auditioning, there were no ages mentioned, and so having lived in Harlem, the name Storm gave me images of a tough guy. So I made him a street guy and totally made my hair spiky. But I was totally not right for the part. I was wrong for what they wanted, but they liked what they saw and what I did."

Nancy Sloan, who was cast as Katie, the youngest Logan daughter, had never acted on television. Nancy, who was a theater major at Kansas

State University, met her agent at a theater festival in Iowa. He arranged to fly her to Los Angeles to audition for *The Bold and the Beautiful.* "I was in Los Angeles for two weeks and had eleven different auditions for the part of Katie," Nancy reveals. She attributes winning her role to a teary-eyed audition. "I remember [director] Bill Glenn pulling me aside before the last audition and telling me the producers wanted to see me cry," explains Nancy, who fretted over whether she'd be able to cry on cue. "I sat at the audition and thought, Great, I'm not going to get the part. This has been a waste of time for everyone." Convinced that she had lost the part, Nancy felt an overwhelming sense of sadness, which stayed with her during the final audition. "I started to cry," she says, "and I got the part!"

Other original cast members included Judith Baldwin, who co-starred in such feature films as *Scarface* and *The Stepford Wives,* as Beth Logan; Teri Ann Linn, who guest-starred on several television series, including *Hill Street Blues, The Fall Guy,* and *Magnum, P.I.,* as Kristen Forrester, Eric and Stephanie's daughter; Clayton Norcross, whose credits included recurring stints on *Santa Barbara* and *The Colbys,* as Thorne, the second Forrester son; and Stephen Shortridge, who was a regular on *Welcome Back, Kotter* as Dave, a police officer who wanted to marry Brooke.

Meanwhile, Caroline Spencer had yet to be cast. It was a pivotal role because Caroline embodied a unique combination of innocence and strength. She was a character who could survive a harrowing experience and ultimately emerge triumphant, with her basic goodness and optimism still intact.

Ironically, at the same time that *The Bold and the Beautiful* was struggling to find Caroline, Joanna Johnson, a young actress, was facing an equal challenge trying to snare an audition for the show. "My agent didn't want me to do soap operas," explains Joanna. "I heard there was a new soap, and that they were going with unknown, young people. I told my agent that I really needed the work and that I wanted her to send me on an audition. She told me she couldn't get me an audition for *The Bold and the Beautiful.* Soon after, Joanna, who was fed up with her agent's stubbornness, switched agents. They immediately impressed Joanna by setting her up with an audition for *The Bold and the Beautiful.*

Joanna initially read for casting director John Conwell and was eventually called back for a screen test. "There were about five girls testing. I went on camera and did a scene," she recounts. "I tested with Stephen Shortridge and I

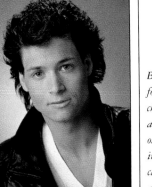

Bryan Genessee originally read for the role of Storm. Based on the character's provocative name, Bryan assumed Storm was a rebellious outsider. But the Bells were so impressed by Bryan that they cast him in a different role, as Rocco Carner.

Nancy Sloan was a college student majoring in theater when she won the role of Katie Logan.

thought I was terrible." Although Joanna felt disheartened by her performance in the screen test, Bill Bell felt differently. "As soon as I finished testing, they wanted me to do an on-camera interview," says Joanna. "That's when I was introduced to Ronn Moss."

Bradley clearly remembers Joanna's first encounter with Ronn Moss. "She walked in, never having seen Ronn before. We were taping something in the rehearsal hall." With a laugh, Bradley adds, "She looked at Ronn and said, 'Wow, you're gorgeous!'"

"I had never seen someone so attractive," says Joanna, who was directed to sit on Ronn's lap. "I got very shy with Ronn," she adds.

Recalling the on-camera interview with Joanna, Ronn Moss says, "I think they wanted to see how would we would relate." Although Joanna felt shy, her demeanor appeared playful on camera. "We hit it off right away," reveals Ronn. "We just had fun. I sat her on my lap like a Howdy Doody doll and we had this banter back and forth."

"Joanna was fresh and natural, and she was inexperienced," observes Bradley. "She was working in an art gallery and had not acted very much before. There was a sparkle in her eye that was really special." Hope Smith concurs, "There was an innocence and naiveté that came across, which played in great contrast to her patrician beauty."

With the search for Caroline at an end, *The Bold and the Beautiful* moved closer to taping its first episode. Meanwhile, John McCook stopped by the show's offices to talk with Bill. Arrangements were made for Ronn Moss, Clayton Norcross, and Teri Ann Linn, who were cast as John's children, to be at

Cast of the Forrester family (clockwise from upper left): Clayton Norcross (Thorne), Ronn Moss (Ridge), Teri Ann Linn (Kristen), John McCook (Eric), and Susan Flannery (Stephanie).

the offices on the same day. "They were going to wardrobe for fittings," says John, who, upon first sight of the three actors, was immediately struck by the realization that he was indeed playing the patriarch of adult children. "My own kids weren't up to my knees yet," John comments, "and two of these three were taller than I was!"

With nearly everything in place to begin production on *The Bold and the Beautiful,* Bill sat in front of his computer to write the first episode. "The scariest moment in my life is when I'm about to do a series and I hit page one of scene one of script one," Bill told the *Chicago Sun-Times*'s Robert Feder. "That's an awesome moment. But then as you write, the characters come alive.

"It's a very exciting, stimulating, adrenaline-pumping experience, believe me," Bill added. "I totally control their destiny—what they do, what they say, how they react, how they don't react. You can't imagine what an exciting thing it is. And, of course, in daytime, like nowhere else on TV, every show is opening night. Every day it comes alive for you. There are no reruns, and, if you're as fortunate as I've been, there are no closing nights."

B&B's first season cast. Back row: Bryan Genessee (Rocco), Stephen Shortridge (Dave), Jim Storm (Bill), Clayton Norcross (Thorne). Middle row: Carrie Mitchum (Donna), Ethan Wayne (Storm), Nancy Sloan (Katie), Katherine Kelly Lang (Brooke), Joanna Johnson (Caroline), Lauren Koslow (Margo), Ronn Moss (Ridge). Front row: Nancy Burnett (Beth), Teri Ann Linn (Kristen), John McCook (Eric), Susan Flannery (Stephanie).

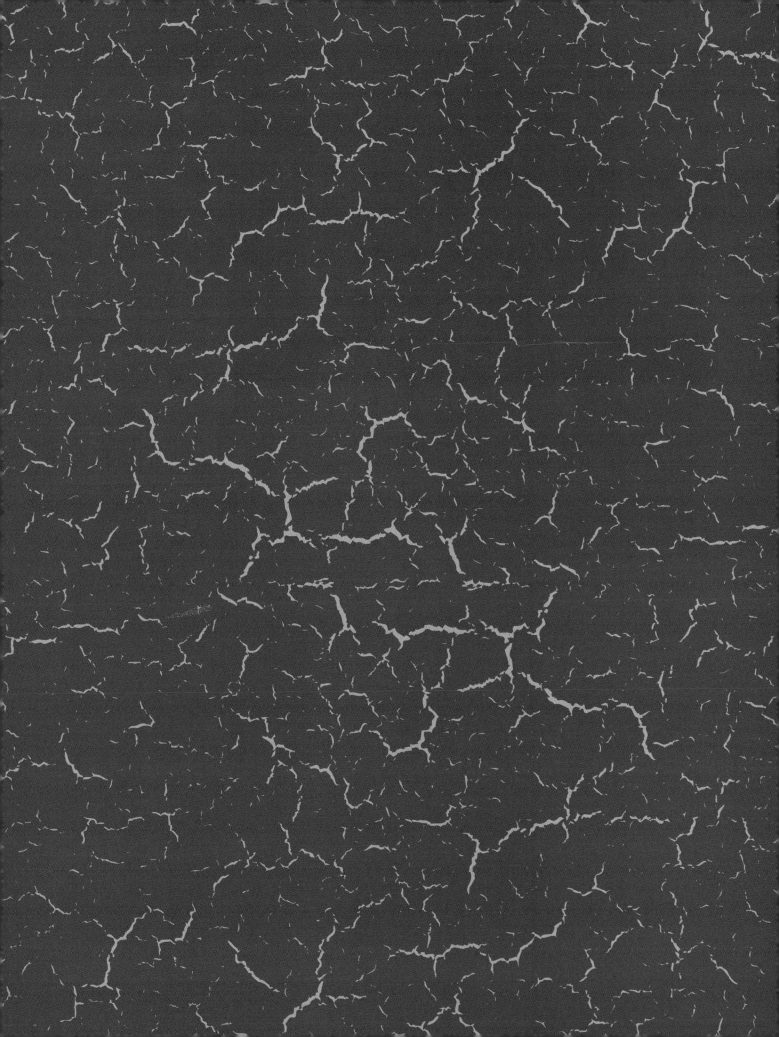

Season One

BROOKE/RIDGE/CAROLINE/THORNE

Beverly Hills playboy Ridge Forrester, one of the fashion industry's top designers, was used to getting what he wanted. Yet Ridge knew the only way he'd get virginal Caroline Spencer into his bedroom was if they wed—so Ridge proposed, much to the chagrin of Caroline's dad, publishing magnate Bill Spencer. Bill felt that Ridge would only give his daughter heartache. Ridge gave weight to Bill's concern when he threw caution to the wind and enjoyed one last fling with Alex, an old flame, shortly before the wedding. Ridge's indiscretion, however, didn't remain a secret, thanks to Conway Weston, a private eye Bill had hired to catch Ridge cheating on his fiancée. Conway quickly snapped several incriminating photographs of Ridge and Alex having just made love in a hotel room.

Bill showed Ridge the photos and ordered the philanderer to walk away from Caroline. Ridge refused, so Bill made good on his threat: He presented the pictures to Caroline as she was preparing to walk down the aisle. A devastated Caroline started to go through with the wedding, but the stress of her fiancé's betrayal and her father's manipulative ways caused her to collapse at the altar. Caroline was rushed to the hospital, where she was befriended by Brooke Logan, a college student from the Valley majoring in chemistry, who was fascinated with Ridge and Caroline's storybook romance.

Brooke spots Ridge and Caroline together as Brooke caters a party at the Forrester mansion.

Disenchanted with both Ridge and her father, Caroline broke the engagement and moved out of her father's apartment. She took a job in an advertising firm and began a new life. In time, Caroline entertained the idea of renewing her relationship with Ridge. But one night tragedy struck: a man named Ron Deacon approached Caroline in a restaurant. He convinced her to let him walk her home. Ron forced his way into Caroline's apartment and raped her.

Feeling she had nothing to offer a man, Caroline stopped seeing Ridge and moved in with Brooke's family. Brooke knew some of the horror that Caroline felt, since several months earlier Brooke had narrowly escaped a similar attack. Ridge's younger brother, Thorne, who had a crush on Caroline, supported Caroline through her ordeal. Bill felt Thorne was much more suited to be Caroline's mate—as well as the son Bill never had. Bill offered Thorne a position in his corporation, but ultimately, with Caroline's prodding, Thorne turned it down.

District Attorney Jeff Talon agreed to prosecute Ron despite the lack of physical evidence that Ron had committed rape. Caroline also found support and friendship with law school graduate Storm Logan, Brooke's older brother. Bill vowed that if Ron wasn't found guilty, he would hand down his own judgment. He fantasized shooting Ron if he were found not guilty. Fortunately, Ron was convicted thanks in part to Ridge, whose testimony revealed Caroline's wish to remain a virgin until her wedding night.

Ridge sent Caroline a letter that professed his love and asked for a second chance. However, Brooke, who had fallen for Ridge, intercepted it and withheld the note because she was in cahoots with Thorne, since they both stood to gain. Unaware of Ridge's true feelings, Caroline accepted Thorne's proposal.

Ridge's mother, Stephanie, who didn't trust Brooke, deduced that Brooke must have kept the letter from Caroline. She demanded that Brooke give Caroline the note. Caroline read the letter on the day of her wedding. Although deeply moved by Ridge's words, she still married Thorne. Brooke served as Caroline's maid of honor. Ridge agreed to be Thorne's best man but decided not to stay for the reception. After the wedding, Brooke realized she was in love with Ridge, so she broke off her engagement to policeman Dave Reed.

Returning with Thorne from their honeymoon, Caroline felt she had made the right decision. Still, she was taken aback when Brooke informed her pal that she had started dating Ridge. On the surface, Caroline appeared to be fine with this development. But when Thorne and Caroline found themselves snowbound with Ridge and Brooke at the Forrester cabin, the young bride found herself wondering if she had truly followed her heart in marrying Thorne.

Caroline found herself torn between two brothers. Ridge offered passion and romance. However, Thorne provided the comfort and love Caroline so desperately needed after she'd been raped.

STEPHANIE/ERIC/BETH

After more than twenty-five years of marriage, malaise had crept into mogul Eric Forrester's relationship with his wife, Stephanie. Although they wed in college to give their child, Ridge, a name, Eric and Stephanie went on to have other children: Thorne, Kristen, Angela, and Felicia. The couple also produced a fashion dynasty. Although their children were involved in helping run Forrester Creations, Eric still remained extremely involved in the daily operations.

Nothing, though, escaped Stephanie's eye—including the fact that other women found Eric extremely attractive, among them his sexy assistant designer, Margo Lynley. Ridge shared a past short-lived romance with Margo. Eventually, Margo professed her love for Eric, who found himself unwilling and unable to return her feelings. Margo offered to quit—which delighted Stephanie to no end—but Eric, who was fond of Margo and recognized her value to Forrester Creations, insisted that she remain.

Eric and Stephanie considered divorce while continuing to entertain fashion industry movers and shakers at their luxurious mansion. Beth Logan, a caterer whom Stephanie hired, coincidentally was Eric's old college sweetheart. Eric had abruptly ended his relationship with Beth when Stephanie announced that she was pregnant with his child.

Eric encounters Beth as she caters a party at his mansion.

Eric came upon Beth twice while she was catering in his home. The first time he experienced a glimmer of recognition. The second time he saw her, Eric realized who Beth was and greeted his former flame with much fondness. They began dating again. Eric revealed why he had left her and Beth explained that she married Stephen Logan on the rebound and had Stephen's son, Storm, and three daughters, Brooke, Donna, and Katie. Beth added that Stephen had walked out on them almost seven years ago.

When Beth's feelings for Eric resurfaced, Storm gently reminded his mother that Eric was a married man. Meanwhile, Stephanie pleaded with Eric to give their union another chance. Grandma Logan, Stephen's mother, pointed out to Beth that Stephen had left because he felt he couldn't match Eric's success. Beth felt anxious about pursuing a second romance with Eric because he was still wed to Stephanie. When a guilt-ridden Beth and Eric, who resolved to give his marriage another chance, decided against pursing their romance, the Forrester children sensed their father's renewed commitment to the marriage and were happy for their parents. Eventually, however, Eric grew discontented and began dating Beth again.

Stephanie's suspicions were aroused by Eric's continued absences. Determined to gain information, Stephanie followed Eric to the Logan house one day. Initially she thought Eric was cheating on her with Brooke but later deduced that since Caroline, while recovering from being raped, was staying with Brooke and her family, Eric was visiting Caroline.

However, before Eric could divorce Stephanie, Beth discovered that she had a lump in her breast. Beth refused to burden Eric with her condition, so she sent him away. He was unaware that Beth had been scheduled for a biopsy and he couldn't believe his former love was lost to him for a second time.

KATIE/ROCCO/DONNA/MARK

Donna Logan felt badly for her younger sister, Katie, who was suffering from acne. So Donna encouraged Rocco Carner, a classmate from school, to date her insecure sister. Rocco happily complied, mainly because he was fond of Donna and wanted to be close to her. Donna sensed Rocco's attraction, but was already dating Mark Mallory.

Donna remained steadfast in her resolve to boost Katie's morale. It was working. Katie felt good about herself, thanks to Rocco, and started to fall in love with the young rebel.

Mark was bad news for Donna. He persuaded her to move in with him and then discouraged her from spending time with her family. On one occasion, Donna had promised to visit her grandmother but—thanks to Mark—didn't keep the appointment. Grandma Logan, who had just cashed a bank check, innocently opened her door expecting to find Donna. Instead, a couple of men broke in and robbed the elderly woman. A miserable Donna was reprimanded by Brooke. Grandma Logan moved in with Beth and the children.

Rocco played the role of Katie's protector, as well as Donna's suitor. Not even Donna's live-in arrangement with Mark deterred Rocco. The Logans and Rocco grew concerned for Donna after they realized Mark was a freeloader who expected Donna to work twice as hard as he did. Storm was particularly worried about Donna. Storm's protectiveness of his sisters and mother stemmed from his father's abandonment.

Rocco helped Donna get a job at Griffey's, a hamburger restaurant that was popular with teens, so she could make some extra cash. Mark grew jealous of the time Donna spent with Rocco. Meanwhile, Rocco's days at Griffey's quickly came to a close. He had saved Ridge Forrester and Caroline Spencer from some muggers and decided to take Ridge up on his generous offer to help him. Rocco phoned the powerful designer and asked him for a job. Donna was happy that Rocco had secured a position in the Forrester shipping room, but sad that her pal was leaving her behind. Rocco flirted with Ridge's sister, Kristen, and continued to date Katie, but his heart belonged to Donna.

At a Logan family dinner, which Mark deemed too "stupid" to attend, Rocco played "footsy" under the table with Donna. Later, he and Donna got a laugh out of the fact that Rocco was actually rubbing up against the leg of—Grandma Logan. Rocco and Donna shared a quiet kiss, which, unfortunately, was witnessed by Katie.

Katie forgave Rocco but blamed Donna for stealing kisses with her boyfriend. Donna felt miserable for hurting her sister. Things grew worse for

Donna encouraged Rocco to date her kid sister, Katie, who was self-conscious about her acne. But Donna didn't count on falling for Rocco herself.

Donna after Mark discovered that she had borrowed rent money from Rocco.

Mark opened up to Donna about his lousy childhood, which drew them close again. But when Donna felt she might be pregnant, Mark chastised her for forgetting to take her birth control pills.

Tired of tips and looking to break away from Mark, Donna sought work as a model. She applied to an agency run by Tommy Bayland out of a seedy studio. But Tommy's smooth charm won Donna over. She posed for some shots, but was told by Tommy that the real money came from wearing provocative clothing. Donna agreed to consider Tommy's advice. Meanwhile, the crafty agent gained Donna's trust by sending her on legitimate assignments.

Eventually Donna realized Mark was not the man for her. Ironically, when she arrived home to break up with him, she found Mark in bed with another woman. Mark tried to talk his way back into Donna's life, but she wouldn't hear of it. Donna threw Mark out and moved back home with her family. She felt great about taking such a positive step in her life.

The holidays were happy ones for Donna and her family now that she was home, but not for Rocco, who had no relatives. He sat alone in his apartment whispering a silent prayer to his missing mom and dad. But Rocco's Christmas turned out to be a happy one after Katie came to his house and invited him to share Christmas with the Logans. Rocco felt loved and cared about. He declared that this was the best holiday ever.

MARGO/BILL

Margo Lynley was a designing woman in many ways. She sketched gowns for Eric Forrester by day, and longed for him during sleepless nights. She endured insults and harassment from Eric's wife, Stephanie, occasionally returning in kind, and even dated Eric and Stephanie's son, Ridge, for a while. Deep in her heart, though, Margo knew that Ridge was no good for her—or any woman who wanted a commitment. Even Ridge's sister, Kristen, backed Margo on that notion.

Margo was pursued both romantically and professionally by publisher Bill Spencer. She kept their relationship a secret from the Forresters, since Bill had tried to woo Thorne away from his family's company. Bill also wanted Margo to work for him. Margo declined the offer, but soon realized that Bill was, in his own way, very devoted to her. Margo passed up an invitation from Ridge to vacation together in Switzerland, sensing that Ridge had only invited her so he could hurt Bill, who was also the father of Ridge's ex-fiancée, Caroline.

KRISTEN/CLARKE

Big brother Ridge's wedding to Caroline prompted an estranged Kristen to return home. Severe, long-festering tension existed between Kristen and Stephanie, who felt that her daughter was too attached to Eric. She suspected Kristen was frigid, so she hired Clarke Garrison, an ambitious designer who worked for rival company Spectra Fashions (which had made much money from knocking off Forrester originals), to romance her daughter. Stephanie encouraged Clarke to continue the charade with Kristen until they could determine whether or not Kristen was frigid.

When Clarke hit a plateau in his pursuit of Kristen, Stephanie impatiently fired him. Sensing that his chance to design for Eric would be lost if he couldn't see Kristen anymore, the gigolo set his sights on a new Forrester: Stephanie. Clarke professed his attraction to Stephanie and gave her a brooch. Stephanie entertained the thought of having an affair with Clarke but decided against it. Kristen, meanwhile, began to warm toward Clarke and showed one of his designs to Eric. Clarke's plan to become a designer at Forrester was taking form.

CLARKE GARRISON
· ·

Six months after *The Bold and the Beautiful* premiered, a new character, Clarke Garrison, was introduced as a potential love interest for Kristen Forrester. Dan McVicar, who was cast as Clarke, originally tested to play Ridge. "I thought Ridge was going to be like J. R. Ewing on *Dallas,* at least that was my understanding of the character," says Dan, recalling his screen test for Ridge. "So I went in and I played that sort of character, a bit of a mischievous guy who was also a womanizer and into business intrigue." Laughing, he adds, "I blatantly stole from Larry Hagman."

Although Ronn Moss was eventually cast as Ridge, Dan's audition made an impression. Six months later, he was brought in to play Clarke. "When they needed a troublemaker, they remembered my test and they created the role of Clarke Garrison," he reveals. "So there wasn't an audition for Clarke."

The first thing Dan did when he heard the news that he'd been cast on *The Bold and the Beautiful* was give up his waiter's job.

"I called the restaurant where I was working," says Dan, "and I told them, 'I won't be in on Saturday to work, but I will be in for dinner.'" That Saturday, Dan adds, "I had the best dinner of my life!" Dan was also touched to learn his

Dan McVicar

meal was on the house. "So they celebrated with me, which I thought was very kind. It was a waiter's dream."

Dan recalls his first scene on *The Bold and the Beautiful.* "It was with Teri Ann Linn. Clarke came into Kristen's office and teased her about her father, Eric Forrester." Clarke pretended not to know that Eric was Kristen's father, and Kristen didn't realize that Clarke was having fun at her expense. "It was a charming, romantic comedy–type of scene," says Dan, "and a great entrance for the character."

Although Clarke eventually became involved with Kristen, he flirted with several women during his first few months on the show.

"Clarke's first screen kiss was with Stephanie," reveals Dan.

When Dan joined *The Bold and the Beautiful* he appreciated that there was an air of mystery surrounding the true nature of Clarke's character. "In the beginning, the audience was always left guessing whether Clarke would be a nice guy or not," he says. Two years later, however, a new woman joined the series who shed a tremendous amount of light on Clarke's history. Her name was Sally Spectra and her entrance marked the beginning of an exciting new chapter for *The Bold and the Beautiful.*

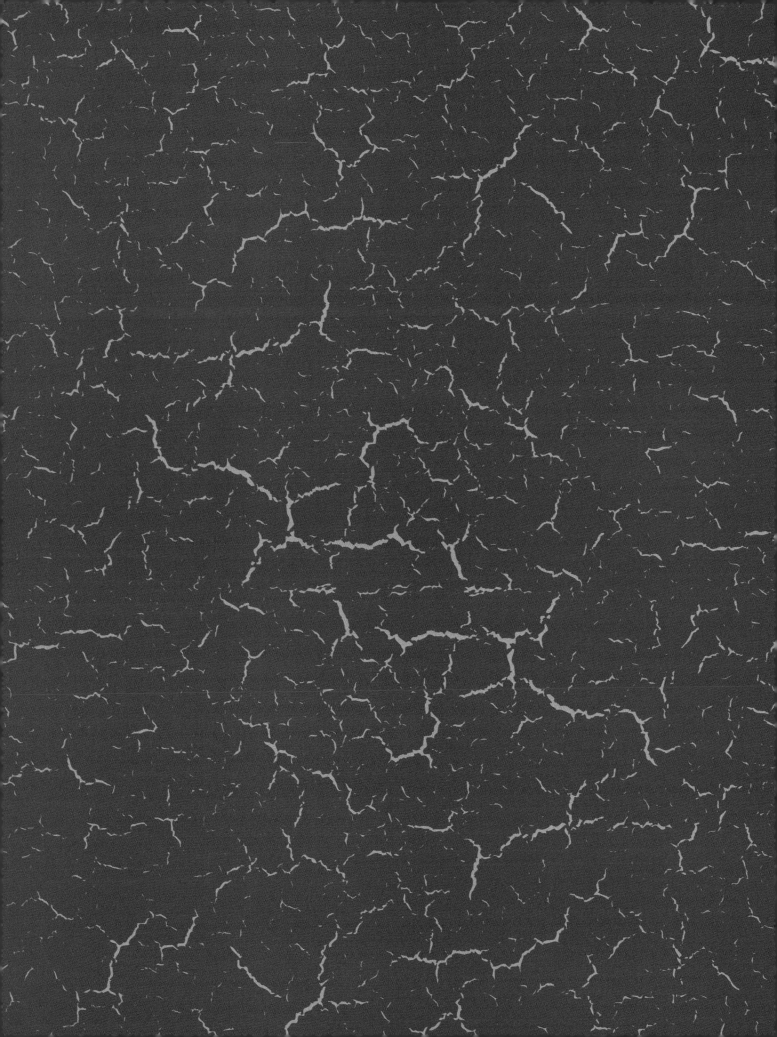

Season Two

BROOKE/RIDGE/CAROLINE/THORNE

Although Caroline and Thorne were married, Ridge still wanted her near him. Both he and Thorne offered Caroline a job at Forrester Creations, but instead she chose to become editor-in-chief of *Eye on Fashion,* a new fashion magazine published by her father.

Meanwhile, Brooke found a surprising ally in her quest to win Ridge. Stephanie supported Brooke, so that Ridge would not be free to steal Caroline from Thorne. Brooke suffered a setback, though, after she came clean with Caroline about withholding Ridge's letter. A livid Caroline announced to Brooke that their friendship was over. Brooke feared she'd lose Ridge if he learned of her duplicity. Caroline felt further betrayed after Thorne told her that hiding the note was his idea. Caroline offered Brooke a deal: She wouldn't tell Ridge about the note—provided she agreed never to see him again. Brooke had no choice but to agree.

At work, Ridge enlisted the aid of Rocco and Margo to mass-produce affordable, funky Forrester fashions, but Eric nixed his son's plan. Forrester originals should hang in the closets of only the very wealthy, Eric argued. Ridge was dealt another blow when he learned that Eric and Stephanie wed because she had become pregnant with Ridge. Caroline consoled Ridge as he dealt with this revelation.

Brooke broke her promise to Caroline and met Ridge for dinner, unaware that Caroline and Thorne would be joining them. But Caroline held her tongue. Meanwhile, Thorne couldn't convince his bride to move out of the Forrester mansion and start their own family. Fortunately for Thorne, Ridge started falling for Brooke, whom he affectionately called "Logan," and asked her to move in with him. Brooke turned him down.

Caroline threw a pool party to celebrate the premiere issue of *Eye on Fashion* at which the champagne flowed a little too freely. A tipsy Caroline retired early. While Thorne made a sandwich in the kitchen, Ridge, as a practical joke, slipped into Caroline's bed. Before a naked Ridge could announce his presence, an amorous Caroline came on to him, presumably unaware it was Ridge and not Thorne. Ridge found himself responding to his former fiancée's passion. Ridge and Caroline made love. The next day, a hung-over Caroline feared the worst when Thorne informed her that she and he hadn't made love the night before. Guilt-ridden, Caroline told Stephanie about her infidelity. Stephanie kept Caroline from running away by telling her if Thorne ever found out what happened, he'd kill Ridge.

Caroline and Ridge acknowledged their mistake to each other. Ridge vowed to respect his brother's marriage. But for Caroline, the promise came too late. She found herself unable to make love to Thorne. Caroline received a short reprieve from Thorne's advances during his recovery from an appendectomy.

Ridge put distance between himself and Caroline by again asking Brooke to move in with him. This time, she accepted. Caroline remained stoic as she looked down from her bedroom window and saw Ridge and Brooke frolicking by the pool.

While Caroline was away on business, Thorne overheard Stephanie tell Eric about Ridge's "adolescent prank" and his having sex with Caroline. A stunned Thorne, who was still taking painkillers to ease the discomfort from his recent appendectomy, began drinking heavily. The combination of pills and alcohol allowed Thorne to shoot Ridge in the back of the head with his mother's handgun. An incredulous Stephanie witnessed the shooting. The Forrester matriarch wiped her son's fingerprints from the pistol and hid the weapon. Thorne passed out in bed with no memory of what he'd done. Fearing Ridge might die before she could profess her love, Caroline flew to his side.

Lt. Burke investigated Ridge's shooting, quickly dismissing Bill and Clarke as suspects. As Burke deduced that Thorne was his man, Stephanie stepped forward and confessed. She claimed she thought Ridge was a prowler and accidentally shot him. A skeptical Burke had Stephanie thrown in jail, hoping she'd 'fess up. But Burke caved before Stephanie did, and he released his prisoner. Still, Burke warned Stephanie that Thorne was a time bomb waiting to explode.

Ridge came out of his coma with no memory of what had happened. Thorne also had no recollection. Caroline sought therapy with Dr. Cameron.

After Ridge was released from the hospital, he told Brooke he loved her. Brooke's joy was overshadowed by Caroline, who reminded Brooke of her duplicitous nature. Brooke countered that Caroline was jealous of her relationship with Ridge. Brooke tried to believe she was special to Ridge, but grew despondent, since Ridge had not given her an engagement ring. She had decided to move out when Ridge whisked her away to the family's cabin in Big Bear. Ridge handed an agitated Brooke a glass of champagne. Brooke was overjoyed to find at the bottom of the goblet an engagement ring. Ridge proposed marriage and Brooke accepted. But Caroline vowed that the ceremony would never take place.

STEPHANIE/ERIC/BETH/STEPHEN

Stephanie suspected that Eric might have become reinvolved with his college sweetheart, Liz Henderson. The Forrester matriarch became determined to find her, unaware that "Liz" was actually Beth Logan. Meanwhile, Brooke told Eric that Beth was facing breast cancer, which was why she sent Eric away. After Eric assured Beth that he would stand by her, she found the strength to undergo a biopsy. Beth's situation had a thin silver lining—Stephanie was actually impressed by Brooke's devotion to her ill mother. Meanwhile, Beth wondered if, after her operation, she'd still be desirable to Eric. Dr. Bailey announced to the Logans that Beth's mastectomy was a success. All the cancer was removed. Meanwhile, Stephanie saw Eric's college yearbook and a photo of Liz. While visiting Beth in the hospital, Stephanie opened Beth's Bible, which was inscribed "Liz Henderson." Stephanie realized the other woman in Eric's life was Beth Logan. Eric asked a devastated Stephanie for a divorce. She agreed. Margo was saddened upon learning that Eric had found love with someone else.

In an effort to keep Eric, Stephanie hired Conway Weston to track down Beth's estranged husband, Stephen. Meanwhile, Eric asked Storm to have his father declared legally dead—a move that was opposed by family members, especially Stephen's mother and Katie. Grandma Logan reminded Beth again that Stephen walked out on the family because he felt inferior to the almighty Eric. Weston located Stephen in Arizona and Stephanie anonymously passed on the information to the Logans. Brooke and, later, Donna flew to Arizona to convince their father to come home. Donna used a photo of Grandma Logan to sway her dad. Finally, Stephen agreed and returned to his family. But the happy reunion was short-lived. Beth and Storm immediately blasted Stephen for deserting the family. However, Katie insisted that her dad be allowed to stay.

Stephen fought hard to regain his family's trust, making headway by saving Katie's life when she choked on some food at a cookout. Stephanie geared up her plan to squash Eric and Beth's affair by asking Bill to give Stephen an overseas job at Spencer Publications. Stephanie even subsidized Logan's salary. Next, the Forrester matriarch informed Brooke that if she didn't encourage Beth to reunite with Stephen, then Stephanie would tell Ridge that Brooke knew all along about Beth's affair with Eric. Brooke feared that if she didn't side with her worst enemy, then she would lose the man she loved. Stephanie didn't leave the convincing up to Brooke alone. She visited Beth herself, and pointed out the virtues of going to Paris with a man deeply in love with her. Unaware of Stephanie's manipulations, Beth agreed to consider her advice.

ANGELA

Manipulating the Logans wasn't Stephanie Forrester's only secret. Eric became aware of Stephanie's mysterious absences two afternoons each week and hired a private eye. He learned that Stephanie had been meeting with Dr. Todd Powell at a home in Santa Monica. The private eye also revealed that Stephanie owned the house under her maiden name (Douglas). Eric confronted Stephanie about her other life. Stephanie lied to Eric and claimed that she and Todd were lovers. But during a search of Todd's house, Eric discovered a fragile, bedridden young woman. Stephanie confessed that the girl was Angela, Eric and Stephanie's microcephalic daughter, whom Stephanie had claimed died at birth. Stephanie explained that she lied about Angela's existence to spare Eric pain.

Devastated by Stephanie's lies, Eric moved out after telling his other children about Angela. But Beth pointed out to Eric that Stephanie's actions were actually quite selfless. Eventually Eric apologized to his wife.

During an evening out on the town dancing with Brooke, Ridge spied an Angela look-alike. He couldn't believe someone who looked just like his sister was so active and alert.

Beth felt Eric slipping away as he and Stephanie bonded over Angela. Later, Eric sadly informed Beth that he'd be staying with Stephanie. Brooke swore vengeance on Stephanie for hurting her mother. Beth decided to go to Paris with Stephen. But for Stephanie, the victory was bittersweet. Eric explained to his wife that while he would not divorce her, he also could not renew the sexual intimacy of their marriage.

Angela, the Forresters' comatose daughter, died as a teenager. Her physician hired an imposter to pose as Angela so he could continue to collect a regular paycheck from Stephanie.

KRISTEN/CLARKE/MARGO

Kristen, who was now designing at Forrester, submitted one of Clarke's designs as her own. Eric was so impressed with it, he decided to use it as the showstopper in a Forrester fashion show. Kristen couldn't help but wonder if she was being used, but Clarke insisted his feelings were genuine. Eric, Ridge, and Stephanie each warned Clarke not to hurt Kristen, but Clarke did just that by secretly dating Margo. Eric was surprised when Clarke revealed that it was his design, and not Kristen's, that was used in the Forrester fashion show. Kristen explained to her dad that she gave him Clarke's design because she loved him. Eric offered Clarke $100,000 for his showstopper, but Clarke said he wanted a job—not a payoff.

Hoping to turn his sister away from Clarke, Ridge invited several eligible bachelors, including Storm, to a party in Kristen's honor. Kristen was touched by her brother's gesture but, while intrigued by Storm, Kristen's heart belonged to Clarke.

Kristen and Clarke eloped to Las Vegas. Upon the happy couple's return, Eric offered Clarke a job.

ABOVE: *Poor, unsuspecting Kristen had no idea that her friend and office mate Margo was having an affair with Clarke, Kristen's boyfriend.*

Just as Clarke was about to achieve his dream of working at Forrester, Margo announced that she was pregnant with their child. Clarke warned Margo that if she told Kristen about the baby, he'd walk out of Margo's life forever. Anxious to protect her rights, as well as her child, Margo hired Storm as her

LEFT: *Against her family's wishes, Kristen eloped with Clarke to Las Vegas, where they were married by a Justice of the Peace.*

ABOVE: *Margo blackmailed Clarke into giving her $100,000 for child support for their son, Mark. Margo had her sights set on another cash box, wealthy publishing magnate Bill Spencer.*

attorney. Storm was thrilled to learn that Margo wanted to sue Clarke because he had always disapproved of Clarke's questionable character. Storm and Margo sent a legal letter to Clarke demanding $100,000 in child support. Kristen deduced that Margo's weight gain was due to pregnancy.

After making love to Kristen, Clarke tenderly asked her for $100,000. She complied, but when Clarke showed up to pay Margo he brought only $50,000. Kristen, who believed that Storm was the father of Margo's unborn baby, invited Margo to live with her and Clarke. As Margo gave birth to a baby boy, Storm informed Kristen he was not the infant's father. Margo asked Storm to be her son's godfather. Meanwhile, Kristen demanded that Clarke tell her what he did with the $100,000 she gave him. Clarke panicked and took Kristen for a ride. As they passed a house under construction, Clarke lied to Kristen and claimed it was their new home. Meanwhile, Storm asked Margo if she would marry Clarke if he were available. Margo wasn't sure.

BILL/DONNA/NICK

Donna had gotten Mark out of her life, but not her desire to model. When Donna needed some money, Tommy sent her out on a quick assignment. But the modeling job turned out to be exchanging sex for money with a guy who was anxious for an encounter with a prostitute. Rocco saved Donna before the man took advantage of her. Donna's next gig—modeling lingerie—was slightly more legitimate. Tommy told Donna that she could make more money if she posed nude. Surprisingly, Donna agreed, provided that the photos appear only in European magazines. Donna met with Nick Preston, the young, handsome head of the magazines, who oversaw the nude layouts. Donna became attracted to Nick.

Donna signed the contract to pose nude. At her request, Tommy shot the photos. Nick informed his boss, Bill Spencer, that he had discovered a fresh new model for their overseas market. Bill saw something unique—and familiar—about Donna. Bill was so entranced by Donna that he published her nude photos in his American publication, *Temptation.* Donna was identified in the photos as "Savannah."

Nick, who had begun to see Donna socially, advised her that their relationship should be kept secret, since his boss told him never to date one of their models. But Bill bugged Nick's office and learned that Nick had feelings for Donna. As punishment, Bill showed Nick the copy of *Temptation* featuring Donna, aka "Savannah." Nick was upset because of his promise to Donna that the photos would appear only in their European magazines. Meanwhile,

Donna informed Brooke that she was giving up modeling, since it conflicted with her and Nick's relationship. Donna felt betrayed when Nick revealed that her photos were used in *Temptation.* Nick bought up every issue, but that only caused Bill to order a second printing. When Donna learned of Nick's gesture, she thanked him with a kiss.

Katie discovered Donna's nude layout. Donna deduced that it was Bill who had betrayed her after she saw Nick leaving Bill's office. Donna vowed that Bill Spencer would pay for hurting her. Using the name Jamie Kensington, Donna approached Bill for a publishing internship. Bill immediately pegged "Jamie" as "Savannah," but he didn't know that Jamie was also aware of his ties to porn magazines. So Bill agreed to let Jamie study with him.

Nick and Rocco tried to give Bill a taste of humiliation by snapping naked shots of him at Bill's health club. Donna suggested the photos be printed in one of Bill's male nude model magazines. Bill, unaware he was being set up, hired Jamie (Donna) to write an article for one of his legitimate publications. The topic? Female exploitation in girlie magazines. Bill argued against the points Donna made in her article about the exploitation of women in men's magazines, but he did concede that she had a talent for writing. Bill asked Donna to be his protégée. She was thrilled, unaware that Nick and Rocco had already arranged to have Bill's nude photo printed in *Stud* magazine. Donna was livid when she found out that Nick and Rocco had executed their plan without consulting her. Caroline discovered the photos of her dad and informed him of the scam. Ironically, it was shortly after Bill received a prestigious honor for morality in publishing. Bill vowed revenge against those who had humiliated him.

KATIE/ROCCO

Determined to marry Donna, a sly Rocco slipped a note with an engagement ring into Donna's coat pocket while they embraced. What Rocco didn't know was that Donna had been wearing Katie's jacket. When Katie found the note, and the ring, she assumed that Rocco wanted her to be his wife. Poor Rocco couldn't bring himself to break Katie's heart. Instead, he tried to show her what a mean dude he was by taunting their waitress pal Stacy while she was waiting on them at Griffey's. Stacy dumped a bowl of chili on Rocco for his smart remarks—which caused Katie to laugh. Rocco skirted the issue for months. Eventually, he found the strength to tell Katie that her engagement ring was meant for Donna. A heartbroken Katie began dating Kurt, a college classmate. Rocco was happy for Katie but was also a little surprised to find himself jealous that Katie's new life wouldn't include him.

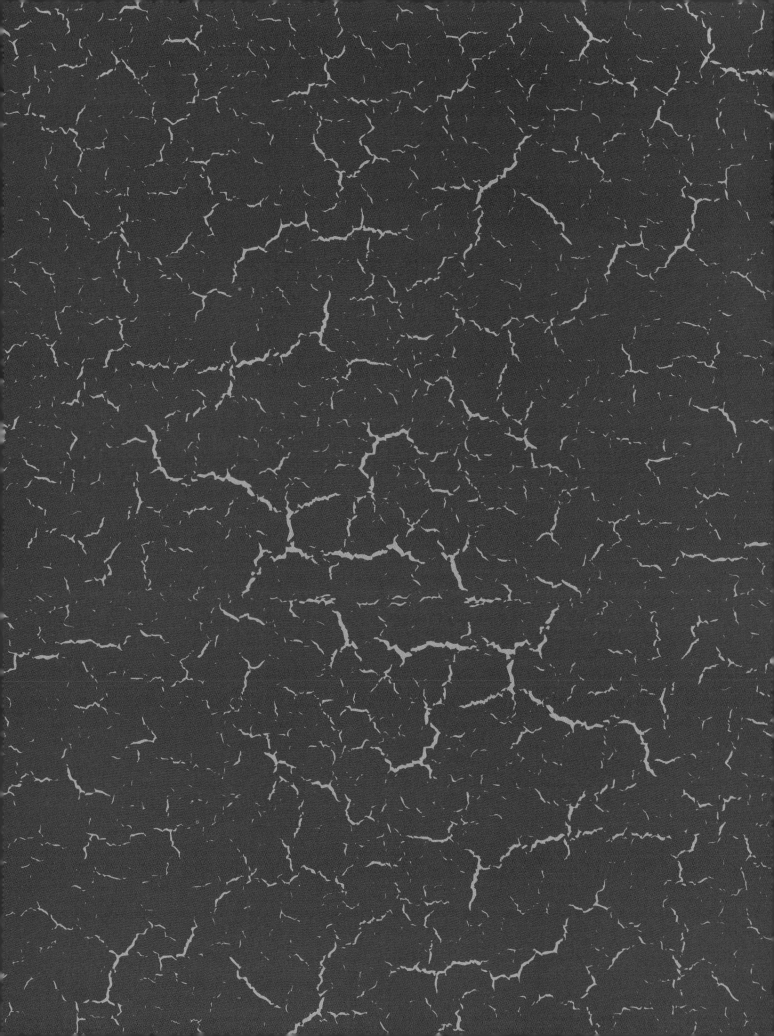

Season Three

THORNE/CAROLINE/RIDGE/BROOKE

Caroline took an aggressive tack in her plan to keep Ridge and Brooke from marrying. Although Caroline was occasionally able to give herself to Thorne, she knew that Ridge was her true love.

Caroline and Ridge finally discussed their drunken night of passion. Caroline acknowledged that although she was drunk, she knew Ridge was the one in her bed and, therefore, was a willing participant in his prank. Caroline admitted to Ridge that she loved him. Ridge was ecstatic, but he knew he had strong feelings for Brooke.

Suddenly Ridge had a new dynamic to deal with: Brooke was pregnant with his child. Ridge was initially less than thrilled with the news but quickly came around.

Stephanie, eager to keep Thorne's marriage intact, informed Caroline of Brooke's condition. Caroline told Stephanie that Ridge and Brooke's wedding would never happen.

Thorne agreed to be the godfather of Ridge and Brooke's baby. The younger Forrester felt slighted, though, when Caroline insisted that Ridge and Brooke join them in her birthday celebration. During the party, Caroline behaved amorously with Thorne, which only riled Ridge.

After Ridge and Brooke set a wedding date, Caroline planted suspicion in the bridegroom's mind. Was Brooke truly pregnant? Caroline asked. When Ridge asked, a furious Brooke moved out. Brooke played a tape of her doctor confirming that indeed the rabbit had died. Ridge cheered Brooke up by telling her Eric would design her gown.

Stephanie ordered Brooke to remove her mother's name from the guest list, since Beth had been involved with Eric. Not wanting to lose Ridge, Brooke reluctantly obliged.

Clarke, Thorne, Ridge, Eric, and Bill in Roman togas at Ridge's bachelor party.

Thorne threw a bachelor party for his big brother with a Roman theme. After crashing the bash with Donna, Brooke mud-wrestled with Ridge. Meanwhile, Stephanie hurt Caroline by suggesting she give Brooke a shower. Ridge told Caroline it wasn't something she had to do.

But Ridge did ask Caroline to accept his future with Brooke. Caroline couldn't. Instead she played her trump card. Caroline blackmailed Brooke into leaving the mansion two weeks before the wedding. Caroline threatened that if Brooke didn't go, she would tell Ridge that Brooke withheld the letter in which he professed his love to Caroline. Again Brooke agreed.

With Ridge to herself, Caroline flirted with him over tennis games and swimming sessions. Caroline told Ridge that she wanted him back and that she'd be divorcing Thorne. Ridge asked Caroline why she waited so long. Caroline blurted out that her "dear friend" Brooke kept Ridge's letter from her until the day of her marriage to Thorne. Ridge was infuriated by Brooke's action. But then tragedy struck: Brooke miscarried. Ridge told Brooke that he still loved her even though she lost their child. The wedding was postponed.

After being released from the hospital, Brooke returned to the Forrester mansion. But Caroline felt Brooke would soon be gone after she spied Ridge sleeping in a guest room. Caroline met with a divorce lawyer.

Ridge found his parents' insistence that Thorne and Caroline stay together bewildering. Eric and Stephanie revealed to their firstborn that Thorne, under the influence of pills and alcohol, was the one who shot him. An incredulous Ridge couldn't believe his own brother had shot him in the head. Eric and Stephanie reminded Ridge that his actions helped motivate Thorne's response. Eric and Stephanie impressed upon Ridge that the only way to keep Thorne from falling apart was if his union with Caroline remained intact.

Ridge, who still had deep feelings for Brooke, convinced Caroline to put her divorce on hold. Eventually, Ridge told Caroline what Thorne had done. They consulted a psychiatrist, Michelle, for advice on how to break it to Thorne that Caroline wanted her freedom. Michelle evaluated Thorne under the guise of being a marriage counselor. As Thorne found himself drifting further away from Caroline, he discovered he had a new—and attractive—friend in Donna.

After therapy with Michelle, Thorne consented to Caroline's divorce request. Ridge told his little brother that he was not the reason Caroline was leaving him.

Despite Caroline's availability, Ridge was unable to decide between her and Brooke. Stephanie taunted Brooke that Ridge would never marry her. When Brooke implied to Stephanie that her feelings for Ridge were unnatural, the Forrester matriarch slapped her. Ridge sadly announced to both Caroline and Brooke that he couldn't marry either of them.

Stephanie verbally abused Brooke as she packed up and left the mansion. Happily, the Logan family was able to come together for Brooke over the holidays. Stephanie berated Beth for seeing Eric and told her that she had been behind Stephen's job transfer to Paris. Stephanie felt justified in her actions since she was fighting for the survival of her family. But Brooke vowed revenge against Stephanie.

Meanwhile, Caroline was devastated to find out that Thorne had learned of her indiscretion with Ridge. Thorne rejected them both. Ridge told Eric that he didn't feel free even though he was unattached. Eric suggested to his son that happiness was his if he could recall when he felt the most free. Ridge considered his father's words and left a message for a special woman asking her to meet him for dinner.

Both Caroline and Brooke received separate messages that a "Mr. Forrester" wanted to meet them. When Brooke arrived at the mansion, presumably to see Ridge, Thorne explained that he was the Mr. Forrester who had left word. He just wanted to talk.

Meanwhile, Caroline arrived at the Ocean Club's private dining room, which was romantically lit and included a violinist. Ridge professed his love for Caroline and proposed marriage. She joyfully accepted. Caroline couldn't believe that she was finally going to become Mrs. Ridge Forrester.

Margo/Clarke/Kristen/"Beau"/Sally

Ridge grilled Kristen about Clarke's "dream house." A suspicious Kristen learned from the builders that Clarke had lied. Meanwhile, Clarke asked his ex-boss Sally Spectra, owner of Spectra Fashions, for a loan so he could pay off Margo. Shrewd Sally gave Clarke the loot in exchange for six Forrester originals that she would sell as her own.

Clarke's efforts were for naught. Kristen knew he had lied. Clarke confessed to his bride that he needed to pay off his pregnant ex-girlfriend—Margo. Kristen blasted Margo, but she also refused to leave Clarke.

No longer needing the money, Clarke went to Sally and told her the deal was off. Sally told Clarke their deal was still on. After all, she had it on tape. Clarke panicked after seeing that Eric had received an audiocassette. The tape was blank, but Sally's threat was real. Sally also demanded that Clarke arrange a meeting between Sally and Stephanie to help Ms. Spectra's work image.

Eric was proud to feature Kristen in his showstopper wedding gown for the fall and winter fashion show because he didn't have a chance to give her away when she married Clarke.

Kristen and Margo conspired to introduce Clarke to his infant son, Mark. When Clarke showed little interest in the toddler, Kristen knew her marriage had been given a reprieve.

When Rocco caught Clarke snooping around Ridge's office for the fashion show sketches, Clarke created his own designs. Clarke gave the designs to Sally and told her they were Forrester originals.

On assignment for *Eye on Fashion*, Caroline examined Sally's designs (that Clarke had done) and agreed to feature them. Sally felt as though she had arrived. The diva snuck into the Forrester fashion show and was livid to discover that Clarke had not given her Forrester originals. He had created separate substitute designs for Sally. She was initially angry because she didn't recognize the designs in the Forrester show. But when Clarke's substitute fashions were well received, she forgave him. Sensing Clarke's stress, Sally (dressed as Mae West!) offered him a deal: he could continue to design for Forrester and, using the name "Beau Rivage," he could also work for Spectra.

SALLY SPECTRA

Darlene Conley remembers with vivid clarity the first time viewers caught a glimpse of Sally Spectra, the woman scorned by the Forresters because she constantly stole their designs and sold them at a discount under her knockoff label, Spectra Fashions. "She showed up in a restaurant one day," says Darlene, "wearing outrageous hair, makeup, and clothing. She sat alone at a table until a very handsome younger man arrived, stood behind her, and opened a bottle of champagne." Darlene smiles at the recollection and adds, "The camera came in for a close-up, and you knew the whole story." In a single scene it was established that Sally was a woman with dazzling style who enjoyed the good life and the amorous attention of handsome young men. In short, a larger-than-life character.

For nearly two years, viewers constantly heard the Forresters refer to Spectra Fashions with extreme disdain. Finally they had a chance to meet the woman behind Spectra Fashions. After taping her first episode, Darlene approached creator William J. Bell and predicted, "The audience is going to love this woman."

Darlene's instincts proved correct. A few days after Sally's memorable first appearance aired, *The Bold and the Beautiful* received hundreds of letters from enthusiastic fans asking when they'd see Sally Spectra again. "She's a very sophisticated woman," observes Darlene. "She's able to speak knowledgeably about a variety of different subjects—literature, theater, or the arts. Sometimes she talks like a Dashiell Hammett character and other times she's like Katharine Cornell in the great Broadway days."

Of course, it takes a skilled actress with a flair for the dramatic and an innate sense of humanity to successfully bring a character with Sally's personality traits to life. "We wanted to bring in a strong leading woman to start a new family that would be in the same business as the Forresters, and compete with them one-on-one," says Bradley Bell. "We brought Darlene in as kind of the dark horse, the villainess. But she has so many levels that the spotlight quickly found its way to her."

Darlene, who previously worked with Bill Bell on *The Young and the Restless,* playing Rose DeVille, a professional criminal with a mean streak, had an immediate grasp of Sally's story. "She was the older woman with the younger

Darlene Conley

man, Clarke Garrison," notes Darlene. "After Clarke dumped her, he came back asking for her money. What could be better to play? I had two great things right off the bat. One was the obvious fact that Sally still loved Clarke, and the other was that she was too tough to let him get away with anything. She was like the women in the movies from the forties that starred Barbara Stanwyck and Joan Crawford. Women who ran their own business, but they had one weakness, some guy. Sally can take on whatever challenge presents itself. It's the thing that makes her so real when it comes to this kind of woman. It's how you have to be in a tough, competitive business like fashion. You have to be able to think on your feet, and then you have to do whatever it takes."

Soon after Darlene joined *The Bold and the Beautiful* as a regular cast member, the writers slowly began adding new characters to her storyline. Two standouts were her assistant, Darla, played by Schae Harrison, and Saul, an immigrant tailor who had worked with Sally for decades, played by the late character actor Michael Fox. "The great thing about the Spectra gang was that it grew on that basis," says Darlene. "Each character that was introduced came in for either a single day or a week. The characters that worked became part of the Spectra unit." Darla, who at first glance seems empty-headed but is actually a very bright, capable worker, and Saul, who had a knack for recognizing when Sally was about to get herself into hot water with a shady guy or a risky business venture, also brought out different facets of Sally's compelling personality, including her fierce loyalty and protectiveness toward the ones she loves. "Don't come near any of Sally's people with the intention of making trouble," warns Darlene, "unless you want your head handed to you. She will fight and defend every one of them. At no time have I ever played her as anything less than an extremely loving woman to the people she loves. And I would rather have Sally Spectra defend me than anybody. She's a powerful, powerful woman, who's intensely loyal and full of life."

"The entire Spectra group is like an entity all its own," says Bradley Bell. "They're so much fun, and they provide a nice counterpoint to the seriousness of what happens with the Forresters."

BILL/DONNA/NICK

Bill was teased about his nude photo, not only by business associates, but also by his own secretary, Miss Crotchet.

Knowing Bill's office was still bugged, Nick and Donna staged an argument over Bill's plight. But Nick's associate, Ramone, tipped his hand and Bill learned that Nick wasn't his loyal ally. Bill ordered Jamie (Donna) to spy on Nick. Donna couldn't get Rocco and Nick to tell Bill the truth.

Caroline hired Storm to go to Washington, D.C., and learn who the publishers of *Stud* were. Caroline was in shock after Storm told her that the stud behind Stud was Bill Spencer. Caroline chastised her dad for his lack of ethics.

Bill invited Jamie to vacation with him in Europe. But Bill grew suspicious after spying Stacy, who posed as a masseuse, working at Griffey's as a waitress. Stacy spied on Bill out of her friendsip for Donna. Stacy warned Donna that Bill was putting the pieces together. Later, Caroline, who saw a photo of Donna, innocently informed her dad that Jamie was really Donna. Soon after, Donna met with Bill and confessed. She told Bill that she wanted to get even with him because he had published her nude photos. Donna left Bill with the necklace he had given her as well as a tearful letter thanking him for all he had shared with her about his legitimate publications.

Donna did ask one final favor from Bill. Would he transfer Donna's dad back from Paris? Bill asked Stephanie, but she refused to let the Logans back into her life.

ANGELA

Now that it was no longer necessary to keep Angela's existence secret, Stephanie insisted that she be moved to the Forresters' home. What Stephanie didn't know was that "Angela" was not her daughter. The real Angela had died in a freak accident years ago. Todd had forgotten to lock Angela's wheelchair brakes and she went careening down a hill. Angela died from the injuries. Not wanting to lose Stephanie's generous stipend, Todd told Stephanie about the accident but said Angela had lived and needed plastic surgery, which explained her new look. Todd had hired a con woman, whose name was never revealed, to play Angela for Stephanie's weekly visits. But now that they were moving into the Forrester home, "Angela" was going to have to play comatose all the time.

Angela and Todd devised a "miracle." Angela slowly moved her hand during one of Stephanie's visits. Stephanie insisted that her daughter be examined, but when Angela murmured, "No hospital," Stephanie knew that she'd been duped. Angela announced that if Stephanie turned her in, she would tell the police that Thorne shot Ridge. Stephanie had forgotten how freely she had spoken around a "comatose" Angela.

Todd and Angela forced Eric and Stephanie to hand over $150,000 and afterward left town. Eric and Stephanie told their children that Angela had died. But Ridge, while gathering Angela's possessions, came upon a very alive Angela. Later, Stephanie and Eric told Ridge that the Angela they knew was an impostor, but they refused to prosecute.

When Angela and Todd drove off, Todd accidentally steered into oncoming traffic. The car crashed. The next day the Forresters read that two bodies had been found in the auto wreck. Todd and Angela were dead. Or were they . . . ?

MARGO/CLARKE/KRISTEN/MICK/MACY

Margo deduced that Kristen had a lover when she lived in New York. Anxious to win Clarke, Margo went to the Big Apple with Bill. There they found Mick Savage, Kristen's ex-lover, a fashion photographer. Margo lied to Mick that she was writing a feature on Kristen. But Mick insisted that he and Kristen were just friends.

Meanwhile, Clarke came clean with Kristen about his deal with Sally and how he hadn't stolen from Forrester. Tired of Clarke's lies, a dissatisfied Kristen turned her thoughts to the past and a happier time in her life when she enjoyed a sexually satisfying relationship with Mick.

Macy Alexander, Sally's only child, returned home after graduating from college. Sally was overjoyed that Macy was back, but Macy felt resentment toward her mother, who had spent the majority of her time running Spectra Fashions. Sally only wanted to provide for her baby. Macy agreed to work for Spectra, on the condition that Sally hire Macy's new pal, Donna, as a model.

Ironically, Clarke recruited Mick as Spectra's photographer. Macy took a liking to Mick, but hoped that Mick wasn't too fond of Donna. To Margo's delight, Kristen was so stunned to find Mick in Los Angeles that she rebuffed Clarke's advances.

When Mick came on to Macy, she demanded to know if he'd been tested for AIDS. Mick later told Macy that he never should have made a move. But then, Mick used Macy to make Kristen jealous. Margo was thrilled to hear that her plan for Mick to win Kristen was working.

Margo was also happy to learn that Clarke acknowledged Mark as his son when the feverish boy was admitted to the hospital. Yet Kristen grew despondent over Clarke's double work life, as well as his involvement with Mark and Margo. Fortunately for Kristen, Margo accepted Bill's marriage proposal. Still, Margo couldn't help but taunt Clarke over the fact that the nude model in some of Mick's photos was Kristen. Clarke slugged Mick. Later, when Clarke observed Kristen in Mick's arms, he thought that their relationship had resumed. But Kristen was actually telling Mick that she had decided to keep their relationship in the past. The embrace Mick and Kristen shared was a symbolic, tender farewell to their bygone romance.

Caroline never thought Margo loved her dad. But Margo surprised her by marrying Bill in a beautiful chapel overlooking the Pacific Ocean. After Caroline moved in with Margo and Bill, Margo quickly grew tired of her. Tensions flared further in the Spencer home after Clarke refused to let Bill adopt Mark.

Kristen warned Mick to stay out of her life. But when Mick grabbed her and kissed her, she realized that he still had a hold over her. Sally didn't like Mick's influence on Macy, so she tried to bribe him into leaving town. Mick had other offers. Although he and Eric got off to a bad start, Eric eventually

Kristen couldn't forget her first love, Mick Savage. Mick had captured her heart and, in his erotic photographs, her likeness as well.

A few months after Sally Spectra became an integral part of *The Bold and the Beautiful,* Sally's only daughter, Macy, arrived in Los Angeles. It was a challenging character to cast because while Macy initially harbored resentment toward her mother for being shipped off to boarding schools at a young age, she was essentially compassionate and kindhearted.

Bobbie Eakes auditioned for the role in 1989, shortly after Big Trouble, an all-girl singing band she was part of, dissolved. "I had never auditioned for a soap," says Bobbie. "As soon as Big Trouble broke up, my agent called and said, 'They're looking for a new character on *The Bold and the Beautiful,* what do you think about doing a soap?'" Bobbie, who guest-starred on several prime-time television series, including *The Wonder Years* and *Cheers,* decided to do the audition for practical reasons. "You usually tend to audition as much as possible, and then if you get offered the job, that's when the decision-making comes into play," she explains. "In the meantime, you've met the casting director, who in the future might want to see you again for other roles that come up. It's also good to keep up your craft by auditioning. So I said, 'Sure, I'll read for it.'"

In the meantime, Bobbie tuned in to watch an episode of *The Bold and the Beautiful.* "The first thing I saw was a scene where Sally, Darla, and Saul were at a factory in the garment district. Darlene was wearing the dress she wears as Sally in the 'Sally says recycle' poster. It was a big flowery dress with a cinched-in waist." Bobbie immediately found herself intrigued by the chemistry the actors shared together and the natural humor that was present in their scenes. "They were having a ball," she says. "I didn't know it at the time, but these characters were also relatively new. I thought it would be a fun show to do."

Bobbie read for the part and was eventually called to screen test, along with two other actresses. "I actually tested with Billy Hufsey, who had been on *Days of Our Lives* and *Fame.* He wasn't on *The Bold and the Beautiful,* but they were testing him for a new role on the show," she reveals. In another test, Bobbie performed opposite Darlene Conley. Before performing her screen test, Bobbie observed the other actresses who were also up for the role. "I watched them and thought, 'Hmm, they're really great.' They had a lot of energy and they were real frenetic." Con-

Bobbie Eakes

sidering the verve and theatrical flare Bobbie remembered in the scenes with Sally and her workers, she understood that the actresses were making acting choices that tried to match the same tone Darlene, Schae Harrison, and Michael Fox possessed. "I thought, well, I could try to outdo that and go way over the top. Or I could bring it way down and play another element, give them something totally different. In contrast to what Darlene plays, I think it really worked. I think it was a nice balance."

Right before Bobbie's test, Darlene introduced herself and generously offered the young actress suggestions on how to approach their screen test together. Bobbie says, "She gave me a couple of little pointers, other than what I had already decided to do. She also said, 'You ought to hit this line and emphasize this line.' I thought she was absolutely right. I was nervous and thinking about a million things; sometimes it takes somebody away from you to really look at the scene and really see your part in it. I took her advice and the scene went well." Smiling, Bobbie adds, "I thought, She must like me; she's helping me. Now that I know her, I realize she probably gave good advice to every one of the actors. But at the time I thought, She wants me to get it!"

Soon after, Bobbie learned from her agent that she had, in fact, won the role. "Maybe Darlene didn't plan on it," says Bobbie, "but I think she really was responsible for me getting the part."

Describing her role on *The Bold and the Beautiful,* Bobbie observes, "Macy has some very real problems. But all those things that are considered her problems make her very real to people who watch the show. I think there are women who identify with her. She's like your sister or cousin, somebody that you know. Macy isn't threatening. She's pretty likable, for the most part. She has goodness and a wholesome quality. I like to try to balance the wildness of Sally and bridge that broad, wonderful thing that Sally does with the Forrester family, which is very subdued and subtle. It's a different style altogether."

Bobbie says that working with Darlene Conley has been an invaluable experience. "She's a true original. She's always prepared and always brings so much more to the script than anybody ever dreams. So much of the character is really Darlene. She makes the character sing."

hired Mick as Forrester's photographer. Meanwhile, Clarke and Kristen accepted that their marriage was not going to survive.

DEVENEY

Months later, a mysterious bandaged woman woke up in a hospital. It was Angela. A bystander had helped her out of the car wreck. When the woman went back for Todd, Angela hit the Good Samaritan over the head with a rock. Angela, disfigured from the crash, ran away as the car exploded.

Meanwhile, Sally barged her way onto Stephanie's charity committee, and her maneuvering led to Spectra and Forrester doing a joint charity fashion show aboard the *Queen Mary*.

Angela, using the name Deveney Dickson and claiming to be a former hospital burn patient who benefited from the Forresters' generosity, conned Sally into letting her speak at the fashion gala.

On board the *Queen Mary*, Queen Sally conspired to lock Macy and Ridge in a stateroom, hoping romance would spark. Her plan took a twist, though. Thorne took Ridge's room. Thorne was enchanted by the towel-clad Macy, having no idea that she was Sally's daughter. They began to date, but the Spectra-Forrester rivalry later forced them apart.

The fashion show was a success until Kristen, representing Forrester, and Donna, modeling for Spectra, walked down the runway in identically patterned showstoppers. An overworked Clarke had inadvertently copied Margo's design. The Forresters were livid. A veiled Angela spoke and almost revealed that Thorne had shot Ridge, but she decided to exact a greater revenge. Angela planned to drug Thorne, hoping he would try to shoot Ridge again.

Angela (Deveney) befriended Thorne and he took her to Dr. Schnell, a plastic surgeon. Angela fell for Thorne, but her hatred for Stephanie was greater. After she had won his trust, Angela drugged Thorne and told him that Ridge had slept with Caroline. Angela gave Thorne a gun, hoping he would shoot Ridge. Meanwhile, a procedure called photo reconstruction tipped Stephanie off to Deveney's true identity. Stephanie came upon Thorne as he waved a pistol at his brother. Ridge told Thorne that he was the one who had shot him before. A repentant Thorne threw the weapon away. Meanwhile, Angela used money that a sympathetic Thorne had given her so that she could have her face restored.

Thorne regretted his violent act but couldn't forgive Ridge. In a way, Angela had won by causing a deep rift in Stephanie's family, and she had Thorne's money.

Newlyweds Bill and Margo didn't get much of a honeymoon. Margo was needed to be Eric's right hand at the first joint Forrester/Spectra fashion show, held aboard the Queen Mary *in Long Beach, California.*

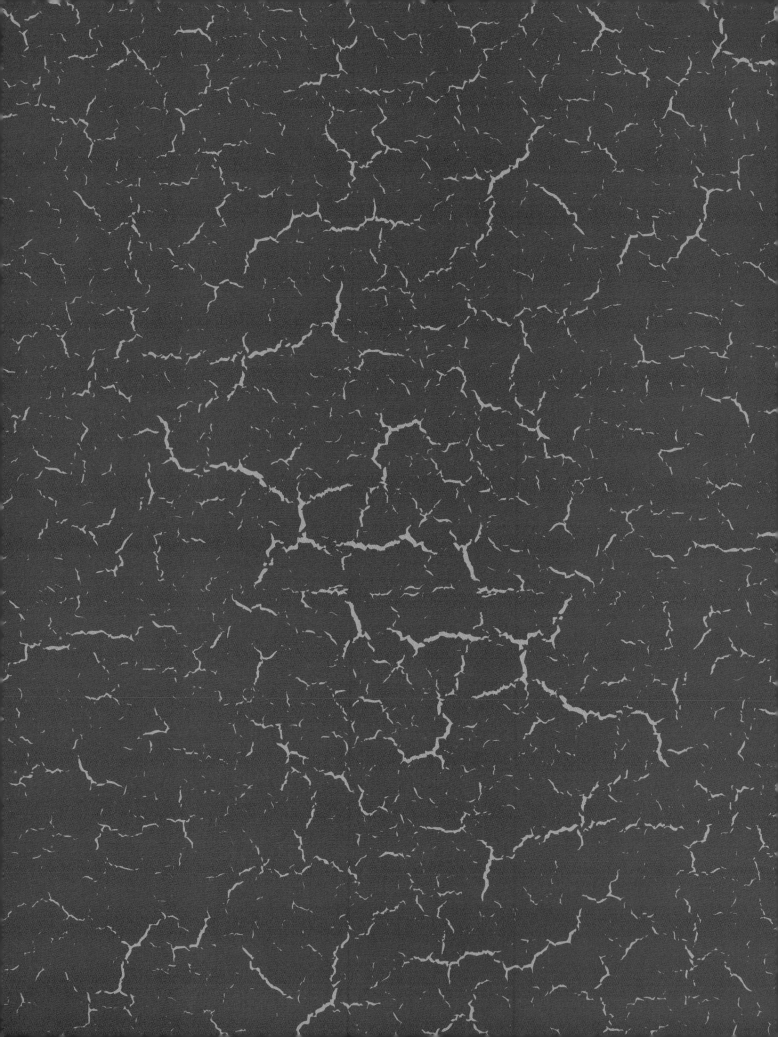

Season Four

Fourth season cast photo. Back row, from left to right: Robert Clary (Pierre, Brooke's Parisian confidant), Jeff Trachta (Thorne), Todd McKee (Jake, Margo's brother, who had a troubled childhood). Middle row, from left to right: Dan McVicar (Clarke), Darlene Conley (Sally), Michael Fox (Saul), Joanna Johnson (Caroline), Colleen Dion (Felicia), Brian Patrick Clarke (Storm, taking over for Ethan Wayne), Katherine Kelly Lang (Brooke), Carrie Mitchum (Donna), Jim Storm (Bill). Front row, from left to right: Bobbie Eakes (Macy), Ronn Moss (Ridge), Susan Flannery (Stephanie), John McCook (Eric), Lauren Koslow (Margo), and Zachariah Koslow-Schillace (Mark, played by Lauren's real-life son).

CAROLINE/RIDGE/BROOKE/ERIC/ STEPHANIE/TAYLOR/STORM

Caroline and Ridge announced their engagement. Thorne declined to be Ridge's best man, but Caroline's co-worker, Valerie, was the maid of honor. On the morning of the wedding, Ridge's thoughts drifted to the first time he and Brooke made love. Ridge, however, was clear about his commitment to Caroline. The couple wed at the mission where Caroline's mother was buried. Brooke watched from afar, but Stephanie spotted Brooke and ordered her to leave.

Eric comforted Brooke over losing Ridge and found himself growing attracted to his son's ex-fiancée. Eric pried the truth from Brooke that Stephanie was responsible for sending Beth and Stephen to Paris. Before he could reprimand his wife, Eric found Stephanie lying unconscious. While Stephanie recuperated from her stress attack, Eric overheard her speak poorly of Brooke. After thirty years of marriage, Eric asked Stephanie for a divorce. Later, Eric and Brooke professed their mutual love and consummated their relationship.

Stephanie assumed a visiting Beth wanted Eric. Beth did ask Eric to reconcile, but he told her that he loved someone else. Brooke announced to a devastated Beth that she and Eric were in love.

Stephanie failed to get Eric to attend marriage counseling, but he did agree to wait thirty days before announcing the divorce. During that time, Brooke discovered that she was pregnant with Eric's child. Thorne implied to Brooke that Eric and Stephanie were going to reconcile. Brooke went to Paris and met Pierre, a friendly restaurant proprietor. After learning of Brooke's decision to terminate her pregnancy, Pierre called Donna, who told Eric of Brooke's whereabouts. Eric flew to Paris and found Brooke before she had the abortion, explaining he was not reconciling with Stephanie. On the way home, Eric proposed to Brooke, who joyfully accepted. Eric was so grateful to Pierre that he set the Frenchman up with his own restaurant in Los Angeles.

Eric and Stephanie's youngest daughter, Felicia, returned home after a three-year absence, just in time for her big brother Ridge's wedding to Caroline.

Eric's attorney advised him to file for divorce in Nevada so that Eric could remarry immediately. Thorne told Stephanie that the other woman in Eric's life was a very pregnant Brooke. After blasting Brooke, a furious Stephanie flew to Nevada and stopped the divorce. Eric chastised Thorne for interfering and warned Stephanie not to stand in his way.

Meanwhile, tragedy lay ahead for Ridge and Caroline. The couple enjoyed only a few months of happiness when Caroline learned that she was dying. Caroline withheld this from Ridge and asked her doctor, Taylor Hayes (Storm's former high school classmate) to look in on Ridge after her death. Caroline also went to Brooke and asked her to be there for Ridge. But Brooke told her she was committed to Eric. Wasn't she?

Brooke asked Ridge to meet her at the Ocean Club's private dining room and told him she had a dilemma. She said a dear friend of hers was dying, but didn't want her husband to know. What should she do? Ridge told Brooke that she should tell the husband. After a tender pause, Brooke told her ex-lover, "I just did." Ridge couldn't believe that Caroline was dying until Taylor appeared to confirm it.

Ridge stayed mum about Caroline's illness because he knew she didn't want him to know. Ridge gave his wife fifty charms for her charm bracelet. The last charm was the symbol of infinity. Ridge said that that represented his eternal love for her. Caroline knew then that Ridge had learned she was dying.

Ridge told Bill that his daughter was dying. Bill called Ridge a liar, but Caroline confirmed it. Then Ridge told his family, but added that Caroline didn't want them to know. Caroline threw a party where she recited a prayer that her mother had once read: "'I shall pass through this world but once. If, therefore, there is any kindness I can show, any good that I can do, let me do it now, let me not defer it or delay it. For I shall not pass this way again.'"

Caroline tells Brooke that she's dying.

DR. TAYLOR HAYES

When Joanna Johnson informed the Bells that she wouldn't be renewing her contract as Caroline, they decided against recasting. Instead, a new storyline revealed Caroline was dying and a new heroine, Dr. Taylor Hayes, was introduced to treat Caroline during her illness. Taylor had a back story with Brooke's brother, Storm. They were childhood classmates. When Taylor returned to Los Angeles, Storm hoped romance would bloom, but shortly after Caroline's death, Taylor became attracted to Ridge.

William J. Bell remembers being immediately impressed by Hunter Tylo, who previously appeared on *All My Children* as Robin McCall and on *Days of Our Lives* as Marina Toscono. "We had a group of actresses come in to read for the part," says Bill. But when Hunter walked through the doors and introduced herself, the role practically became hers on the spot. "You couldn't believe this stunning woman," marvels Bill. "As she was about to leave, I remember saying to her, 'Has anyone ever told you that you're attractive?' It was a little facetious on my part. I purposely didn't say 'gorgeous' or 'beautiful.' Hunter looked at me, smiled, and then turned to leave."

Meanwhile, Hunter put the reading out of her mind and proceeded with plans to move back east with her husband, Michael Tylo, their son, Mickey, and Hunter's oldest son, Christopher, by a previous marriage. Michael, whose previous credits included *Another World, Guiding Light, All My Children,* and *General Hospital,* had just finished filming the TV series *Zorro* and Hunter was preparing to put her acting career on the back burner so that she could return to school for premed courses. "We had our bags packed and we were ready to move back to New York," recalls Hunter.

When *The Bold and the Beautiful* approached Hunter about taking the role as Taylor, she assumed it would be short-term and told them, "I'll do it for the summer and then I have to leave in the fall."

By midsummer, fan mail indicated that viewers were entranced by Hunter's performance, particularly in her scenes with Ronn Moss. Taylor was helping Ronn's character work through his grief over Caroline's death. The producers met with Hunter to discuss signing her to a long-term contract. "They came to me and said, 'People really

Hunter Tylo

enjoy this character, and they enjoy seeing you with Ridge.'" Since Hunter was having a great time on *The Bold and the Beautiful,* she postponed her plans indefinitely to go back to school and signed a contract with the show.

With Hunter committed to the show on a long-term basis, new facets of Taylor's personality slowly emerged. "Taylor started out as very clinical," says Hunter. "She didn't have a sense of humor. She was always trying to do everything just right. She had a track record of sacrificing herself for other people. Since I didn't really plan on staying, in the beginning, I wasn't really developing anything in my performance of the character," she adds. "But when they asked me to stay, I thought, Well, I have to develop a character who's going to stick around and be interesting for me to play." Hunter drew on a quality from her own personality, her sense of humor. Meanwhile, Bradley Bell, who was taking on more responsibilities as a writer, also looked for ways to feature her and move her character to the forefront.

Hunter's playful interplay with Ronn surfaced in a scene where they were becoming romantically involved. "Ridge was supposed to take Taylor out dancing," recalls Hunter. "Brooke saw them together, which was the whole point of the scene." Between dances, Ridge and Taylor sat at a table, drank martinis, and exchanged clever banter. "We were supposed to be getting a little tipsy," explains Hunter, "so I sucked the olive out of the glass and blew it across the table. It hit Ronn in the chest." The producers enjoyed the improvised bit of flirtatious play so much that they kept it in the scene. "It was fun to see Taylor getting a little silly," says Hunter. "And in the history of the show, we had never seen Ridge burst out laughing, which he did then. It was real and it was fun."

"Hunter is extremely professional. She's always on top of her dialogue," observes Ronn Moss. "She always thinks about the scene beforehand and she jots down notes about her scene, which I appreciate. It makes things easier when an actor comes to the scene with a point of view. I've been extremely lucky with the three women—Hunter, Joanna Johnson, and Katherine Kelly Lang—I've worked with most on the show. They bring an intelligence to what they're doing, a professionalism, and a fun attitude to the work that always makes it so much easier."

As the party progressed, Caroline got Stephanie to make peace with Brooke (for at least one evening). Bill asked Caroline to go away with him, but Ridge told him there wasn't time. The two men put their animosity aside for Caroline. Later, Caroline paired everyone off for a dance: Eric with Stephanie, Ridge with Brooke, and herself with Thorne. (Bill danced with Felicia.) Caroline encouraged Thorne to reunite with Macy. Before leaving, Caroline asked everyone to be good to one another. Ridge carried a weakened Caroline home. That night, Caroline died in Ridge's arms.

After Caroline's funeral, Brooke spent time with Ridge, giving him emotional support. Stephanie figured out that Caroline wanted Brooke to be with Ridge after she died. Brooke fibbed to Eric about being with Ridge because she wasn't sure of his feelings—or her own.

Brooke wasn't Ridge's only friend. Taylor gave Ridge a farewell letter written by Caroline. Meanwhile, Storm grew concerned over Taylor's friendship with Ridge because he was hoping that they'd find romance. Taylor and Storm continued to date, but she also found Ridge very attractive.

Eric and Brooke moved into a condo. As Ridge tended to Caroline's garden, he recalled his late wife's wish that Ridge spend his future with Brooke. Pressure from Stephanie and Storm and her own doubts drove a pregnant Brooke to San Diego so she could decide her future.

Stephanie was uninterested in Bill's advances. Instead, she got close to Eric by working at Forrester. Stephanie told Eric that she'd divorce him if he and Brooke moved into the mansion and shared the living space with her. Eric refused.

During Brooke's absence, Ridge began to see more of Taylor. Stephanie pointedly thanked Taylor for helping fulfill Caroline's dying wish: reuniting Brooke and Ridge. Ridge gave Taylor an opal bracelet as a birthday gift. Eric pointed out to Stephanie that a Ridge/Brooke reunion was moot, since Ridge had grown close to Taylor. Stephanie suggested to Taylor that if she truly cared for Ridge, she'd let him go to Brooke. But Taylor continued to see Ridge as a friend while she dated Storm.

A pregnant Brooke returned home just in time for the Forrester fashion show. Before she could see Eric, Brooke went into labor. Ridge rushed her to the hospital. Brooke gently told Ridge that she'd be staying with Eric. Eric was angry that Ridge didn't tell him Brooke had gone into labor.

Eric begged Stephanie for a divorce so he could make his and Brooke's child legitimate. Stephanie refused. Brooke gave birth to a baby boy and named him Eric Jr.—which stung Stephanie. Against Storm's wishes, Brooke asked Ridge to be Eric Jr.'s godfather. Eric didn't like it much either.

Stephanie's lawyer informed her that Eric's divorce petition would soon be granted. Knowing it was inevitable, Stephanie won points with Eric by "consenting" to the breakup—in exchange for Eric's and Brooke's friendship. Eric and a suspicious Brooke agreed to Stephanie's request.

After the divorce, Eric and Brooke made wedding plans. Thorne agreed to be the best man. Meanwhile, a bitter Beth returned and asked Brooke to move to Paris. Brooke refused. Then Beth offered herself to Eric, but he told her that Brooke was his future.

OPPOSITE: *As Eric and Brooke's wedding neared, Ridge found himself increasingly attracted to his future stepmother. Brooke, however, remained committed to Eric. After all, he was the father of her son.*

RIGHT: *Eric Jr.'s christening (left to right, godmother Donna, godfather Ridge, Eric Jr., minister, Brooke, Eric, and Storm). Storm wanted to be the godfather to his nephew, but Brooke felt that Ridge was a more appropriate choice. Eric initially agreed to the idea, but couldn't help wondering if Brooke was looking for a way to keep Ridge in her life.*

BELOW: *Stephanie finally agreed to give Eric his divorce on the condition that he and Brooke agree to become her friends. What Stephanie didn't tell them was that her lawyer had informed her that the divorce was about to go through anyway. Here, Stephanie visits Brooke and Eric at their new condo.*

Stephanie visited Eric and Brooke and asked to see the baby. The parents fibbed that he was asleep. Then the infant started to cry. A stoic Stephanie praised Eric's son. After leaving, her facade crumbled and Stephanie wept over having lost the only man she had ever loved.

Stephanie attempted to use Beth as a wedge between Eric and Brooke. If Brooke felt guilty enough over taking Eric away from Beth, perhaps she'd give him up, Stephanie hoped. At Brooke and Eric's Christmas party, Brooke apologized to her mother for falling in love with Eric. Beth returned to Paris.

Meanwhile, Storm proposed to Taylor and gave her an engagement ring. He told Taylor not to answer. She could wear the ring to see how it felt. Taylor and Ridge went to the Forrester cabin. When they arrived, they ran into Stephanie as well as Brooke and Eric. The five found themselves snowbound. Brooke told Taylor that she was wrong to wear Storm's ring and still date Ridge. Was Brooke looking out for her big brother, or was she jealous that Ridge had found someone else?

SALLY/CLARKE

Kristen ended her marriage to Clarke and left town with Mick. Clarke was left frustrated at home and without an ally at Forrester.

In the market for a designer and a husband, Sally offered Clarke a deal: She'd give him half of Spectra if he married her. Sally offered him his own label: Clarke Garrison Originals. Margo was amazed that Clarke would even consider the deal. With both Kristen and Margo out of his life, Clarke agreed to think over the merger.

Saul disapproved of Sally and Clarke's marriage, which, frankly, was more like a merger. Saul had been with Sally since the beginning and was not about to let her be taken advantage of by anyone, least of all Clarke.

Sally pointed out to Clarke that sexual relations would be part of their union. At the same time, Clarke asked Margo to leave Bill for him. But after Bill told his wife that he'd set up a trust fund for Mark, Margo told Clarke that while he could see more of Mark, she wouldn't be getting a divorce.

Clarke was promoted to senior designer at Forrester, but his mood soured when his design was pulled as the showstopper. Clarke quit after telling Eric he'd received an offer from Spectra. But Sally felt Clarke had waited too long to marry her and said that their deal was off. Eric refused to rehire Clarke.

Clarke planted an item in the society page that he and Sally were engaged. When reached for comment, Sally confirmed the news. Clarke felt uneasy after discovering that Sally ordered a sofa for his office. His intention was to design fashions during the day, not have afternoon romps with Sally. Sensing a detachment from Clarke, Sally feared he would cheat on her, so she had Sybil, a model, try to seduce Clarke. Darla warned Clarke, though, so he reprimanded Sybil in earshot of Sally. Clarke eventually agreed to a June wedding and sketched Sally's wedding dress.

Meanwhile, Sally hired Storm to draw up a premarital agreement, which Clarke grudgingly signed. To avoid publicity, Sally had the wedding at her home. The ceremony came to a sudden halt when Sally announced she couldn't go through with it. In a moment of heartfelt honesty, Sally revealed her vulnerability by quietly saying she couldn't marry a man who didn't desire her. But Clarke, who had his mind on his lucrative deal with Spectra Fashions, changed Sally's mind by making passionate love to her. The smiling couple soon exchanged wedding vows. Sally was now Mrs. Clarke Garrison.

Sally made good on her goal to publicize Clarke by getting him the cover of *Eye on Fashion.* Since Sally knew that Bill also published pornographic magazines, she blackmailed him into running the feature. Bill retaliated by having his public relations executive Julie Delorean infiltrate Spectra. Under the guise of being a fashion book author writing a story on Clarke, Julie wormed her way into Clarke's and Sally's lives.

When Clarke's *Eye on Fashion* cover came out, the Forresters suspected that Sally had used unethical means to get it published. Bill refused to confirm the suspicions. Meanwhile, Clarke made moves on Julie, who had fallen for him. She tried to stay focused on her goal of obtaining dirt on Sally and Clarke, but she soon found herself ruled by her desires and she made love to Clarke.

Later, Bill ordered Julie to write a scathing review of Clarke's fashion show. (But an unwitting victim would have been caught in the crossfire because Felicia Forrester's designs were also featured in the fashion show.) To appease Bill, Julie scribed the nasty critique, but at the last minute, she swapped her scathing story with a favorable article. Julie convinced Bill they would have been laughed at if the bad review had run, since everyone else loved Clarke's showing. Bill bought her story, but then told Julie to drop the review—and Clarke.

Julie was in love, though, and found it impossible to leave Clarke. A suspicious Darla spied Clarke romancing Julie. Clarke told Darla that Sally would only be hurt if she blabbed. Darla remained mum.

Julie Delorean infiltrated Spectra per the orders of her boss Bill Spencer. What Julie hadn't counted on was falling in love with Sally's husband, Clarke.

JAKE

Hoping to get Stephanie's mind off her divorce, Ridge hired a tennis pro to give Stephanie a workout. The instructor, Jake Maclaine, rented the Logans' garage apartment. Donna fell for the handsome stranger, as did Felicia Forrester, who had come home after a three-year absence for Ridge and Caroline's wedding.

Both young women were surprised that Jake had little interest toward them in any romantic way. In fact, Jake particularly found Felicia's attitude abrasive. Later, Jake and Felicia shared a laugh when they realized their mutual hostility was unfounded. Still, Jake kept Felicia at arm's length and refused to open up about his past.

Felicia learned that Margo knew Jake, but Margo asked Felicia not to mention his name. Margo visited Jake and ordered him to leave town before he hurt Felicia just as he had hurt "her" family. When Felicia discovered Jake and Margo together, she demanded to know how they knew each other. Jake revealed that Margo was his older sister. Margo refused to hear Jake's feeble excuse for running away as a teen and never communicating with his parents again.

Jake couldn't make love to Felicia. Felicia was nothing but lovingly patient with Jake, even after he lied to her and said he didn't find her attractive. Jake turned down Margo's offer of $5,000 to leave town. Meanwhile, Felicia asked her pal Heather to see if she could seduce Jake. Heather also struck out.

Taylor suggested to Felicia that a problem from Jake's past may have left him impotent.

Soon after, Margo flew home to Wisconsin to visit her parents, Helen and Ben. Margo denied hearing from Jake. After returning to Los Angeles, Margo visited her brother and begged him to see their parents. Jake finally told Margo why he had left home. To Margo's amazement, Jake explained that their father had sexually molested him. Eventually, Margo believed her brother. Jake begged Margo not to confront their dad. Meanwhile, feeling that the walls were closing in on him, Jake made plans to run away with Donna, but Storm persuaded them to stay in Los Angeles.

Margo and Jake arrived in Wisconsin just as Helen and Ben were about to have a memorial service for their presumed-dead son. Both Helen and Ben were thrilled that Jake was alive. But Jake tried to strangle his father after Ben denied ever abusing him.

Taylor advised Jake to confront Ben again. Jake revealed to his mother what Ben had done. Helen left town to process the news. Ben had a heart attack and phoned his brother Charlie for help. Charlie phoned Margo and Helen to let them know about Ben. Taylor urged Jake to resolve the abuse issue with Ben before he died. Jake stated that he wasn't going to let his past ruin his future. He asked Felicia to hang in there with him, and she agreed to his request.

During Ben's illness, Charlie moved into the Maclaine house. Helen commented that Charlie's presence reminded her of when Charlie used to live with them. Ben changed the subject by quizzing Helen about Jake's accusations of sexual abuse and asked if she truly believed in Ben's innocence. Although Helen reassured her husband that she had faith in his innocence, she had doubts, which she didn't share with him.

MACY/THORNE/DONNA

After his divorce from Caroline, Thorne played the field, dating both Macy and Donna. Macy, who was looking for love after Mick dumped her, kept her background as Sally Spectra's daughter a secret, fearing that if Thorne found out, he'd end their romance.

Donna and Macy were pals, but neither told the other the name of her new beau. Socialite Betty Burns asked Sally to preside over the next fund-raiser. Matchmaking Sally suggested to Betty that Thorne and Macy run the event.

Thorne and Macy put together a variety show. Darla, as Marilyn Monroe, sang "Diamonds Are a Girl's Best Friend." Sally slid into a duet of "Let's Call the Whole Thing Off" with Eric. Macy, who told Donna that she'd be singing with her boyfriend, performed "What's Forever For" with Thorne. A stunned Donna couldn't believe that she and Macy had both fallen for Thorne. Thorne ended his relationship with Donna. Stephanie liked Macy, but wondered about her past.

Bill hired photographer Tommy Bayland to take pictures of Sally's private wedding to Clarke for one of his magazines. Macy was caught in the photos. Thorne asked Macy to marry him. She joyfully accepted, but after Stephanie and Eric showed an incredulous Thorne a magazine picture from Sally's wedding that identified Macy as Sally's daughter, Thorne broke off the engagement. Soon after, Thorne and Macy reunited.

Eric, Stephanie, and Ridge told Thorne they couldn't attend the wedding because of Sally. But Felicia said she would. Sally got wind of the Forresters' reservations and, disguised as a man, visited Thorne at his office. Sally panicked when she heard Stephanie's voice and ducked into a nearby office. Unfortunately, the room happened to be Eric's office, which contained the designs for their upcoming fashion show. Stephanie caught Sally and had her arrested. Sally hired Storm to defend her.

Despite the family strife, Thorne and Macy got married on October 23, Macy's birthday. They sang "Here and Now" as part of the ceremony. Ridge showed up at the last minute to be Thorne's best man. The rest of the Forresters came, too. At Thorne's request, Stephanie withdrew the charges against Sally.

Macy and Thorne happily shared their first Christmas alone and away from their warring families.

Darla chipped in to help Thorne and Macy out with their variety show fund-raiser by impersonating screen legend Marilyn Monroe and performing a rendition of "Diamonds Are a Girl's Best Friend."

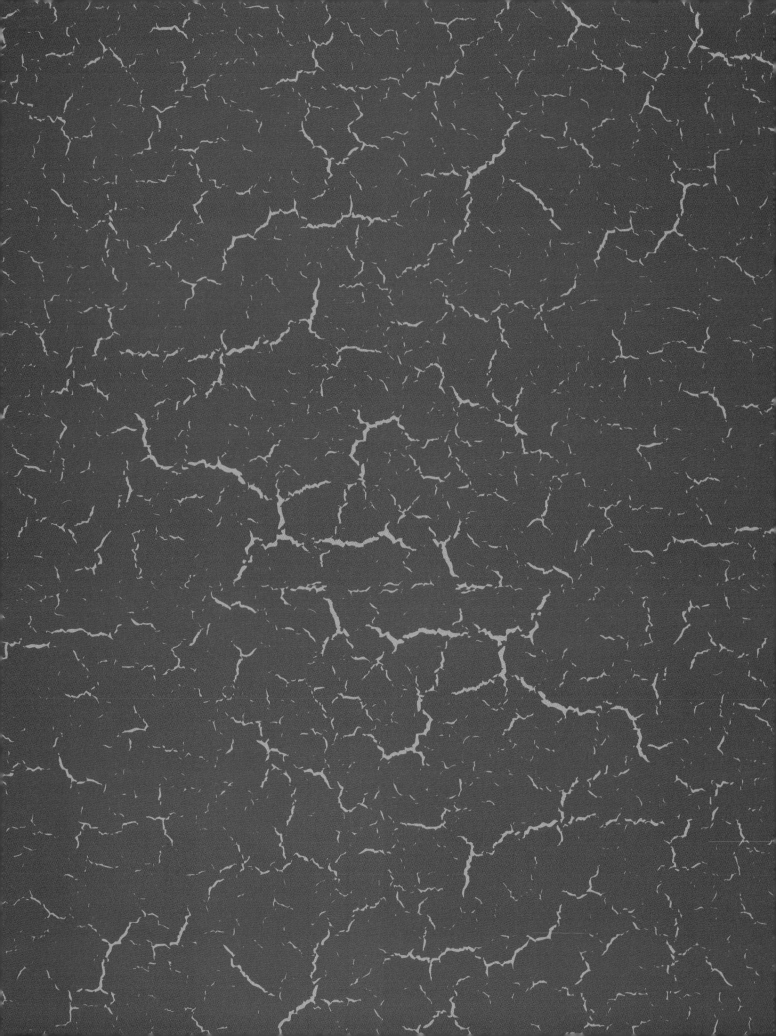

Season Five

Fifth season cast photo. Back row, from left to right: Rod Loomis (Adam), Jeff Trachta (Thorne), Peter Brown (Blake), Michael Fox (Saul), Schae Harrison (Darla), Robert Clary (Pierre), Todd McKee (Jake). Middle row, from left to right: Michele Davison (Ruthanne), Bobbie Eakes (Macy), Hunter Tylo (Taylor), Colleen Dion (Felicia), Jane Rogers (Julie), Darlene Conley (Sally), Dan McVicar (Clarke). Front row, from left to right: Lauren Koslow (Margo), Ronn Moss (Ridge), Susan Flannery (Stephanie), John McCook (Eric), and Katherine Kelly Lang (Brooke).

STEPHANIE/ERIC/BROOKE/RIDGE/TAYLOR

Forrester family and friends prepared for Brooke and Eric's wedding. Stephanie and Margo were sad to be losing Eric. However, Brooke agreed to let Stephanie attend the ceremony.

Eric and Brooke exchanged vows in Palm Springs, California. Bill, Margo, Donna, Katie, Storm, Felicia, Stephanie, Thorne, and Macy all attended. But Thorne took ill just before the ceremony, so Ridge stepped in as best man.

As Brooke prepared to walk down the aisle, she fantasized that Ridge asked her to elope. A dreamy Brooke accepted and she and Ridge exchanged vows. But she came out of her reverie and wed Eric after exchanging a last glance with Ridge.

Eric and Brooke took off in a hot air balloon and spent a romantic honeymoon in the desert. They rode horses to a beautiful oasis that included an Arabian Nights–style tent that Eric had prepared.

Back in Los Angeles, Taylor advised Stephanie that befriending Eric and Brooke was unhealthy. But Stephanie couldn't let go of her faith that someday she and Eric would reunite.

Stephanie prepared to go on a trip, but while she was packing, she had a minor stroke that caused her to forget who she was—and to leave her purse behind with all of her money and identification when she set out. Unfortunately, Stephanie's car broke down and she was stranded in a dangerous section of Los Angeles. Some homeless people attacked Stephanie and stole her jewelry—except her wedding ring. Stephanie was befriended by two homeless individuals, Ruthanne Owens and Adam Banks, who helped her survive a brutal existence living on Los Angeles's mean streets. Stephanie told Ruthanne that she didn't know her own name. Yet Stephanie showed recognition when Ruthanne happened to mention the name "Liz" (perhaps because Stephanie's rival was Beth Logan, aka Liz Henderson). During her harsh time on the streets, Stephanie went by the alias "Liz."

While homeless, Stephanie used hotel bathrooms to clean herself and ate discarded scraps from garbage cans for sustenance. Ruthanne told her pal that she wasn't always so destitute. But hard times fell on Ruthanne, a college graduate. She was divorced, laid off, and subsequently evicted from her apartment. Ruthanne lived in her car until it was stolen.

Stephanie pricked her finger while handling a rose and found that the word "thorn" resonated with unexplained meaning for her. Meanwhile, Ridge and Thorne, after initially disregarding Maria's (the family housekeeper) concerns, finally acknowledged that their mother was missing.

Sally spied Stephanie when she and Ruthanne were rummaging through a trash bin outside of Spectra. Even though the Forresters knew their matriarch was unaccounted for, they dismissed Sally's concerns. The Forrester clan was infuriated when Sally distributed a flyer with a picture of the missing Stephanie.

In poignant contrast to the current bleakness of Stephanie's life, Adam took her on a date. During their date, Adam revealed that he had once been an English teacher before eventually hitting hard times. After exchanging a tender look, he and Stephanie kissed. Later, Ruthanne and Stephanie were forced out of their abandoned hotel by a thug. The two women slept on the street in a cardboard box.

Adam found one of Sally's flyers and sent a resistant Stephanie home in a cab. A confused Stephanie arrived at the mansion and was warmly greeted by her family, none of whom she remembered.

Brooke became upset by Eric's concern for his ex-wife. She decided to take a break in the Forrester steam room. However, the break was anything but relaxing. She became further agitated when Ridge, who was once again back to his nefarious pranks, entered the steam room naked and pretended to be Eric. Brooke angrily left before anything happened.

One night, while Eric was helping Stephanie regain her memory, Ridge took Brooke dancing at Pierre's. Taylor, along with her ex-husband, Blake (who, unknown to Taylor, was still suffering from a medical condition that caused violent outbursts), spied the couple having a wonderful time. Meanwhile, a skeptical Brooke suspected that Stephanie's memory loss was a ploy to win back Eric's affections.

Stephanie did regain her memory but pretended not to remember so that she could effectively manipulate her family and foes. First Stephanie befriended Brooke. Then Stephanie feigned disgust when Eric revealed her underhanded participation in having the Logans transferred to Paris.

Meanwhile, Stephanie's circle of skeptics continued to grow. Bill, after unsuccessfully trying to convince Stephanie that they had been lovers, also suspected that Stephanie had regained her memory. As Stephanie continued to play her memory loss to the hilt, she focused her attention on exposing Brooke's marriage to Eric as a sham. Stephanie's scheme included hiring Ken, a private eye, to install hidden video cameras inside the lab where Brooke worked at Forrester Creations. A determined Stephanie hoped to catch Brooke in the arms of another man.

Meanwhile, Ridge and Taylor began to see each other more seriously, especially after he advised her against marrying Storm. After Taylor dumped Storm, the lawyer decked Ridge and took a job at a law firm in San Francisco. Donna went with him when she discovered that a job offer from Bill had more to do with romance than journalism.

Ridge enjoyed Taylor's availability but told her he wasn't ready for marriage. While dating one night Blake and Taylor were spotted by Ridge and Brooke, who were having a platonic dinner. Jealous at seeing Blake and Taylor kiss, Ridge kissed his stepmother, Brooke—just as Eric showed up with Stephanie. Ridge and Brooke tried to explain they were just trying to annoy Taylor, but Eric wasn't convinced.

Eventually, Brooke and Ridge realized that their time together was only going to make Eric jealous, so they agreed not to see each other. They soon realized that wasn't very practical, especially since Eric insisted that Ridge work with Brooke on developing a formula that would make fabric wrinkle-free.

Stephanie confided in Adam that she had recovered her memory. Ironically, Brooke's suspicion that Stephanie was faking her memory loss to win back Eric was lessened after Brooke spied Adam giving Stephanie a kiss.

Ruthanne passed on Stephanie's generous offer to move into the mansion. Soon after, Stephanie enlisted Eric's help in reuniting Ruthanne with her ex-husband and children. Eric located Ruthanne's ex-husband, Mitch Owens, and their children, Jason and Yvette. Stephanie and Eric visited Mitch and clued him in on Ruthanne's misfortune. After seeing the rundown hotel where Ruthanne lived, Mitch reached out to his ex-wife and the Owens family reunited.

Stephanie told Ridge she had regained her memory but felt she needed to continue her charade because she believed Eric was falling in love with her.

Ridge proposed to Taylor, but she turned him down after deducing that he had only popped the question to make himself unavailable to his stepmother. Still, Ridge presented Taylor with an engagement ring. Taylor was furious when Ridge told Eric they were definitely getting married. Taylor called off the so-called "engagement."

At Eric's birthday party, Brooke learned from Stephanie that Taylor and Ridge might not be getting married. Brooke comforted Ridge on the anniversary of Caroline's death. Brooke admitted to Ridge that she didn't want him with any other woman. After acknowledging that her memory had returned, Stephanie urged Brooke to pursue Ridge. But Stephanie was crushed after Eric thanked her for helping him become closer than ever to Brooke.

Later, Brooke, with Ridge's supervision, was successful in creating a miracle formula that would make fabric wrinkle-free. They celebrated by making love on the lab floor, unaware that their betrayal was being captured on Ken's hidden cameras. Ken gave Stephanie the tapes.

Hoping to reunite the Forrester matriarch and patriarch, Ridge and Brooke jumped at Eric's idea that Stephanie return to work at Forrester Creations. Taylor deduced that Ridge wanted his parents back together so that Brooke would be free for him.

Ridge felt guilty about making love to his father's wife, but his guilt was assuaged when Brooke told him that Eric knew she was torn over whom to be with before their marriage. Ridge grew bitter toward his dad.

While Eric was on a business trip to Europe, Stephanie had a handwriting expert write a phony note from "Eric" to her proclaiming his love for Stephanie and his desire to divorce Brooke. Stephanie showed Ridge the letter. An incredulous yet overjoyed Ridge told Brooke and the two went off to make

Eric and Brooke's marriage lasted a short six months before he realized that she'd fallen in love with Ridge again. Here, Stephanie implores Brooke to divorce Eric and go to Ridge so that Eric would become available for her.

love at the Forresters' Big Bear cabin. Meanwhile, Stephanie hid an authentic letter from Eric to Brooke that professed his commitment to their marriage.

Eric was hurt in a car accident on his way home from the airport. Brooke visited him at the hospital and couldn't believe Eric made no mention of wanting a divorce. Stephanie admitted to Ridge and Brooke that the note was fake. But Ridge and Brooke had made a commitment to their future, so Brooke told Eric that she was in love with Ridge. Eric trembled at the thought of losing his beloved wife. A furious Eric ordered Ridge not to talk about Brooke in his presence.

A stunned Stephanie couldn't believe Eric's unwillingness to divorce Brooke. Meanwhile, Eric resumed his role at work and conducted business as if everything was okay in his life. Eventually Eric told Brooke that if she lived with him for two months, he would give her a divorce. Ridge didn't like the plan, but Brooke assured Ridge it wouldn't be forever.

A determined Eric made the most of his two-month arrangement to win back Brooke. Ridge confided in Taylor that he wasn't sure if he could ever love anyone the way he had loved his late wife, Caroline. Meanwhile, Brooke tried to make Eric's life unpleasant. Still, Ridge informed Brooke that as long as she played Eric's wife, he would play the field. Ridge made love to Taylor. Was Brooke's plan to live with Eric for two months going to cost her a lifetime of happiness with Ridge?

BILL/JULIE/CLARKE/FELICIA

Felicia contractually agreed to design for Spectra Fashions after Sally promised the ambitious young Forrester her own label. Once she signed the contracts, Felicia was devastated to learn that her father was planning to offer her the same deal. Eric was hurt by Felicia's defection.

Neither Storm's legal expertise nor Eric's generous offer of $250,000 to Sally could free Felicia from her ironclad deal with Spectra Fashions. Macy's relationship with the Forresters, especially with Thorne, began to suffer because of Sally hanging on to Felicia. Felicia purposely designed some awful sketches hoping Sally would fire her, but her strategy backfired. To Felicia's dismay, Sally produced Felicia's dreadful designs!

Once Felicia realized that Sally was going ahead with the fashion show, Felicia changed the music that accompanied the fashion presentation, and substituted it with music that had a harder edge. Surprisingly, the fashion press applauded Ms. Forrester's offbeat style.

Meanwhile, Clarke tried to back away from his union with Julie, but she wouldn't hear of it. Julie confessed to Bill that she had been in a relationship with Clarke. Bill, surprisingly, supported the affair. Julie wormed her way into Sally's confidence by telling her that she wanted to write a book on Clarke and Sally.

Clarke conned Darla and Saul into believing that he was through with Julie. Meanwhile, Julie submitted the completed manuscript of her tell-all book about Clarke to Bill, which he decided to publish without Clarke's knowledge.

Clarke was furious to discover that Sally was pregnant. Sally let Clarke believe that she went through with his command to have an abortion. Meanwhile, Julie was furious to learn that Clarke had slept with Sally. Clarke calmed his lover by swearing he'd never do it again. Julie held off publishing the book, but Bill sent a copy of the manuscript detailing Clarke's misdeeds to Sally, who started to read it but stopped before realizing that the lead character was her husband.

Clarke learned that Bill was interested in Julie, so he asked her to go away to Hawaii with him. Julie agreed. An unsuspecting Sally flew to Hawaii to inform Clarke that he had won a design award. Sally was shocked to discover a nude Julie on the balcony next to Clarke's. Sally thought Bill was with Julie but then learned she was with Clarke.

A betrayed Sally returned home and had Clarke's name removed from her building. Sally had Clarke's office trashed and fired him. Julie tried to crash Sally's next fashion show. Sally grabbed Julie and had her thrown out, but not before Julie overheard that Sally was still pregnant. Clarke showed up uninvited, too. However, an empowered Sally realized that she no longer needed him. Felicia was now designing for her successfully.

When a reporter grilled Clarke about why his name was no longer on Sally's building, Clarke lied and claimed the Santa Ana winds blew it down. Clarke tried to get some money from Sally, but Sally reminded Clarke that their prenuptial agreement stipulated that they had to be married for two years before he'd acquire any assets.

Neither Eric nor Bill was interested in hiring Clarke. Julie lost interest in Clarke after he turned down a lucrative deal to work for another designer. Bill did have one offer for Clarke. He'd give him $100,000 if Clarke gave up his parental rights of Mark. Clarke flatly refused.

A pregnant Sally tripped over the spilled contents of Darla's purse. Sally recovered without injury, but Darla felt guilty. Saul offered to wed Sally, but she gently told him that they should remain just pals. Meanwhile, Julie told Clarke that Sally was still pregnant.

Clarke wormed his way back into Spectra after Felicia's next fashion line failed. Taylor, as his therapist, pointed out to Clarke that his marriage must have had some good points since he was so creative during his time with Sally. Clarke tried to con Sally into a reunion, but she held firm about the divorce.

Later, though, Sally told Clarke that she was still expecting. Clarke feigned surprise and delight. Clarke and Sally bonded during childbirth classes. Clarke, with Sally present, broke off his relationship with Julie by telephone.

Clarke stood by Sally as she gave birth to their son, Clarke Jr. A spiteful Julie tipped Macy off to the fact that Clarke knew about Sally's pregnancy for months. Macy told her mom, but later Julie back-pedaled and "confessed" to Macy that she lied about Clarke knowing that Sally was still pregnant.

Sally assembled her staff and told them that Clarke would save Spectra Fashions from the near-financial ruin they faced, thanks to Felicia's failed line of fashions. Clarke informed a disappointed Felicia that he was Spectra's top designer.

Spectra's money woes appeared to be over after an envelope containing the Forresters' innovative formula was delivered to Sally. Clarke told Sally that while he had the means to steal the profit-making invention, he didn't do it. Who did steal it? Was it Jake? Macy? Or was Clarke lying?

FELICIA/JAKE/MACY/THORNE

Jake couldn't believe that his father, who had taught him so much, could also have sexually abused him. One sound Jake could not force from his mind was a haunting, clinking noise. He had heard it each night as his father entered his room to molest him. Jake, along with Margo, returned to Wisconsin, where his father was recovering. Jake fell ill because he was staying in the same room where the abuse had occurred. Uncle Charlie entered Jake's room to bring his nephew some juice. Just then, Jake heard the clinking sound. The noise was being caused by Charlie's military dog tags. Jake realized that his Uncle Charlie had been his abuser, not his father.

Jake snuck out of his family's home and confronted Charlie at his house. Charlie knocked Jake out and tied and gagged his nephew. Charlie told Jake that he couldn't live to expose him, so Charlie dragged Jake to the exhaust pipe of his truck and started the engine. Margo, having deduced that Charlie could have been Jake's molester, went to Charlie's house and rescued her brother. Before they could turn Charlie in to the police, Charlie shot himself to death.

Jake and Felicia share a happy moment around the holidays. However, Jake's involvement with Felicia's sister-in-law Macy eventually led to the couple's breakup.

After Charlie's burial, Jake and Ben reunited. The Maclaine family was finally able to begin the healing process. Jake briefly got back together with Felicia, but then told her he needed to see other women. Shortly after Macy and Thorne's separation, Jake hit it off with the depressed Macy over a tennis lesson. After a subsequent tennis lesson, the couple made love. Soon Felicia and Thorne arranged a double date so they could tell their respective loved ones that it was time for new beginnings. Still, Macy and Jake continued to see each other. Sally encouraged her daughter to go after her new guy and forget Thorne. But Macy told Jake she wanted to stay committed to her husband. Thorne knew there was another man, but Macy wouldn't reveal Jake's identity.

Jake dated Felicia, yet he carried a torch for Macy. As Spectra's newest designer, Felicia found inspiration by being with Jake. Just before Felicia's first fashion show, she spied a beautiful necklace in Jake's apartment. Assuming it was for her, Felicia was devastated to see Macy wearing the necklace at the fashion show. Felicia ordered Macy to tell Thorne about Jake, or else she would expose the truth. However, Jake convinced Macy to remain silent. Macy found herself backed in a corner when Felicia ordered Macy to end her affair with Jake.

Macy worked at her marriage, but when Forrester business kept Thorne from home, Macy found solace with Jake and also from alcohol. Later, Macy ended her affair with Jake. Felicia was delighted to learn that Jake had arranged for Macy to spend time with Thorne. Felicia let Jake know that although she was a little guarded, she really wanted them to be together. Meanwhile, Macy admitted to Thorne that she had a lover, whom she still encountered.

Jake accepted Eric's job offer at Forrester before he realized that it would mean working for Thorne. When Felicia spied Macy and Jake kissing, she told Thorne about Macy's affair. Thorne decked Jake after the tennis bum admitted to the adulterous liaison. Macy came upon Jake in his apartment and couldn't believe what Thorne had done.

BLAKE/MARGO/BILL

Margo's marriage to Bill was falling apart. Bill blasted his wife for keeping him in the dark about her family problems. Jake confronted Bill over his shabby treatment of his sister, but Bill didn't sympathize with him over the abuse he had suffered at Charlie's hands. Margo remained in her miserable marriage to Bill only because Mark needed a father.

Blake, having hit a roadblock in his pursuit of Taylor, ran into Margo at the Taxi Bar. Margo was intrigued by the handsome stranger. When Blake learned that Margo worked at Forrester, he pumped her for information about Ridge.

Blake fell for Margo but couldn't let go of Taylor. He rented the apartment across the street from Taylor and kept tabs on her with binoculars. Unaware that he was spying on her, Taylor was grateful for Blake's moral support, especially since Ridge was still in love with Brooke. Taylor and Blake made love after he claimed he hadn't had any violent attacks in years. Taylor gave Blake a key to her apartment. But later Blake suffered a panic attack after he called Taylor's apartment and Ridge answered the phone.

After Sally blabbed to Margo about Bill having an affair with Julie, Margo wanted out of her marriage with Bill. When Bill saw Blake giving Margo a supportive embrace, Margo teased Bill that she and Blake were lovers. Bill started to give Margo more attention.

After learning that Stephanie had videotaped Ridge and Brooke making love, Blake snagged the cassette and showed it to Taylor. Taylor was

furious with Blake until Stephanie confessed that she, not Blake, had the tape made. Still, Blake suggested to Taylor that they go their separate ways after he proposed to Margo and he noted that Taylor was in love with Ridge.

However, when Blake spied through his window that Taylor was being attacked by a former patient, he sped to her rescue and chased the intruder away. Blake told Taylor he couldn't always be with her unless she could give him a commitment. Taylor couldn't.

Ridge, Taylor, and Blake. Ridge found competition for Taylor in the form of her ex-husband, Blake Hayes, a wealthy oil tycoon. Blake rented the apartment across the street from Taylor so that he could keep tabs on her comings and goings.

Bill walked in on Margo and Blake kissing. After Bill made a few insulting remarks to his wife, a berserk Blake attacked Bill. A worried Margo started to have second thoughts. Soon she and Blake mutually agreed to end their romance after realizing that Bill and Taylor were still very much a part of their respective lives.

Blake spied Taylor having dinner with Ridge at Pierre's. When Ridge went to get the car, he was jumped from behind and brutally beaten. Taylor accompanied Ridge to the hospital, where she reminded a concerned Brooke that she was Eric's wife—not Ridge's. Brooke retaliated by confirming to Blake that Taylor was on a date with Ridge on the night of the attack. Margo asked Taylor if Blake could have beaten Ridge. Taylor responded that it was a possibility she hadn't considered.

FAITH

Realizing he wouldn't have a future with either Taylor or Margo, Blake decided to leave town. As he said good-bye to Margo, Blake learned that Bill's deceased daughter Caroline had an identical twin named Karen who had been kidnapped as an infant.

Blake left Los Angeles and coincidentally landed in Starlight, Texas, and came upon Karen Spencer, who was going by the name Faith Roberts. Faith worked as a waitress and lived with her "mother," Bonnie. Blake befriended Faith, hoping that she would ultimately be the key to his winning back Taylor.

KAREN SPENCER

Joanna Johnson left her role as Caroline on *The Bold and the Beautiful* in 1990, intent on trying her hand at film writing and directing. Although Joanna did write two screenplays, including one entitled *Sister Sarah*, which explored the friendship between a deeply religious girl and a rebellious teenager from the punk scene, Joanna had trouble getting a foothold in the film industry.

A year and a half after Joanna departed from *The Bold and the Beautiful*, the opportunity arose for her to return. But this time around she'd be playing a different character, since Caroline had died. In the storyline, it was revealed that Caroline had a twin sister, Karen, who, as an infant, was kidnapped from the Spencer nursery. Karen ultimately ended up in the care of Bonnie, a protective and impoverished country-woman, who renamed her Faith.

Joanna looked forward to returning to *The Bold and the Beautiful*, particularly because of her admiration for Bill Bell and the positive working relationship she shared with Ronn Moss in their storyline together. "Ronn and I had a good time working together,"

Joanna Johnson

she says. "He's extraordinarily professional and generous. He has an enormous amount of class. Working with him was always a joy."

Returning to *The Bold and the Beautiful* presented Joanna with several significant challenges. For starters, there was the memory of her emotional portrayal as the vulnerable Caroline, a character viewers continued to miss. "People used to ask what the differences were between myself and Caroline," says Joanna. "I'd tell them, 'I'm not as innocent as Caroline.'" But after leaving *The Bold and the Beautiful*, Joanna realized that Caroline made an impact on her life. "I think I do have an innocence," she concedes. "I don't know if it's an innocence or a certain optimism. But Caroline certainly brought out that aspect of my personality. She was innocent, and that was how I played her." Meanwhile, Joanna, who dyed her hair brown to play Karen, looked forward to the challenges of playing a character with a rougher edge, who hadn't gotten the same breaks in life as her sister, Caroline.

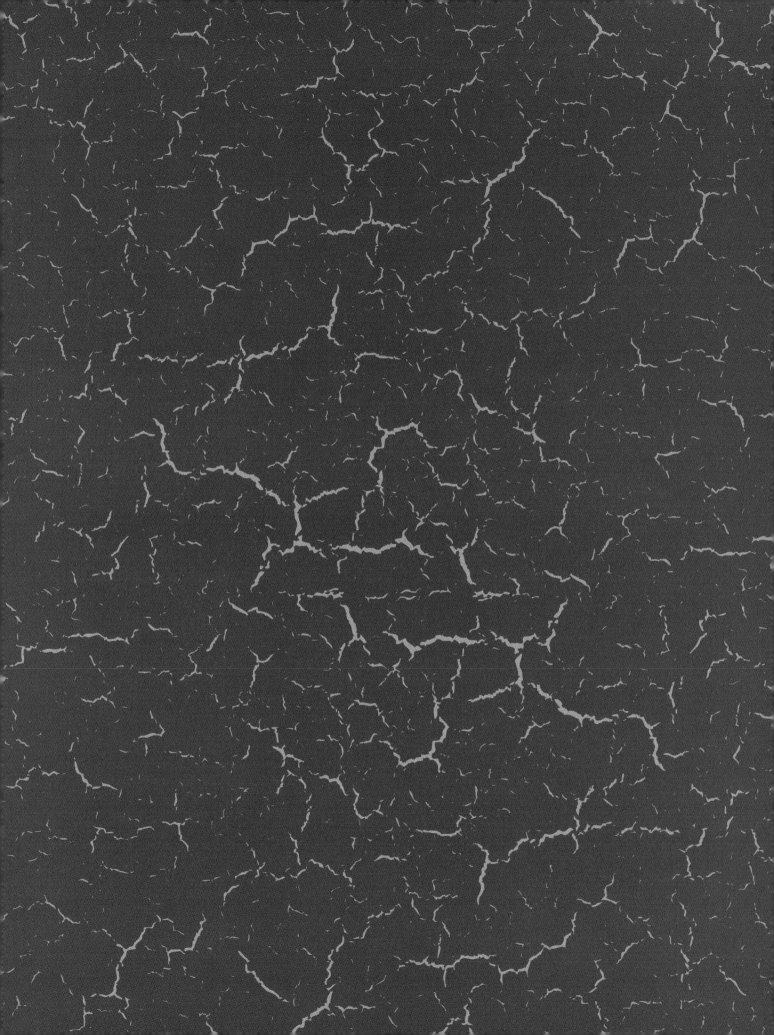

Season Six

TAYLOR/RIDGE/BROOKE/ERIC/STEPHANIE

Brooke continued to make herself unappealing to Eric by breaking an expensive vase. Eric laughed when he realized Brooke's plan.

Ridge received an anonymous letter from a man who claimed responsibility for Ridge's beating. The mystery man told Ridge he mistook him for a man with whom his wife was having an affair. Ridge accepted the letter at face value and had no reason to believe his attacker was Blake.

At the end of their two-month trial period, Eric and Brooke shared a romantic dinner and said farewell. Brooke promised Eric he could see Eric Jr. whenever he wanted. Brooke and Ridge decided to postpone living together in order to give Eric Jr. time to adjust to the separation.

Eric named the anti-wrinkle formula BeLieF after Brooke's initials—Brooke Logan Forrester. Brooke told Eric that she enjoyed the limelight as BeLieF's creator.

Taylor advised Eric to spend more time with Eric Jr., since the boy was having trouble adjusting to the separation. Brooke accused Taylor of giving the advice so Ridge would be more available. Ridge was not pleased to learn that Brooke withheld from him the fact that Eric had moved in again with her and Eric Jr.

One night, Eric saw a bookcase about to crash down on Eric Jr. The senior Forrester pushed his son out of the way but took the impact. Eric was blinded. Ridge grew uneasy after noticing Brooke's attentiveness to Eric. Still, Ridge and Brooke continued to make love. Eric confided in Ridge his fear that once his eyesight returned he would lose Brooke. Eric's vision returned, but he kept it a secret, until Sally saw Eric catch a falling vase. But Ridge had already decided to step aside. Ridge let Brooke "discover" him in bed with Heather, an old girlfriend. Heather later admitted to Brooke that Ridge had lied for Eric's benefit.

Taylor needed to get away by herself to sort out her conflicting feelings for Ridge. She headed for St. Thomas and was furious upon discovering that Ridge had followed her. Still, a charming Ridge romanced Taylor and proposed marriage. She accepted.

Back in the States, Brooke confronted Ridge over his scheme with Heather. Brooke was shattered to learn of Ridge and Taylor's engagement. Taylor's father, Jack, flew in for the wedding.

Brooke danced with Ridge to their song, "Unforgettable," but the next day he wed Taylor. That same day Brooke learned she was pregnant. Brooke raced to the chapel, but she was too late. Stephanie tried to throw Brooke out

ABOVE: *Brooke and Ridge announce the creation of BeLieF at a press conference.*

OPPOSITE: *A Forrester family portrait. Clockwise from top right: Eric, Kristen, Ridge, Felicia, Thorne, and Stephanie.*

of the reception, but Brooke informed her she was pregnant. After Ridge and Taylor's honeymoon, Brooke gleefully told Ridge that he was going to be a dad. Brooke was crushed when Ridge asked that the baby be subjected to a paternity test since, he bluntly pointed out, Brooke had also slept with Eric.

Taylor blasted Brooke for getting pregnant. Thinking Ridge didn't love her, a devastated Brooke decided to leave town. But she mysteriously collapsed before she could depart. Stephanie came upon Brooke just before Sheila, Forrester Creations' new nurse, could inject an unknown serum into her veins. After being released from the hospital, Brooke changed her mind about leaving.

Brooke decided not to chase Ridge anymore. She felt that he'd come back to her on his own. One night, though, Brooke dropped by Ridge's house only to see him and Taylor kissing. Brooke lied, stating she only wanted to talk business, but Taylor viewed Brooke's obsession with Ridge as a mental disorder.

TOP: *Eric pushed Eric Jr. away from a falling bookcase and took the impact himself. Here, Ridge checks on his unconscious father.*

ABOVE: *Ridge followed Taylor to romantic St. Thomas, where he proposed marriage.*

Ridge entertained the notion of taking Brooke on a tour of Europe to promote BeLieF. Taylor asked Ridge not to go but in the end supported his decision. While Ridge was away, she confided to Stephanie her fears that he would leave her for Brooke. Stephanie had become fond of her new daughter-in-law.

Ridge returned home early without Brooke to tell Taylor that several investors wanted to fund an international branch of Forrester Creations. Taylor reluctantly agreed to let Ridge move to Europe, but Ridge decided his marriage was more important. Brooke returned home as her due date was approaching. Ridge was shocked when Brooke announced that she still loved him. Unhappy with Ridge's reaction, Brooke rushed off to the Forrester cabin in Big Bear. Ridge arrived just as Brooke was going into labor. Ridge acted as midwife, as Taylor, via telephone, guided him through the delivery. Brooke gave birth to a baby girl.

FELICIA/JAKE/MACY/THORNE

Jake landed a position at Forrester Creations. But the job didn't last long. Thorne fired Jake for sleeping with Macy. Meanwhile, Felicia found a letter from Forrester Creations among Macy's mail and deduced that Spectra was indeed stealing from her family's company. Felicia showed Eric the contents of the envelope, which contained a copy of the BeLieF formula. Sally believed in her daughter's innocence but decided to cancel their plans to market BeLieF in order to save her daughter's marriage. Sensing her marriage was over, Macy moved in with Jake, now a platonic friend.

Clarke was happy to learn that Sally's plan to slash Spectra's prices was working but was dissatisfied to hear that Sally wanted to resume their sexual relationship.

A steamed Sally confronted Stephanie over remarks she made about Spectra's inferior products in a fashion publication. Sally lunged at Stephanie but ended up falling into the Forrester pool.

Clarke suggested Sally get revenge against Stephanie by shipping out BeLieF-treated dresses that Spectra had made. Sally insisted that those gowns be destroyed, but it was too late. The outfits were somehow already distributed.

Eric had Lt. Burke arrest Macy for stealing the formula. Thorne posted bail, but Macy went home to Jake. Lt. Burke suspected that Clarke was the culprit. Clarke decked Jake after he suggested that Clarke stole BeLieF.

Thorne realized that he had left his keys in the lock of his file cabinet the night the BeLieF formula and the note that Macy had sent Thorne, professing her love for him, were stolen. Jake realized that he'd never win Macy's heart and confessed to stealing BeLieF. The charges against Macy were dropped. Jake denied to Macy that he was just protecting her by taking the blame.

Margo, however, knew that Jake was lying. As a favor to Margo, Eric refused to prosecute Jake. Jake told Margo that he didn't take BeLieF. Margo returned to Wisconsin with Jake after she ended her loveless union with Bill.

Clarke feigned impotence to avoid having sex with Sally. Macy got Darla to come on to Clarke, but, sensing he was being set up, Clarke resisted Darla's advances. One woman Clarke couldn't get out of his mind was his ex-wife, Kristen, who had come home for Ridge and Taylor's wedding. The only way Clarke could make love to Sally was by fantasizing she was Kristen.

Darla overheard Clarke plot to leave Sally after their second anniversary when he received half-ownership of Spectra, per their premarital agreement. Sally ordered her lawyer to nullify the deal, but the attorney said that could be done only if Clarke were unfaithful. The Spectra gang set all of Clarke's clocks ahead on the day the deal was scheduled to close. When Clarke thought that he had reached the five o'clock deadline giving him half-ownership of Spectra, he made love to Kristen. Sally and Saul burst in the door videotaping Clarke's infidelity. Kristen left Clarke.

Sally realized that Spectra was lost without Clarke as its designer. She agreed to let him come back, but Clarke had a list of requirements, to which Sally agreed. However, when Clarke ordered Sally to change her son's name, Sally torched his contract and had security throw him out of the building.

BLAKE/FAITH/RIDGE

Bonnie couldn't believe that Blake knew Faith's true identity. Bonnie confessed that "friends" of hers kidnapped infant Karen Spencer. Fearing for Karen's safety, Bonnie took her away and raised the infant as her own. Faith was devastated to learn her true origin. Blake told Faith about her twin, Caroline, and her brother-in-law, Ridge Forrester. Faith bid her mother a teary good-bye and left for Los Angeles with Blake.

Blake's plan was to transform Faith into the image of Caroline, hoping that Ridge would fall in love with her and forget Taylor. Faith, though, had fallen for Blake.

Blake took Faith to Pierre's, where they saw Taylor having dinner with a handsome man. Blake informed Faith that Taylor's date was Ridge, her brother-in-law.

Blake received an invitation to a masquerade charity ball at Stephanie's mansion. Knowing Ridge would be there, Blake had a voice teacher coach Faith on how to lose her Texas accent. At the gala, Ridge kissed the hand of a masked Faith. Blake whisked Faith away before masks were removed.

The Spectra gang gathered at the Taxi Bar to celebrate Darla's birthday. Faith, who was dining at the Taxi that evening, was accidentally captured in a Spectra group photograph. Sally was amazed at the girl's resemblance to Caroline. Blake was thrilled to hear that Faith had fallen for Ridge. Blake urged Faith to use her birth name, Karen Spencer. He also hired a stylist to dye Karen's hair to match Caroline's color.

Karen, now the image of Caroline, visited her father. Bill was stunned. After he compared Karen's fingerprints to those taken from his daughter's crib, Bill realized his daughter had finally come home.

Next, Karen saw Ridge, who couldn't believe he was looking at his dead wife's twin. Bill confirmed Karen's identity to Ridge. Ridge accepted Karen into his life as a friend.

BLAKE/KAREN/THORNE/MACY/SLY

As Blake's obsession with Taylor grew out of control, he ordered Karen to remain in her room while he figured out how to break up Ridge and Taylor. Karen phoned Bill for help. Blake gagged Karen and tied her to a chair before she could escape.

Thorne accompanied Bill and they rescued Karen. Thorne, who had never met Karen, was amazed at how much she looked like Caroline. Macy felt threatened when she saw how protective Thorne was of Karen. Later, Karen met privately with Taylor to discuss how she felt incapable of living up to Caroline's image. Blake eventually threw in the towel and moved back to Texas.

Thorne fell in love with Karen. He asked her to move in on the same evening that Macy announced she wanted a reconciliation. The trio agreed to all live together, since there were three bedrooms in his apartment.

Macy and Karen each tried to get Thorne to choose between them, but Thorne admitted he cared for both of them. Macy made inroads with Thorne by getting him to join her in a duet at the Bikini Bar.

After Karen's and Macy's competitiveness had reduced them to the point of having a food fight, they ordered Thorne to choose. Thorne decided on Macy, but on his way to tell her, Thorne spotted Macy giving an innocent farewell hug to a visiting Jake. Thorne assumed that Macy had been seeing Jake and therefore told Karen that he'd be staying with her. Macy was devastated.

Karen learned from Ridge that Thorne had always been fond of Christmas. That Christmas, Karen turned their home into a winter wonderland, filled with holiday decorations. Karen gave up her virginity and made love with Thorne. Meanwhile, Macy cried on Sly's shoulder at the Bikini Bar. Sly sent an anonymous note to Macy, requesting a New Year's Eve date. But an excited Macy assumed the letter was from Thorne. When Macy discovered Sly wrote the letter, she chastised him for lying his way into her life.

ZACH/FELICIA/SLY

Jack Hamilton came to Los Angeles for his daughter Taylor's wedding. Stephanie showed some romantic interest in Jack, unaware that Jack had taken a job as Spectra's accountant. Jack and Stephanie began dating. Jack also gave Sally moral support now that Clarke was out of her life.

Meanwhile, Felicia met Taylor's estranged brother, Zach, and his buddy, Sly, while at a bar. Zach, who didn't tell Felicia who he was, allowed himself to be hit by Felicia's car so that he could get closer to her. Stephanie advised her daughter to get a lawyer in case Zach tried to sue, but instead Felicia convinced Zach to recuperate at the mansion.

Zach took a job managing the Bikini Bar, where he originally met Felicia. Taylor deduced that Felicia was dating Zach after Taylor saw the young Forrester wearing her mother's earrings.

Felicia and Zach made love. Zach confessed to Felicia that he had killed a man to avenge his mother's death. Zach feared he might have to kill again, after a man named Ganz told Zach that his father owed him a $100,000 gambling debt. Ganz ordered Zach to kill Jack, since Zach had murdered one of Ganz's pals. Ganz told Zach that if he refused, then Ganz would murder Felicia.

Zach placed an anonymous call to Taylor seeking advice about his dilemma, but he didn't reveal that he had been ordered to kill his father. Instead he approached it as a general discussion about the moral and ethical implications involved in murdering someone, even if it was for a higher purpose, such as saving someone else's life. Taylor responded that murder was never the answer. Later, having made contact with his father, Zach ordered him not to ask Taylor or the Forresters for money to pay Ganz. Zach lied to Ganz that he killed Jack. Meanwhile, Jack "borrowed" $20,000 from

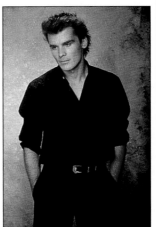

Taylor's rebellious younger brother Zach came to Los Angeles and took up with Felicia, much to Stephanie's dismay.

Spectra's accounts and left for Las Vegas, hoping to make a killing before he himself was killed. Stephanie was devastated by Jack's sudden departure, but he asked her not to give up on him.

Zach informed Felicia that his father's gambling had destroyed his family. One night Zach's mother was trying to escape from her husband's gambling buddies and was killed in a car wreck. Zach was relieved to hear that Jack won the money, but it was too late. Ganz had already found Felicia and tried to rape her. Sly attempted to save Felicia, but Ganz decked him. Zach rescued Felicia and got Ganz to admit that Jack never owed him any money. Felicia stopped Zach from killing Ganz. They let Ganz go because they knew that he would turn Zach in for killing Ganz's pal.

Jack replaced Sally's money with interest before she noticed it was missing. Zach and Jack agreed to start anew. Still unaware that Jack and Zach were father and son, Stephanie, having heard of her daughter's ordeal, demanded that Felicia have nothing to do with Zach or his father. Zach and Taylor shared a joyful reunion at a chapel with Jack on the anniversary of their mother's death.

Zach informed Felicia that his father was Jack Hamilton. Sally told Stephanie that Jack was her boyfriend. Before Stephanie could confront a two-timing Jack, he admitted that he'd been dating Sally, having had no idea about the animosity between the two women. After Jack purchased an engagement ring for Stephanie, he learned that Stephanie hated Zach and "Zach's father" for endangering Felicia. Stephanie ordered Jack out of her life when he told her that he was Zach's father. Stephanie sought solace from Eric. Later, Stephanie persuaded Sly to watch out for Felicia. Felicia told Stephanie she was moving in with Zach. Stephanie slapped Felicia after she suggested that her mom was jealous because Felicia had a man and Stephanie didn't.

Felicia was stunned after Stephanie attempted to have Zach arrested for endangering Felicia's life. But Stephanie backed off because of her daughter's pleas. Zach assured Felicia that he had never been convicted of a crime. Realizing they needed a fresh start, Felicia and Zach left town, after sharing tearful good-byes with their families.

On the outs with Stephanie, Jack turned to Sally, which made Saul jealous. Jack gave Sally the $100,000 he had won, enabling her to keep Spectra operational. Sally's joy was short-lived after she learned that that money would only keep the company afloat for a week.

SHEILA

With a history in Genoa City that included baby-snatching, kidnapping, and attempted murder, Sheila Carter needed a new start. She found it in Los Angeles, where she accepted a job as a nurse at Forrester Creations. Meanwhile, as far as the people in Genoa City knew, Sheila had been killed in a fire. Sheila started the fire to keep Lauren Fenmore, whose baby she had snatched, and her own mother, Molly, from turning her in to the police. At Forrester Creations, Sheila felt an immediate attraction to Eric and cunningly surmised that she could get close to him by baby-sitting for his son. Sheila didn't mind sitting for Eric Jr.

After all, she had always liked kids. But Eric Jr. already had a full-time nanny, Judy. So Sheila purposely spilled some liquid soap on the floor, causing Judy to take a nasty fall. Sheila stepped in as Eric Jr.'s temporary caretaker.

Judy read about Sheila's heinous crimes in a Genoa City newspaper and confronted her. Sheila threatened Judy's family, which prompted the frightened ex-nanny to flee Los Angeles.

SHEILA CARTER

William J. Bell describes Kimberlin Brown's addition to *The Bold and the Beautiful* cast in 1992 as "a very important, pivotal moment in the development of the show."

Previously, Kimberlin appeared on *The Young and the Restless* as Sheila Carter, a nurse who wreaked havoc on Lauren Fenmore's life. Sheila's misdeeds included stealing Lauren's husband, Dr. Scott Grainger, kidnapping Lauren's baby and passing it off as hers and Scott's, covering up the baby-snatching by surgically removing a telltale Fenmore birthmark on the child, and, finally, kidnapping Lauren at gunpoint and leaving her to die in a burning farmhouse, along with Sheila's mother, Molly. "I couldn't go on with her at *The Young and the Restless*," explains Bill Bell. "She would've been arrested." But Bill hated losing the character and the actress because of their immense popularity with viewers.

"Suddenly, I thought, What if Sheila leaves Genoa City and ends up in Los Angeles? It gave the character a new lease on life. After leaving the farmhouse where she was presumed to have died in the fire, we saw Sheila in a roadside diner. There happened to be a newspaper and she looked in the want ads. The one that appealed to her was a position as company nurse at Forrester Creations in Los Angeles. She called Forrester Creations and stated that she wanted a job. Boom, there's a whole new connection with both shows!"

Meanwhile, Kimberlin Brown was delighted to continue her role as Sheila on *The Bold and the Beautiful*. "I had a wonderful experience on *The Young and the Restless*, so to be able to go to *The Bold and the Beautiful* and continue with my character was icing on the cake," says Kimberlin.

Kimberlin Brown

Kimberlin also grasped the impact Sheila's move would have in bridging the two shows together. "There were a lot of loyal *B&B* viewers who had never heard of Sheila. But for those fans, basically, what they witnessed was the bringing on of a new character. For *Y&R* fans who followed Sheila to *The Bold and the Beautiful*, they were introduced to an entirely new cast of characters." And the fans followed in legion. With Sheila's arrival, *The Bold and the Beautiful* shot up to second place.

Kimberlin also enjoyed the opportunity to play different sides of Sheila's personality that weren't explored on *The Young and the Restless*. "The wonderful thing about *The Bold and the Beautiful* is that it gave Sheila a chance to be somebody else. It allowed her to do things that she had never done before. In a sense, it was a whole new Sheila, one who was trying to get away from her past and start fresh. When Eric Forrester showed an interest in Sheila, it was the first time any man expressed an interest in her because of who she was as person and a woman. She didn't have to manipulate him to make something happen. It was also wonderful that Eric was truly attracted to Sheila, without having to be drugged or manipulated."

Although some viewers, understandably, see Sheila as twisted, bordering on psychotic, Kimberlin understands why the character, nevertheless, continues to hold appeal for the audience. "Regardless of what's happening, you sympathize with Sheila, because you see motives for what she's doing. She's always trying to attain love or to help someone that she loves. How can you hate someone who simply wants to be loved or help the people that she loves?"

Eric and Sheila soon began dating and eventually became romantically involved. Stephanie tried to ally herself with Sheila once she saw that Sheila was interested in Eric. Stephanie became suspicious of Sheila upon learning that she had withheld telephone messages for Brooke from Judy.

Wanting to be a good mate for Eric, Sheila asked Taylor to recommend her to a therapist. Taylor suggested her colleague, Dr. Jay Garvin. Jay advised Sheila to seek forgiveness from people she'd harmed. Sheila didn't think Lauren Fenmore, who still lived in Genoa City, would ever forgive her. They shared an adversarial relationship from their first encounter because Sheila was attracted to Lauren's husband, Dr. Scott Grainger.

When Lauren and Scott separated, because of Lauren's friendship with her ex-husband, Paul, Sheila had decided to take advantage of the situation. She plied Scott with alcohol and pills and seduced him. Soon afterward, Scott and Lauren had reconciled, until Sheila announced to Scott that she was pregnant with his child. Feeling trapped, he had divorced Lauren, the woman he loved, and married Sheila. Shortly thereafter, Lauren had discovered that she, too, was pregnant with Scott's child. Not wanting to disrupt Scott's life any further, she decided to keep her pregnancy a secret from him. Sheila, however, learned that Lauren was pregnant.

Sheila then suffered a miscarriage. Knowing that she would lose Scott without their baby, she pretended to still be pregnant. When Lauren gave birth to her son, Sheila bought a baby boy from a baby broker and used that baby to substitute for Lauren's in the hospital nursery. Sheila then went out of town and told Scott that she had given birth to their son while she was away. Meanwhile, as Scott and Sheila were raising their infant son, Lauren's baby, whom everyone believed was fathered by Paul, had become critically ill and died. Lauren had been devastated by the loss of the baby she believed to be hers.

Lauren's eventual discovery of the truth had led to Sheila's hasty departure from Genoa City. So after Eric informed Sheila that Lauren, who owned a successful department store in Genoa City and ordered clothes from Forrester Creations, was coming in for a fashion show, Sheila knew the two of them were fated to meet again.

On her way to Lauren's hotel suite, Sheila crashed her car and landed in the hospital. She fantasized that she met with an unforgiving Lauren and hit her on the head with a vase. In Sheila's dream, Lauren recovered and had Sheila arrested as she modeled Eric's showstopper gown at the fashion show. In reality, Lauren left without ever meeting Eric's new lady friend, although she did cringe when she learned that her name was Sheila. With Lauren back in Genoa City, Sheila felt safe, but she knew Lauren would someday return.

Sheila phoned her mother, Molly, pretending to be a pal of Sheila's named Sara. Sensing her mother would be forgiving of her crimes and disappearance, Sheila left town to be with her. Sheila brought Molly to L.A. so she could see firsthand the happy new life she had built for herself. Molly advised Sheila to have her friend Sara intercede with Lauren. Sheila's evasiveness led Molly to realize there was no "Sara."

Sheila felt that Eric would not finalize his divorce from Brooke if he turned out to be the father of her daughter. Eric introduced Sheila to his friend Dr. Tracy Peters, who would be conducting the paternity tests. Sheila volunteered her services at the hospital—so she could alter the tests.

DARLA/BILL

With his marriage to Margo over, Bill started dating Darla. Sally's perky assistant felt out of place when Bill took her to the Cafe Russe, just as Bill appeared awkward when Darla took him dancing at the Bikini Bar. The couple found a happy medium at the Taxi Bar. Darla confided in Bill that she was an orphan.

With Spectra on the brink of bankruptcy, Darla asked Bill to bail out the company. Bill agreed, provided that Karen oversee his investment. Darla was less than thrilled by Karen's hiring.

Livid that Thorne had dumped Macy for Karen, Sally ordered Darla to go undercover and take a job at Forrester Creations. Darla, using the name Camille Howard, snagged work in the mailroom.

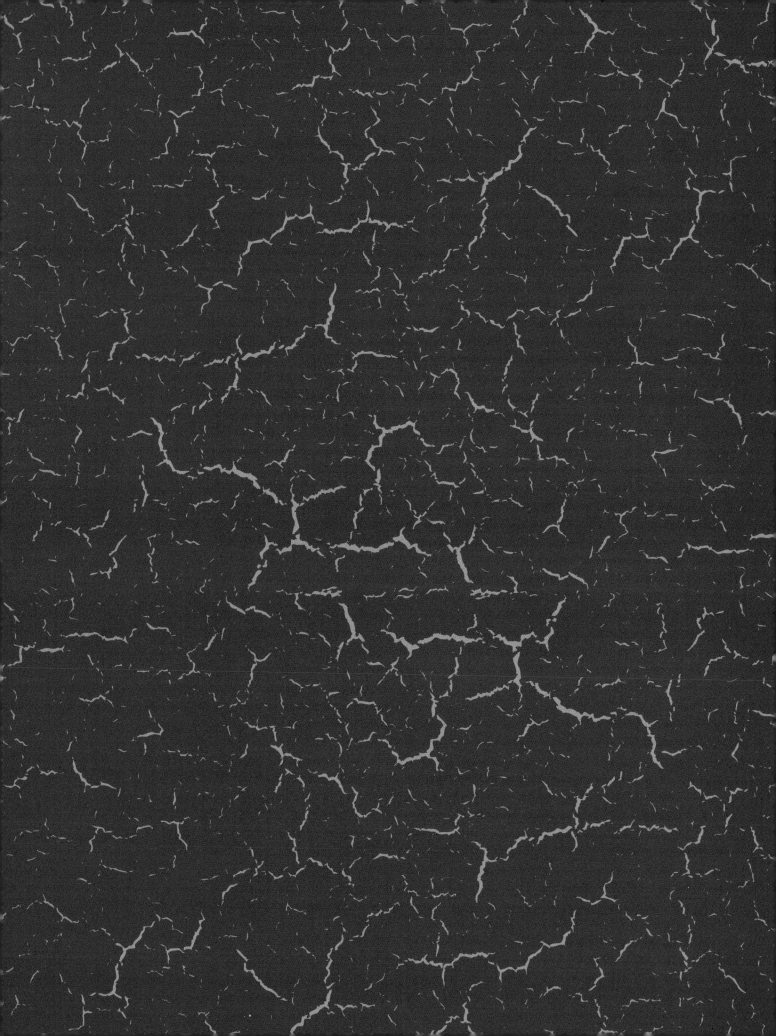

Season Seven

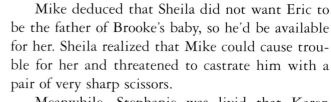

TAYLOR/RIDGE/BROOKE/ERIC/SHEILA/LAUREN/STEPHANIE

Ridge accompanied Brooke and her baby girl to the hospital, where the infant was diagnosed with jaundice. The doctors suggested that the paternity test be delayed until the baby recovered. Brooke held off on naming her child.

Stephanie accused Brooke of using her pregnancies to trap the Forrester men. Meanwhile, Brooke pushed Taylor too far when she admitted that her love for Ridge would never die.

Sheila conned a hospital security guard named Mike Guthrie into getting her access to the paternity test lab. In order to keep Lauren Fenmore from ever revealing the truth about their past association, Sheila hatched an elaborate scheme. She began blackmailing Lauren by sending her pieces of a photograph that showed Lauren committing adultery with Brad Carlton, a former boyfriend of Lauren's who continued to be a strong presence in her life. Sheila knew that no court would allow Lauren to have custody of her son if Lauren was a known adulteress.

Brooke feared that Eric was her baby's father, since she and Eric had made love nine months earlier. But Dr. Peters pointed out to Brooke that it takes forty weeks for a baby to come to term, not nine months. Still, Eric remained a likely candidate.

Sheila overheard Brooke's theory, so she snuck into the lab and began to switch the tags that identified Eric's and Ridge's blood samples. Just then Mike entered and spun the carousel that held the unlabeled vials. A furious Sheila quickly reaffixed the labels, uncertain as to which vial contained Eric's blood.

Security guard Mike Guthrie was not to be underestimated. Using his knowledge of Sheila's attempt to influence the outcome of the paternity test on Bridget, he blackmailed his way into a security position at Forrester Creations.

Mike deduced that Sheila did not want Eric to be the father of Brooke's baby, so he'd be available for her. Sheila realized that Mike could cause trouble for her and threatened to castrate him with a pair of very sharp scissors.

Meanwhile, Stephanie was livid that Karen gave Ridge Caroline's diary, which included an entry expressing Caroline's wish that, after she died, Ridge would spend his life with Brooke. Stephanie told Karen that she couldn't be both her and Brooke's friend, which angered Karen.

Brooke, Eric and Sheila, Ridge and Taylor, and Stephanie met in Dr. Peters's office to hear the paternity results. Dr. Peters announced that Ridge was the father. Brooke revealed to Ridge that she was naming their daughter Bridget, a combination of their names.

Eric divorced Brooke and proposed to Sheila. She accepted.

Brooke invited Ridge and Taylor to visit Bridget. Brooke feared Taylor's insecurities would keep Ridge from his daughter, but Ridge said that would never happen. Taylor became unsettled after reading Caroline's diary, and her wish that Ridge be with Brooke. But Ridge gently told Brooke that he was committed to Taylor.

Eric suggested to a disappointed Sheila that they wed after Forrester Creations' fall showing. Afraid that she might lose Eric, Sheila drugged Eric's wine with a mysterious powder that appeared to be an aphrodisiac. Eric passed out after drinking the wine and missed a dinner date with Stephanie. Sheila taunted Stephanie with Eric's devotion.

Brooke dropped by Ridge's office with Bridget—and a romantic picnic lunch, but when Taylor spied Brooke and her basket of goodies, she told her to take a hike.

Lauren arrived for the Forresters' show and was shocked to discover that Eric's Sheila was the same Sheila who had once kidnapped her baby, Scotty. Sheila warned Lauren that if she told Eric about her, then Sheila would show proof of Lauren's marital infidelity with Brad to Scott.

At a Forrester dinner in her honor, Lauren started to expose Sheila. But when Eric announced that Sheila was his fiancée, Lauren clammed up, for fear of breaking Eric's heart. Stephanie sensed the tension between Lauren and Sheila, but Lauren refused to come clean.

After a successful show, a reporter asked Brooke who was Bridget's father, Eric or Ridge? Hoping to score points with Ridge, Brooke lied that Eric was the tot's dad. Meanwhile, Sheila placed a phony call to Lauren luring her back to Genoa City before she could tell Eric about Sheila's sinful past. Eric blasted Stephanie for filling Lauren's head with "lies" about Sheila, but Stephanie sensed that Lauren's mistrust of Sheila was well-founded.

TAYLOR/RIDGE/BROOKE/CONNOR/KAREN/STEVE

Forrester's patent attorney, Steve Crown, wondered where the contracts were that gave Forrester ownership of Brooke's BeLieF formula. Eric explained to Steve that since Brooke had invented BeLieF while she was his wife, there were no contracts. Steve pointed out to Eric and Ridge that since Forrester's future profits hinged on BeLieF, they should get Brooke to sign over her rights. Ridge kept it secret from Taylor that Brooke was in a powerful position.

Brooke was thrilled to receive from Ridge an antique family rattle for Bridget. Stephanie blasted Ridge for not saving the heirloom for his and Taylor's firstborn.

Taylor and Ridge spotted Brooke on a date with Ridge's old high school rival, Connor Davis.

Ridge visited Brooke and was unhappy to find Connor holding Bridget. Brooke told Ridge that if he didn't like the fact that she was dating, then he should marry her. Taylor appreciated Connor's commitment to keeping relations between everyone civil.

Stephanie threw a dinner party and invited Brooke so that she'd be amenable to signing over control of BeLieF. But Connor grew suspicious of Stephanie's kindness. Meanwhile, Ridge told Brooke that he and Taylor were going to start a family.

Per Eric's request, Steve ingratiated himself into Brooke's life by posing as a masseur. Connor recognized fellow attorney Steve but didn't realize he'd seen Steve at the courthouse.

Connor and Ridge came to blows over Brooke. Brooke ordered them to stop fighting. Eric sent Ridge to Monte Carlo so he wouldn't interfere with Steve's plan to win Brooke's trust.

Taylor advised Ridge to examine his feelings for her while in Monte Carlo. Ridge agreed to reach a decision while he was away whether to stay with Taylor or divorce her and go to Brooke.

After Connor requested a copy of the BeLieF patent, Steve suggested to Eric that he get Brooke to sign over her rights to BeLieF immediately. Ridge, upon his return, volunteered to get Brooke to sign. Meanwhile, Brooke told Connor she didn't want him bad-mouthing Ridge anymore and ordered him out. Connor became involved with Karen. Ridge handed Brooke the patent contracts and offered to explain them. But Brooke, who trusted Ridge, signed away. Ridge took his copy of the contract and left, after announcing to Brooke that he was remaining married to Taylor.

Stephanie lorded it over Brooke that not only had she lost Ridge, but she had also signed away all rights to BeLieF. Connor examined Brooke's copy of the contract and wondered why it was signed. Brooke said she signed only one copy and Connor deduced that Ridge left with the unsigned document. Brooke still owned the BeLieF formula and as a result had the upper hand at Forrester.

Connor urged Brooke to make the Forresters pay for trying to deceive her. Brooke shredded the signed document in front of the Forresters and vowed that there were going to be some big changes. Sheila tried to mediate between Brooke and the Forresters, but only alienated herself from Eric's family.

Eric informed Brooke that he was to blame for deceiving her and asked her to renounce her claim to BeLieF. Brooke agreed to sign over all rights to BeLieF, provided that Stephanie apologize and that the family agree never to deceive Brooke again. Stephanie begrudgingly apologized, but just before Brooke signed the contract, Steve entered. Brooke wondered what her masseur was doing at Forrester. Connor realized that Steve was an attorney and Steve admitted that he was the Forresters' lawyer. Feeling duped, an enraged Brooke slapped Steve and refused to sign. Stephanie smacked Brooke, and for the first time ever, Brooke struck Stephanie back, announcing that she would be claiming her rights as BeLieF's creator.

Later, Brooke and Connor met with the Forresters and their new attorney, Elliott Parker. Elliott advised Eric to pay Brooke ten million dollars in exchange for BeLieF.

After analyzing the reports, Connor informed the Forresters that Brooke would sign over BeLieF in exchange for the office of her choice, an expense account, a full-time driver, and, finally, 51 percent of the stock in Forrester Creations. The Forresters balked at the last demand. Brooke was unaware that Connor was going to ask for so much. Elliott advised the Forresters to consider the offer.

The Forresters agreed to Brooke's demands but were shocked when Brooke announced that her personal assistant and liaison between herself and Forrester would be Sheila. Later, Connor and Brooke celebrated their win at the Ocean Club's private dining room, where Connor presented Brooke with a diamond necklace.

Brooke ordered Stephanie to move out of her office, since Brooke would be its new occupant. Stephanie was livid when Sheila arrived to facilitate the move. Meanwhile, Connor was hurt when Brooke turned down his marriage proposal but expressed interest in continuing their romance.

Brooke ordered the Forresters to speed up production for the next fashion show. She insisted that the company be run like a business. Sheila was disappointed to see that her duties at Forrester included secretarial work.

Shutterbug Sheila snapped a photo of Connor kissing Karen at the Bikini Bar and presented the photo to Brooke as proof that Connor was cheating. Sheila told Ridge that she had put an end to Brooke and Connor's romance. A trusting Brooke, however, believed Connor's claim that he and Karen were just pals. Meanwhile, Ridge was furious at Sheila.

Brooke was now in charge of Forrester. Here, she visits Stephanie in Stephanie's new, and less glamorous, office.

Ridge told Taylor that he'd have to rebuild his relationship with Brooke so that Eric wouldn't stress out over losing the company. Brooke proposed that Forrester Creations start producing fashions for men. Ridge agreed to design the new line, but a furious Eric argued that Forrester stood for elegant women's fashions. Connor couldn't believe that Brooke didn't consult him on this new venture. Connor wished Brooke were more like Karen.

One day, Ridge "playfully" pushed Brooke into the pool, but she hit her head and fell unconscious. Ridge rushed Brooke to the hospital and told her that he was sorry. Still harboring feelings for Ridge, Brooke forgave him.

Connor suggested to Karen that Ridge was pretending to be Brooke's pal so that he could win back Forrester.

Stephanie's neighbor, Charlton Heston, asked that the Forresters' next fashion show benefit the American Film Institute. Stephanie agreed but was berated by Brooke for not first presenting the idea to her.

The Forresters invited the AFI's Jean Firstenberg along with Hollywood celebrities Carol Channing, Steve Allen, and Jayne Meadows. But the

Forresters weren't expecting the Spectra gang, who crashed the showing with Anthony Armando's designs. After the show, Brooke informed Ridge that she was considering giving the Forresters back their company. Ridge was so happy that he kissed Brooke. The spontaneous and innocent kiss was captured by a photographer.

Karen apologized to Ridge for her role in crashing the Forresters' fashion show and also told him that since she was seeing Connor romantically, Brooke could use Ridge's friendship.

Ridge and Brooke joined together to celebrate Bridget's birthday while Taylor was in Scotland helping an old friend, James, cope with a very emotional situation (see page 84).

ERIC/SHEILA/LAUREN/BRAD

Sheila received a visit from Genoa City's Brad Carlton—Lauren's fellow adulterer. Brad feared that if the photo was made public, he would lose visitation rights to his daughter, Colleen. Brad threatened Sheila into giving up the prints and the negatives.

Lauren flew in for Eric's wedding, as did his daughter Kristen. But all the Forresters—except Brooke—refused to support the upcoming union.

Lauren confronted Sheila the night before the wedding while Sheila was trying on her wedding gown. Sheila taunted Lauren and boasted that all men—even Lauren's son, Scotty—preferred Sheila to Lauren. The two women engaged in a savage catfight, which left Sheila's wedding gown, personally designed by Eric, ripped to shreds. Lauren left feeling victorious, but the next morning she found evidence that Sheila still had photographs proving Lauren's infidelity.

Thorne refused to be his father's best man, but Brooke agreed to stand up for Sheila. Lauren gave Sheila an ultimatum: Either call off the wedding or face the consequences when Lauren told Eric the truth about Sheila. Lauren, Stephanie, Kristen, Ridge, and Thorne all wore dark colors to the ceremony to show their protest. Before the vows could be exchanged, Sheila ran away. Stephanie was thrilled. A satisfied Lauren returned to Genoa City.

Later, though, Sheila returned and told Eric that she didn't feel comfortable getting married in a room filled with people who hated her. Sheila and Eric wed in private. Later, Sheila bragged to Stephanie that Eric and she were husband and wife. Sheila flaunted her ring in front of Stephanie. Soon after, Eric and Sheila moved into their new home in Holmby Hills. The realtor told Eric and Sheila that their home was once owned by Harry Houdini.

ERIC/SHEILA/LAUREN/SCOTT

Sheila and Eric's marriage suffered extreme stress after Sheila accepted the position as Brooke's liaison. All the Forresters felt that Sheila was siding with Brooke. Sheila argued that she was their only hope of placating Brooke.

Sheila hit another snag when Mike Guthrie, the guard who knew that Sheila had attempted to switch Bridget's paternity blood samples, showed up and demanded a job at Forrester. Sheila tried to take Mike out by having a doberman attack him in an elevator, but Mike tamed the dog and blackmailed Sheila into hiring him as Forrester's head of security.

After visiting Genoa City and an ailing Scott Grainger, whom she had once wed, Sheila returned home, only to have Eric inform her that he wanted a divorce because he felt he could no longer trust her, mostly because of her association with Brooke. Sheila convinced Eric to take a vacation to Catalina Island to renew their union. Eric agreed. The couple ran into Lauren and Scott, who were also on a romantic retreat. Scott was stunned to see that Sheila had married Eric. Lauren and Sheila faced off, while Scott bought some medication from the pharmacy for his critical medical condition.

Sheila visited Scott in his hotel room to beg his forgiveness, while Lauren met with Eric to tell him about Sheila's past. Before she could fill Eric in, Scott

Catalina (left to right: Eric, Lauren, Sheila, and Scott). Sheila convinced Eric to visit Catalina Island with her to try to repair their troubled marriage. When Eric saw the compassion Sheila felt for a dying Scott, he decided to give their marriage a second chance. What Eric didn't know was that Sheila and Scott had once been married.

Sheila finally felt victorious over Lauren after Scott, who had forgiven his scheming ex-wife, made a deathbed plea that Lauren promise to keep quiet about Sheila's past.

summoned Lauren to his room. With his final breath Scott begged Lauren not to tell Eric about Sheila's past and to give her a second chance. Lauren agreed as Scott passed away.

Lauren went back to Genoa City to bury Scott. Eric was so touched by Sheila's compassion for the dying Scott—a man whom Eric wrongly assumed Sheila hardly knew—that he canceled the divorce.

Taylor and James. Taylor took on her former mentor, Dr. James Warwick, as a patient.

TAYLOR/JAMES/DAMON

Taylor received a surprise visit from her former mentor, Dr. James Warwick, who requested that Taylor accept him as a patient.

During their sessions, James described to Taylor his fear of losing a woman he loved named Sophia, who was dying. He also talked to her about his mother who lived in Scotland and his deceased father.

Taylor began to let her desire to help James infringe on her marriage to Ridge. Taylor sternly chided Ridge after he accidentally came across some notes about James's condition. Taylor tried locating James's mother's address in Scotland for insurance purposes, but could only locate Damon Warwick, James's "deceased" dad.

After intense therapy, James revealed that he hated his father as a result of years of physical and mental abuse and that his father hated him as well. Taylor went to Scotland for answers. Taylor told Ridge that James wouldn't be going with her, but at the last minute, James decided to go. James confessed to Taylor that his father, Damon, was alive and that he owed his mother his life.

Due to a lack of rooms, James and Taylor were forced to share a suite. Maggie, the innkeeper, assumed that James and Taylor were a couple, and when Ridge called for Taylor, Maggie innocently told him that Taylor and James were registered in the same room. James comforted Taylor with a kiss after Taylor learned from Stephanie that Ridge had stayed over at Brooke's place.

Taylor and James met with Damon, who lied to Taylor about how much he cared for his son. Later, a drunken Damon allowed his hatred for James to show as he contended that James killed his own mother. Damon tried to hit James with a fireplace poker, but James knocked Damon down and ran off with Taylor.

After a very emotional and cathartic session with James, Taylor deduced that James's mother died in childbirth and that Damon blamed James. Taylor surmised that James created wonderful memories of his departed mother so that he could endure his father's abuse. Taylor encouraged James to confront his father one last time.

DR. JAMES WARWICK

Dr. James Warwick came to *The Bold and the Beautiful* shrouded in mystery, particularly in regards to his childhood in Scotland. Viewers later discovered his mother had died in childbirth and that her loss was so traumatic for James's father that he mentally abused the young James. Ultimately, the abuse left James unable to have any kind of relationship with a woman until he became reacquainted in Los Angeles with Dr. Taylor Hayes, a star student from his days as a college professor. Ian Buchanan, who plays James, explains that "initially, James was described as a sort of gothic psychiatrist who had been Taylor's mentor. I liked playing him because he was very dark and mysterious. Gradually, the character started to lighten a bit."

Though Ian was no stranger to soaps, having starred as Duke Lavery on *General Hospital*, he'd enjoyed great success in prime time on *Twin Peaks* and *On the Air*. He still looked forward to returning to daytime in a regular role. "It's really nice to be coming back to soaps with no thought about what it's like to do movies or prime-time series," he told *Soap Opera Digest*. "I

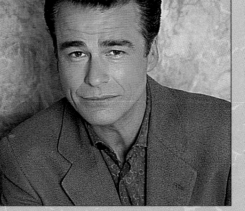

Ian Buchanan

also wanted to work regularly again. I love to be exhausted when I go to bed at night and wake up thinking about the character. And I knew the only place I could do that would be on a soap if the character was right."

After being away from soaps for four years and working in film, which has only one camera, Ian initially found it difficult readjusting to working with several cameras again. "When I started on *The Bold and the Beautiful*, I remember being more nervous than I had ever been in my life. I was completely frozen. It took me about two weeks to actually conquer it."

Before joining *The Bold and the Beautiful* in 1993, Ian occasionally wondered what it would be like returning to *General Hospital*, where his character enjoyed a hot storyline with Finola Hughes, who played Anna Scorpio, who he counts as one of his closest friends. "As I got older, I thought it might be interesting to see what Duke was doing when he got older, if he had lived," Ian told *Soap Opera Digest*. "But now that I'm doing *The Bold and the Beautiful*, all of those thoughts have completely vanished."

KAREN/THORNE/MACY/SLY

When Karen informed Macy that she heard Jake was back, Macy clarified that Jake was in town for only one day to pack his things and say good-bye. Karen deduced that Thorne chose her only because he thought Macy was unavailable. Karen confided this revelation to her dad, but Bill told his daughter not to tell Thorne. Meanwhile, Thorne told Macy that he didn't care if she dated Sly, a friend of Taylor's brother, Zach, who continued to work at the Bikini Bar after Zach left town. Macy and Thorne filed for divorce.

Sly courted Macy with poems, which, unbeknownst to her, were written by his good-natured co-worker Keith, who also worshipped Macy. To Sly's delight, Macy sang "Poetry Man" to thank him for his sonnets and surprised Sly with her vocal skills, which she had developed since her musical debut at the variety talent show a few years earlier. Macy told Darla that she had sent Thorne a tape requesting a meeting. However, Bill intercepted the cassette and kept it from Thorne.

Depressed over Thorne's unresponsiveness, Macy got drunk on tequila. Keith brought a drunken Macy home and tucked her into bed. Sally thanked Keith for taking care of her daughter.

Macy accepted a job singing at the Bikini Bar from Sly. Keith tried to point out to Sly that Macy was drinking too much, but Sly told Keith not to interfere or else he'd be fired. Macy passed out while performing on stage.

Sly took advantage of Macy's alcoholism to pursue a relationship with her.

Thorne tried to help her, but Sly told him to take a hike. Stephanie's pal Ruthanne, who was also Keith's aunt, assured her nephew that he was good enough for Macy.

Macy returned her wedding ring to Thorne and lied to Sally that she had stopped drinking. Later, Keith saw Sly plying Macy with alcohol at the Bikini Bar. Macy knocked into Keith's brother Kevin, a busboy trainee, which caused him to drop his tub of glasses. Sly blasted Kevin for being stupid. Keith informed Sly that his remark was insensitive, since Kevin was mentally handicapped. Sly apologized but refused to let Kevin bus tables.

Thorne was unable to give Karen a commitment because of his feelings for Macy. Thorne and Macy agreed to meet and discuss their relationship, but Sly plied Macy with alcohol so that she would miss her date, which Thorne saw as Macy's lack of interest in him and their relationship. Karen said good-bye to Thorne after pointing out to him that he wasn't over Macy.

Keith informed Sally that her daughter was still drinking. Sally, Saul, Jack, Darla, and Keith staged an intervention. Sly, though, remained silent about Macy's problem so that she would remain dependent upon him. Sally ordered Macy to leave Spectra after smelling liquor on her breath. Macy continued her downward spiral until Thorne found her lying in an alley and brought her home. Macy learned from Thorne that he had chosen Karen because he saw Macy embracing Jake. Macy clarified to Thorne that she was just giving Jake a good-bye hug. Thorne and Macy agreed to stay together.

Meanwhile, a gunman named Earl broke into the Bikini Bar. Kevin tackled Earl from behind. Sly showed his appreciation by hiring Kevin as a busboy.

Macy and Thorne celebrated their reunion by singing at the Bikini Bar. Kevin spied Macy sneaking a drink. Macy swore Kevin to secrecy. Sometime later a drunken Macy was driving with Kevin in the car when she caused an accident, which left Kevin hospitalized. He soon recovered and was released. Thorne learned from Macy's doctor that she was legally drunk at the time of the "accident" and chastised his wife for her behavior. As Kevin recovered from his injuries, Macy contacted Alcoholics Anonymous.

Keith, Kevin, and Sly visited Macy to check on her recovery. Kevin informed Macy that Keith was responsible for all of Sly's love poems. Macy embraced Keith and thanked him for all of his kind words.

THORNE/MACY/ANTHONY

The Forresters threw Macy a party to celebrate her sobriety. But Macy suffered a setback at the Taxi Bar after Sheila, who was angry at Thorne for not supporting her marriage to Eric, spiked her orange juice with vodka. A mysterious newcomer, Anthony Armando, helped Macy home and into bed. As Anthony kissed her good-bye, Thorne entered and punched out the Casanova. Macy was livid that Anthony had taken advantage of her.

Unknown to Macy, Karen hired Anthony to be Spectra Fashions' newest head designer. When Thorne found out, he began to suspect something was going on between Macy and Anthony. Anthony teased Macy that she had behaved amorously toward him when he helped her home. Macy deduced that Anthony was lying and shredded one of his sketches. Thorne attempted to have Anthony fired, but Macy admitted that Spectra needed him. Anthony scored points with Macy after he hired Keith and Kevin to work at Spectra.

Thorne told Macy that if Anthony wasn't fired, their reconciliation was off. Macy was tempted to drink, but Anthony convinced her to stay sober. Meanwhile, Sally told Anthony that his name would not go on designs produced by Spectra as he had requested. But Sally changed her mind after she realized that the Armando label could more easily infiltrate Stephanie's AFI fashion show.

Wrongly assuming that Macy was involved, Thorne asked her for another separation after the Spectra gang shanghaied their way into his family's fashion gala.

STEPHANIE/JACK/SALLY/SAUL

Sally confided in Darla her fear that Jack still cared for Stephanie. Indeed, Jack did, but Stephanie had ended their relationship over Zach's involvement with Felicia.

Darla, in her Camille disguise, appropriated three Forrester sketches for Spectra to copy. Karen, unaware of where the designs were coming from, approved of Sally using them to make a profit. Later, Sally cut short a meeting about stealing from Forrester when she spied Jack eavesdropping on the conversation. Darla was saddened after Bill made a pass at "Camille," but was later happy when Bill turned down advances from her alter ego. Still, the couple eventually drifted apart when Bill's business dealings took him away from Los Angeles.

Saul was all set to take Sally out to dinner, but when Jack became available, Sally told Saul that she'd be going with Jack instead. Jack thrilled Sally by giving her an engagement ring. She accepted his proposal.

Sally boasted about her engagement to Stephanie while Jack noticed a Forrester design in his fiancée's office. Jack threatened to walk out on Sally if she dared to present the Forrester gowns as her own. Sally ordered Saul to yank the designs just as their fashion show began. Karen was livid that Sally had sunk to such low measures.

Thorne explained to Stephanie that Jack was responsible for Sally not using the stolen Forrester gowns. Stephanie dropped by to thank Jack for his aid. Saul spied the encounter and told Sally.

Sally looked forward to her wedding to Jack. But when she caught Jack kissing Stephanie, Sally found herself unable to go through with the ceremony.

Karen, Darla, Taylor, and Macy threw Sally a bachelorette party. Macy invited romance-cover model Fabio to drop by and wish Sally well. When Sally spotted Fabio, she proclaimed, "Oh, my Fabio, it's God."

Saul grudgingly agreed to be Jack's best man. Later, though, Saul overheard Jack plan to meet Stephanie at the Cafe Russe. Saul arranged for him and Sally to spot the rendezvous, where Sally saw Jack give Stephanie a kiss. Sally informed Jack that the wedding was off. Later, Sally confronted Stephanie, but Stephanie let her rant and rave, since she knew that Jack was watching from a distance. Jack comforted Stephanie and professed his love for her. After Sally learned that Jack and Stephanie were back together, Sally lied that she was pregnant. When Jack demanded that Sally take a pregnancy test, she had Juanita, a pregnant employee, fill in for her. Jack bought Sally's lie.

Suspecting that Sally wasn't really pregnant, Stephanie had a spy drop by Sally's office selling baby furniture. After Sally told the salesman she had no use for baby furniture, Stephanie's suspicion that Sally wasn't really pregnant was confirmed. Stephanie convinced Saul to reveal Sally and Jack's whereabouts. Stephanie barged in on Sally and Jack just as he was about to impregnate her for real. Jack quit Spectra after Stephanie exposed Sally's con job.

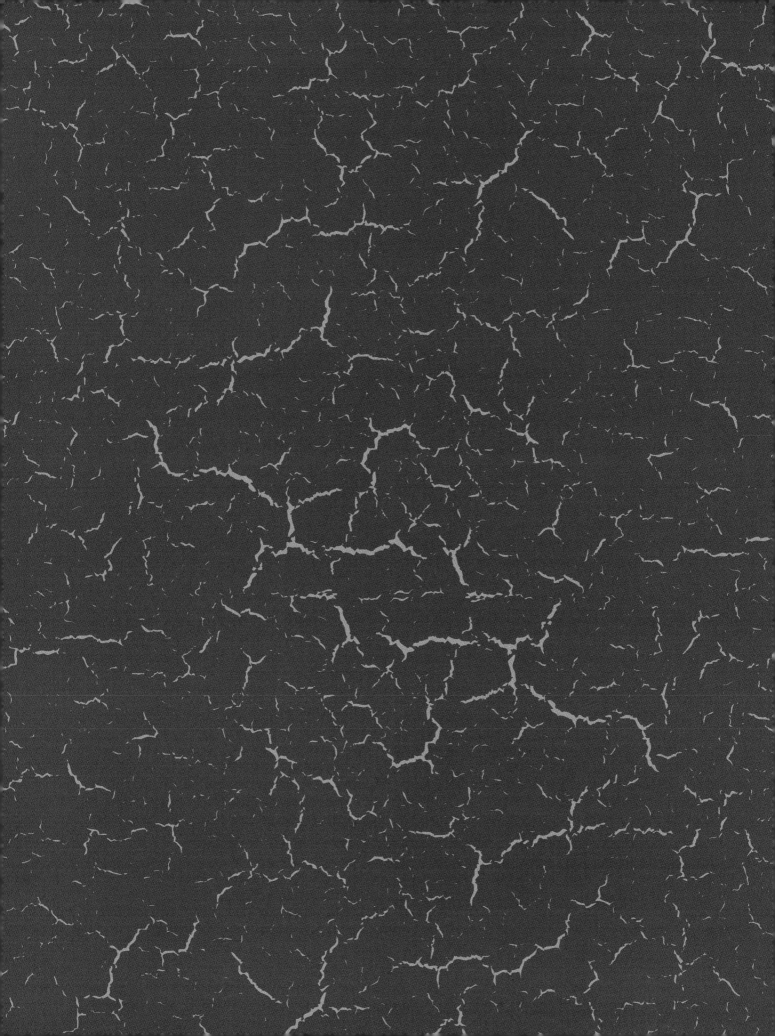

SEASON EIGHT

TAYLOR/JAMES/DAMON

James had a final showdown with his abusive father. During the heated confrontation, Damon told James that his mother, Mary, died in childbirth so that James could live. Damon said he felt that James had conjured up images of his mother to torment Damon. But James countered that he only created false memories of his deceased mother to combat Damon's anger. Realizing neither meant to truly hurt the other, James and Damon embraced.

Maggie showed Taylor an American newspaper with a photo of Ridge and Brooke embracing at the Forrester fashion show. After James kissed Taylor, the good doctor warned her former mentor not to fall in love with her. Taylor flew home, leaving James in Scotland to spend some much-needed time with his father.

BROOKE/JAMES/TAYLOR/RIDGE

Ridge admitted to Brooke that he felt he and Brooke and Bridget and Eric Jr. made a great family. But Brooke suspected Ridge was being nice to her so she'd give the Forresters back their company.

Upon Taylor's return, she and Ridge cleared up the misunderstandings about Taylor and James having shared the same room in Scotland and about Ridge kissing Brooke. Upon his return, James balked at Ridge's idea that he find a new therapist. Taylor taunted Brooke that Ridge was only getting close to her so the family could win back Forrester. Ridge assured Brooke it wasn't true. Taylor and Ridge agreed to put their recent woes behind them. However, Taylor continued to see James as a patient.

James asked Taylor to think of him as a man and not as a mentor. Taylor sadly informed James that she'd have to end their doctor-patient relationship. James found a new friend in Brooke, though. Soon they began dating.

However, when the international division of Forrester was ready to be set up, Brooke told Ridge that if he went with her, she'd return controlling interest of Forrester back to the family. Ridge agreed. Taylor was incredulous at her husband's decision and found refuge at James's apartment. An angry Ridge punched out James for moving in on his wife.

Just as Ridge was about to board the plane, Thorne arrived and announced that he'd be taking his place so that Ridge could avoid putting his marriage in jeopardy. Ridge refused, so Thorne punched Ridge and took his ticket. Brooke was furious when Thorne boarded the plane instead of Ridge. Assuming that Ridge was on his way to Paris with Brooke, Taylor and James left for the Forresters' cabin. After they arrived, a powerful earthquake hit the area. The cabin was in ruins, without running water or electricity, and James's leg was badly injured. He and Taylor began to freeze because of the frigid winter weather. After an aftershock hit, James expressed to Taylor his desire not to die a virgin. Out of compassion and fondness, Taylor allowed herself to make love to James.

Soon after, Ridge arrived with a rescue squad. Taylor and James decided to keep their lovemaking a secret. Ridge insisted that James recuperate at the Forrester mansion. Meanwhile, Brooke returned from Paris after Bridget and

Eric Jr. became ill. After seeing James, Brooke sensed that he and Taylor had been physically intimate. James denied it. Soon James and Brooke began dating again and made love.

Taylor was invited to attend a medical conference in the Middle East. Ridge gave his wife a personally designed outfit to wear on her trip. She left behind a letter for Ridge detailing her betrayal.

Stephanie found the unopened letter from Taylor to Ridge and read it. She and Jack agreed that the letter should be hidden.

Soon after Taylor departed, Brooke and James heard a tragic radio news bulletin. Taylor's plane had crashed. There were no survivors. Ridge couldn't believe that he was again a widower. Taylor's charred outfit was sent to Ridge as proof that she was dead. Ridge, James, Stephanie, and Jack lauded Taylor at her funeral.

Ridge eulogized Taylor after she was presumed dead in a plane crash. Unbeknownst to Taylor's loved ones, she had exited the plane before it had taken off.

On the rebound from Ridge, Brooke fell for James and even made plans to marry him. But when Ridge proposed marriage to Brooke, James was out of Brooke's life as quickly as he'd entered it.

Despite Ridge's availability, Brooke continued to date James and, as their romance progressed, he proposed marriage. She accepted. Meanwhile, Ridge found friendship with Rhonda, a Bikini Bar waitress. Brooke fibbed to Ridge that Eric Jr. was thrilled about getting James as a stepdad. When Ridge found out that Brooke was lying, he insisted that he remain part of the kids' lives.

Brooke and Ridge were drawn together after Bridget was hit by a stray bullet in a drive-by shooting at a neighborhood park. Dr. Santana told a relieved Ridge and Brooke that Bridget would recover. Later, Ridge accused James of marrying Brooke on the rebound, since he had loved Taylor. Rhonda pointed out to Ridge that if he truly loved Brooke, then he should tell her. Ridge burst into Brooke's hotel suite on the eve of her wedding and told her not to marry James. Ridge stunned Brooke by proposing marriage. James countered that Ridge would only give Brooke heartache. But Brooke ignored James's warning and ultimately accepted Ridge's proposal.

Meanwhile, Prince Omar of Morocco supervised a medical team to watch over a beautiful woman who had been found injured. The woman turned out to be Taylor, who had gotten off the plane before it had crashed. Taylor, who had amnesia, informed Omar that she had been attacked at the airport. Taylor's attacker must have switched clothing with her and then occupied Taylor's seat on the plane. Omar realized that Taylor's family must have assumed Taylor died in the crash. Omar, who began to fall in love with Taylor, treated her like a princess. Omar chose to call Taylor "Laila."

Meanwhile, James was surprised to receive in the mail Taylor's lecture notes (postmarked Morocco), which she had undoubtedly carried with her on the plane. James felt that if Taylor's papers survived, then perhaps so did Taylor.

Omar's assistant, Moustafa, discovered that Laila's real identity was Dr. Taylor Hayes and told Omar, who, fearing he might lose her, kept the news from Taylor. Omar forbid Moustafa from telling Taylor the truth. Later, Omar proposed marriage to Laila and she accepted.

The Logan family arrived in Los Angeles for Ridge and Brooke's wedding. Meanwhile, Laila came upon the file that Moustafa had put together on Taylor, which included news of Ridge and Brooke's upcoming wedding, and she began to regain her memory. Taylor tried calling Ridge to stop the wedding, but Omar cut the phone lines just as Ridge picked up the phone. Not knowing that Taylor was alive, Ridge married Brooke on the beach in Malibu. Storm was Ridge's best man and Kristen was Brooke's maid of honor.

Ridge and Brooke sailed to the Canary Islands on their honeymoon. Omar arranged for Moustafa and his aide, Imane, to keep an eye on the couple. A storm forced Brooke and Ridge to land in Morocco. Omar invited them to be his guests so that Taylor could see how happy they were.

Omar, who was holding Taylor prisoner, arranged it so that Taylor observed Ridge and Brooke from behind a one-way soundproof wall. Taylor was furious at Omar and deeply saddened to see how contented Ridge was in his new life. Taylor later tried to reach Ridge in his room, but several guards grabbed her. Finally, a despondent Taylor accepted that Ridge was committed to Brooke.

As Ridge and Brooke departed, a veiled and defeated Taylor kissed Ridge's hand and told Brooke to take care of her husband. Later, a Moroccan orphan girl comforted Taylor. Back in the States, James was intrigued by Brooke's story about the veiled Laila.

Taylor wed Omar after he agreed to let her work in the orphanage. Omar was sad that Taylor did not want a sexual relationship with him. Later, James spotted a newspaper photo of Omar and the veiled Laila. Thinking that Laila strongly resembled Taylor, he shared his theory with Connor that Laila and Taylor were the same person. Posing as a biographer, Brewster MacKensay, James traveled to Morocco and met with Prince Omar.

THORNE/MACY/ANTHONY/SALLY

Anthony recruited Karen in his quest to win Macy. But Macy saw through Anthony's plan and sang to him "You're Never Gonna Get It" at the Bikini Bar. A confident Anthony said he felt up to Macy's challenge.

Anthony had Saul and Keith make bathing suits out of a fabric that became invisible when wet. He then got Connor to invite Macy and Karen, wearing the see-through suits, into the hot tub. But Keith turned the tables on Anthony and Connor by giving them transparent garments instead. Later, Anthony chastised Keith for his double-cross.

Meanwhile, Sally fell in love with Anthony and asked him to move in with her. Unaware of Sally's feelings for him, Anthony accepted after Sally informed him that Macy often visited. Macy began to fall for Anthony. A concerned Darla advised Thorne to pursue Macy, or he'd lose her to Anthony. Darla also suggested to Sally that she was falling too quickly for Anthony, but Sally wouldn't listen. Thorne asked Macy for a reunion, but she tearfully declined.

Soon after, Macy received Thorne's divorce papers. Anthony was happy to learn that Macy was a free woman and asked Sally not to mention that they had shared a kiss. But Sally had already told Macy. Believing that Sally was involved with Anthony, a loyal Macy said she wanted nothing to do with him. In the meantime, Anthony began to play surrogate dad to Sally's son, C.J.

Sally arranged a surprise birthday party for Anthony. Meanwhile, Anthony convinced Macy that he and Sally were just pals. As Macy and Anthony made love, Sally, C.J., and Darla realized that Anthony wouldn't be attending their surprise party. Later, Anthony's heart broke when he realized that C.J. wanted him to be his dad. Macy asked Anthony to tell Sally that they were dating.

Thorne returned for Taylor's funeral. He and Macy met and agreed to remain friends. Upon Macy's insistence, Anthony moved out of Sally's,

Macy's affair with Anthony created heartbreak for Sally, who was in love with Anthony. Feeling betrayed by Macy, Sally fired her daughter from Spectra Fashions. Eventually, Macy and Sally reconciled.

Sally couldn't believe her eyes when she spied her longtime rival Stephanie Forrester at her "Grand Diva" fashion show. Sally dragged Stephanie up onstage with her and made the crowd think that Stephanie gave her stamp of approval to Sally's new line.

under the pretext that he needed to help his pal Connor, but when C.J. became ill, Anthony again stayed at Sally's home. Before Sally could ask Anthony to marry her, she overheard Macy and Anthony profess their love. Sally fired Macy from Spectra, despite Macy's insistence that she never meant to hurt her mom. Sally stoically suggested Anthony move out so he could lend moral support to Connor.

Anthony impressed Sally by creating fashions for larger-sized women. Spectra called Anthony's new line Grand Diva. Later, Anthony told Macy not to stop by and visit Spectra because of Sally. Meanwhile, Anthony shared several kisses with a depressed Darla, while still pretending to be Sally's pal.

After Macy sang for Anthony at the Bikini Bar, record producer Don Navarone suggested she pursue a singing career. Macy, who was hurt by Anthony's lack of interest in her, focused her attention on her musical talents and invested in a demo tape to promote her singing.

Anthony and Macy had another fight, and he decided to end their relationship. Darla promised Anthony that she'd be there for him if he stayed at Spectra. Anthony wanted Macy back, but Macy insisted that they take their relationship slowly.

Don explained to a surprised Macy that the record producers were only interested in her if she and Thorne agreed to perform as a duet. Thorne tried singing a love song with Macy but stopped halfway through the ballad and said that the feelings just weren't there. Macy was glad when Sally asked for a mother-daughter reconciliation. After encouragement from Ridge, Thorne gave singing another chance. Macy and Thorne signed a record deal. Meanwhile, Ivana, a beautiful model at Forrester Creations who had a crush on Thorne, conspired with Anthony to keep the songbirds apart.

Macy and Thorne were invited to perform at a concert in Rotterdam. Before they left, Macy, who had developed a sore throat, learned it might be cancerous. Rather than jeopardize the concert, a gallant Macy kept her illness a secret. Sally, Eric, and Don accompanied Macy and Thorne to Rotterdam. An ill Macy disappeared just before the concert began. Sally and Eric performed as a last-minute opening act while everyone searched for Macy. Thorne found Macy, who managed to sing despite her illness. The crowd loved all four singers, but after the concert Macy collapsed. Meanwhile, Anthony offered to conspire with Stephanie to keep Thorne and Macy apart, but Stephanie passed on his offer.

Back in the States, Macy underwent throat cancer surgery, while her family kept a vigil during the operation.

ERIC/SHEILA/JAMES

Sheila had her marriage back on track, thanks to Scott's dying wish that Lauren give Sheila a second chance. But when a sickly Molly phoned Sheila and asked her to stay with her while she recuperated, Sheila left town—and Eric.

During Sheila's absence, Eric grew close to Stephanie. Jack was jealous that Stephanie was spending time with her ex-husband. After Molly recovered from her illness, Sheila returned home and pumped Mike for a status report on Eric and Stephanie.

Sheila's insecurities about Stephanie continued to grow, which only made her unattractive to Eric. As the tensions mounted in their marriage, Eric informed Sheila that they wouldn't be making love again until she dropped her resentment toward Stephanie.

Meanwhile, Stephanie suggested to James that Sheila had a mysterious connection to Lauren. Sheila confided in Mike about her life in Genoa City and that only three people, Lauren, Molly, and Brad, knew that she had survived the fire. Sheila realized her former therapist, Jay, knew, too. James tried to get information about Sheila from Jay, but he refused. Later, Sheila argued with Jay about keeping her secrets. At one point Jay grabbed Sheila's arm. She instinctively pushed him away. Jay tumbled off his balcony and fell to his death. Sheila escaped, unseen, with her medical file.

Lt. Burke questioned James about Jay's death, but no charges were filed against him. Sheila told Mike what happened and bought his silence with a kiss. When questioned, Sheila told Lt. Burke that she had no idea who would want Jay dead.

James tried to point out to Brooke that Sheila was evil, but Sheila professed her innocence. Desperate to keep her marriage alive, Sheila tried a new tack to keep Eric—she offered to let him go if that's what he truly wanted. Eric was touched by Sheila's offer.

Later, Sheila got Mike to steal a copy of Eric's will. Sheila ran the document by Connor, who told her that her financial future would be more secure if she had Eric's baby. Sheila used her wiles to get Eric to make love to her, but she didn't become pregnant. Unbeknownst to Sheila, Eric had had a vasectomy. Stephanie allowed Eric to recuperate at her house. Meanwhile, Eric lied to Sheila, stating he was on a business trip. Sheila suspected that Eric was having an affair, since nobody knew his whereabouts.

Upon Eric's return, Sheila informed her husband that she had a spare room turned into a nursery. Sheila made love to Connor, hoping to get pregnant and pass the baby off as Eric's.

Sheila lied to Eric that she was pregnant, but Eric snapped back that the baby couldn't be his, since he'd had a vasectomy. Connor pointed out to Sheila that Eric's having a vasectomy without telling her might get her a hefty divorce settlement.

Sheila got Eric to stay with her for thirty days by promising not to sue. Eric coerced Sheila into getting therapy from James. James advised Sheila that if she opened up to him, Eric might be amenable to a reconciliation. Sheila was saddened to hear Eric agree with James's theory that Eric had wed Sheila because he was rebounding from Brooke.

Sheila confessed her wicked past to therapist Dr. Jay Garvin. During a struggle with Sheila, Jay accidentally fell off his balcony and died.

Sheila felt her marriage slipping away after Eric agreed to attend Thorne and Macy's Rotterdam concert without her. James felt Sheila needed an intensive therapy session, so Eric suggested the Forresters' Big Bear cabin, which had been restored since the earthquake. But Stephanie warned James to watch his back, since Sheila might have had a hand in Jay's death. Once James mentioned to Sheila the names "Lauren" and "Genoa City," Sheila attempted to flee. But James informed her that if she didn't stay, Eric would divorce her. Sheila was about to murder James with a fireplace poker, but she backed off when James received a phone call and abruptly left for Morocco to search for Taylor.

CONNOR/KAREN

Connor resumed his romantic relationship with Karen, but before they had sex, Karen insisted that Connor take an AIDS test. Connor reported to Karen that he tested negative for HIV, but Karen gently told Connor that she wasn't ready to make love. Connor loosened Karen up with a few drinks and seduced her—without using a condom.

The next day a guilty Connor confided in Macy that he didn't use protection while he was with Karen. Macy told Karen. But Karen informed Macy that she had used her diaphragm as an added precaution against pregnancy. Meanwhile, Karen decided to let Connor think that he had gotten her pregnant.

During a double date with Macy and Anthony, Karen pretended to have cravings for unique food combinations. A nervous Connor suspected that Karen was pregnant. Later, Connor apologized to Karen for plying her with alcohol so she'd be more receptive to having sex. Determined to teach Connor a lesson, Karen told him that she was expecting.

Connor threw Karen a surprise wedding at his home because he thought she was pregnant with his baby.

Karen spotted airline information in Connor's belongings and feared he was going to skip town. Instead, Connor arranged a surprise wedding ceremony and invited Sally, Saul, Darla, Keith, and Kevin to his home. Karen and Macy showed up and didn't understand what was going on—until the minister arrived.

Connor confided in Anthony that he was only marrying Karen because of her pregnancy. Karen and Connor exchanged vows, but their union wasn't legal, since they hadn't signed the marriage license. Karen confessed that she wasn't really pregnant and that she wanted to teach Connor a lesson. Connor responded that he needed time to think before he'd sign the certificate.

While he was deciding, Connor took Darla out on a date, which upset Karen. Reviewing her life in Los Angeles, a despondent Karen decided to return to Starlight after receiving a call from Bonnie. Since Bill had recouped his investment in Spectra,

Karen signed the company back over to Sally. Connor visited Karen on her last day in Los Angeles and they parted as friends.

Connor took Darla out on a few dates, but a serious relationship between the two never truly formed.

Ivana/Dylan/Jessica/Sly

Eric's brother John and his wife, Maggie, sent their introverted teenage daughter, Jessica, to live with Stephanie due to marital strife and financial hardship. But Stephanie and Eric were surprised by Jessica's arrival, since John and Maggie didn't let them know she was coming.

Meanwhile, college student Dylan Shaw interviewed with Eric and Ridge for a summer internship. The Forrester men were impressed with Dylan's knowledge of the design world. Ridge hinted that Dylan might even have a job at Forrester after he graduated.

Dylan was informed that Forrester had a strict company rule: No dating the models. But when Forrester model Ivana Richards Vanderveld invited Dylan out to the beach, he couldn't help but accept.

Ridge and Thorne took Jessica to the Bikini Bar, where she struck up a friendship with Sly. Jessica also hit it off with Dylan when she met him at Forrester Creations. Ivana taunted Dylan for kissing up to the boss's niece, but Dylan asserted they were just pals.

Forrester Creations model Ivana Vanderveld didn't adhere to Forrester's policy on interemployee dating after she spotted attractive new intern Dylan Shaw.

Sly was aware that Jessica had a crush on Dylan and felt slighted. Sly was aware of Forrester's "No dating the models" policy, so when he and Jessica spotted Dylan and Ivana kissing, he visited Eric and mentioned Dylan's date with Ivana. Dylan was chewed out by Eric. Ivana accused Jessica of having snitched, but Jessica told Dylan she hadn't and then filled him in on Ivana's rudeness. Later, Jessica was disappointed to see Dylan flirt with Ivana. Dylan and Ivana threw Jess a party for her seventeenth birthday. The Forresters let Dylan accompany Jessica to her party.

At the celebration, Jessica cried after hearing Dylan say that Eric had asked him to keep an eye on her. Jess gave in to peer pressure and consumed several gelatin cubes that contained vodka. Sly whisked a tipsy Jessica off to Ivana's bedroom. Dylan pulled Sly away from Jess before he could "seduce" her. Dylan brought Jessica home from the party and gave her a birthday kiss.

The next day Stephanie explained to Jessica that her parents had asked her and Eric to become Jess's legal guardians. Eric's first parental assignment was to send Jessica off for a day of fun at Universal Studios with Dylan. Later, Dylan gave Jessica a necklace as a gift. She thanked him with a kiss. Jessica and Dylan were falling in love. Soon after, in Dylan's dorm room, Dylan and Jessica made love.

Stephanie spied some flowers that Dylan anonymously sent to Jessica and wondered who they were from. Not wanting to jeopardize Dylan's position at Forrester, Jess remained mum. Jess informed Dylan that they needed to lay low. Later, though, Jessica blurted out to Stephanie that Dylan was her boyfriend. When Stephanie found some condoms in Jessica's dresser, she raced over to Dylan's dorm room and found Jessica and Dylan together.

JESSICA FORRESTER AND DYLAN SHAW

Season eight marked the first chapter in a new, young love story on *The Bold and the Beautiful*. Eric's niece, Jessica, arrived unexpectedly from Iowa when his brother John's marriage to Maggie was falling apart. Meanwhile, at Forrester Creations, Eric had accepted a new college intern, Dylan Shaw. It was inevitable that Jessica's and Dylan's paths would cross. To play the roles of Jessica and Dylan, *The Bold and the Beautiful* hired two newcomers to daytime television, seventeen-year-old Maitland Ward and Dylan Neal.

Before Maitland joined the cast of *The Bold and the Beautiful*, she'd been up for one other role, on *Saved by the Bell*. Although Maitland was an inexperienced actress, her desire to act dated back to her early childhood. Maitland's parents enrolled her in acting classes when she was nine years old, but a professional career was put on hold when she started wearing braces as a teenager. Once the braces were off, however, Maitland was ready to pursue her dream. A few months later she landed the role on *The Bold and the Beautiful*.

Recalling her first few months on the show, Maitland told *Soap Opera Digest,* "I was very naive, especially about the acting business when I got this job. One of my first days on the set, John McCook said, 'You're going to learn more about acting in the next few months than you ever

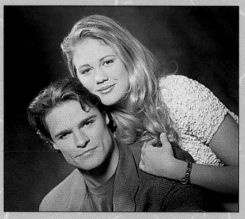

Dylan Neal and Maitland Ward

could in class.' I was, like, 'Oh, yeah, whatever,' but he was so right."

Maitland credits her more experienced castmates with helping her adjust to her new role. She especially appreciated the protective role Dylan Neal adopted in her interest. "Dylan is so great! He really watches out for me," she says.

Although Maitland enjoyed her first break soon after pursuing an acting career, it was a different story for Canadian-born Dylan Neal. He arrived in Los Angeles from Canada in 1992 and came close to landing roles on such soaps as *Days of Our Lives, The Young and the Restless,* and *Guiding Light.* But when it came down to the wire, the nod ultimately went to another actor. Dylan finally got his shot with *The Bold and the Beautiful.* Recognizing the opportunity he has to hone his acting skills on the show, Dylan paraphrases a quote from an actor he admires, Kevin Costner. "He once said 'I always believe I have the right to get better.' I loved it. You can't start at the level of Robert De Niro. You have to grow as an actor, and that means you have to grow as a person because that's where your acting comes from; who you are. Also, everyone will tell you that you have to get worse as an actor before you get better, which is what acting is all about; to make your mistakes and learn what you're doing."

Stephanie had Dylan arrested for statutory rape, since Jess was only seventeen years old and Dylan was twenty when they had sex. Eric fired Dylan, who spent the night in jail, unable to post a $25,000 bond. The next day Ivana put up the funds.

Jessica implored Eric not to prosecute Dylan. Eric agreed to let Dylan escort Jessica to Ridge and Brooke's wedding, but told him he'd better watch his step.

Sally overheard Dylan and Jessica discuss their dilemma and invited Dylan to drop by her office. Later, Dylan accepted Sally's offer to work at Spectra. Meanwhile, District Attorney Teresa Emerson met with the Forresters to discuss Jessica's case. Jessica informed the authorities that she willingly went to bed with Dylan. Still, the DA's office decided to proceed with its case against Dylan.

Despite Jessica's supporting testimony, the grand jury handed down an indictment against Dylan. Sally hired Connor to defend Dylan. Stephanie ordered Jessica to stop seeing Dylan, at least until after the trial.

Ivana brightened Jessica's mood by asking her pal Jose Eber, a famous hairstylist, to give Jessica a makeover. Jessica loved her new look. Later, the judge ordered Dylan to stay away from Jessica, but Dylan told Connor nothing could keep them apart. When Stephanie got wind of a secret meeting between the two lovebirds (arranged by Sally), Sally told Jessica to hightail it back home. Upon discovering that Dylan was working at Spectra, Stephanie deduced that Sally was bankrolling Connor on Dylan's behalf. Eric chastised Sally for encouraging Dylan and Jessica's romance.

Later, Dylan, against the court's orders, visited the Forrester mansion to see Jessica. Eric and Dylan got into a fight as Dylan attempted to go up the stairs. Jessica came upon the two men and ordered her uncle to stop. When Eric tried to explain to Jessica that she was too young to understand love, Jessica pointed out to her uncle that he had been married to three women in the last five years, so therefore what kind of expert was he? Eric was deeply hurt by Jess's words.

Eric testified that Dylan took advantage of his innocent niece. Then Jessica took the stand. Trying to keep Dylan out of jail, Jessica told the court that she didn't think she should have to say whether or not they had had sex.

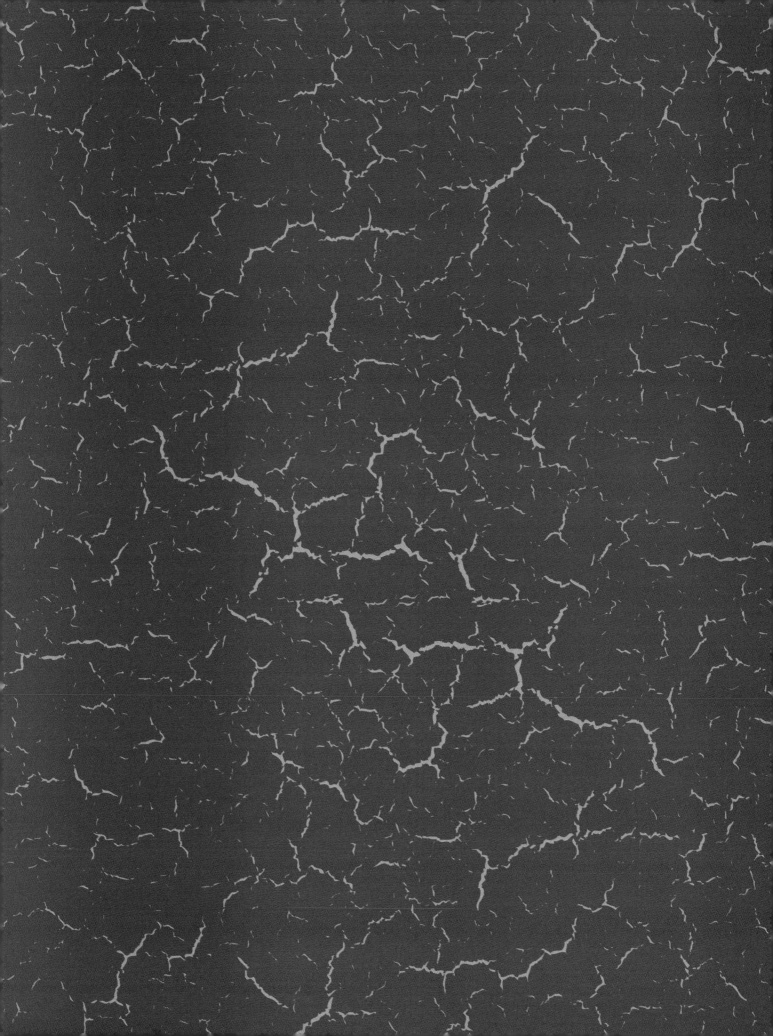

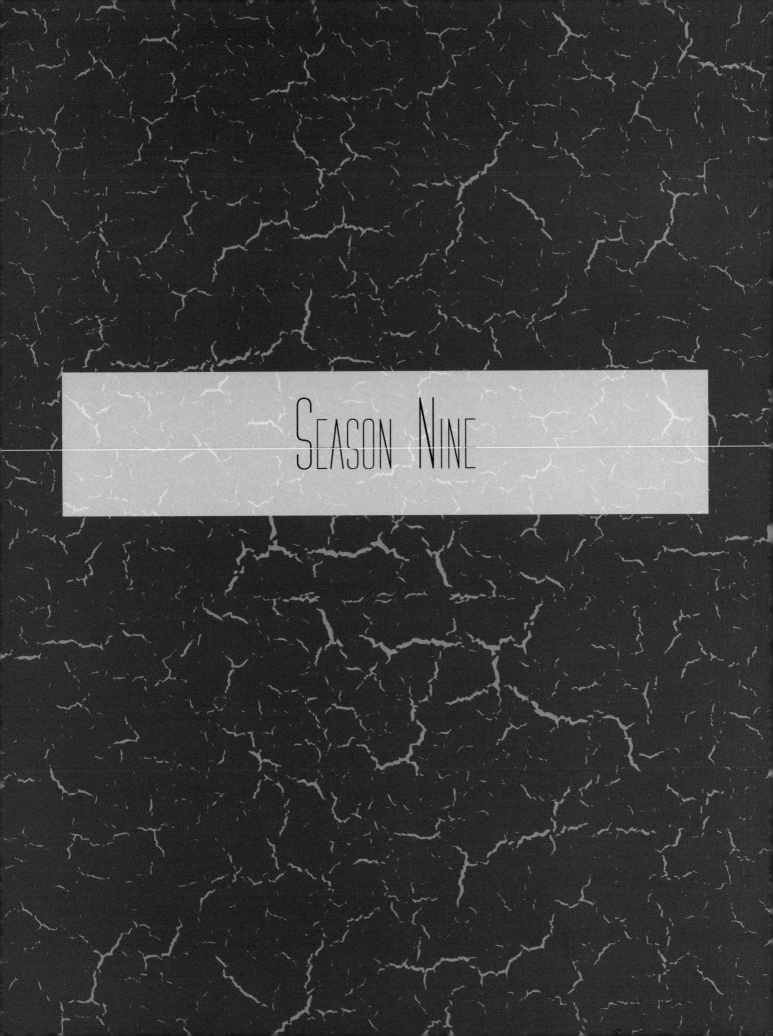

SEASON NINE

Ninth season cast photo. Back row, left to right: Michael Fox (Saul), Maitland Ward (Jessica), Dylan Neal (Dylan), Lindsay Price (Michael), Lark Voorhies (Jasmine), Jeff Trachta (Thorne). Middle row, left to right: Scott Thompson Baker (Connor), Barbara Crampton (Maggie), Bobbie Eakes (Macy), Schae Harrison (Darla), Darlene Conley (Sally), Ian Buchanan (James). Front row, left to right: Katherine Kelly Lang (Brooke), Ronn Moss (Ridge), Susan Flannery (Stephanie), John McCook (Eric), Hunter Tylo (Taylor).

JESSICA/DYLAN

As Dylan's statutory rape trial proceeded, Jessica testified that she and Dylan had only made love once. After Connor discussed with Dylan the likelihood that he'd be convicted, Jessica suggested to Dylan that they run away. Dylan initially agreed, but he changed his mind and drove back to Los Angeles while Jessica was asleep.

After Teresa concluded her closing statements at Dylan's trial, Stephanie told the court that Dylan acted responsibly in not running away with Jessica. The jury returned a verdict of not guilty. Jessica made up with Eric and Stephanie. Meanwhile, Jessica and Dylan decided to put their relationship on hold.

MAGGIE/JESSICA/DYLAN/MICHAEL

Jessica's mother, Maggie, newly divorced, pulled up to the Forrester mansion in her RV. Maggie informed Stephanie that she wanted Jessica to move back to

Iowa, but Jess didn't want to leave, since she had just been accepted to the University of Southern California on a full scholarship.

Maggie moved into the Forrester guest house. Meanwhile, since Dylan's romance to Jessica was on hold, they agreed to see other people. Dylan shared several kisses with Darla. He also moved into his new apartment, where he learned that his sight-unseen roommate, Michael, was actually a girl.

One night Dylan met Maggie, unaware that she was Jessica's mom. The two hit it off and began dating. Dylan and Maggie kissed on the beach after a day of boogie-boarding. Sly spied the kiss and told Jessica, who darted off to Dylan's, where she found him setting up a romantic dinner for two and left. Jessica poured her heart out to Maggie, who urged her to fight for her beau. Meanwhile, neither mother nor daughter realized they were involved with the same man.

When Jessica brought Dylan home for dinner, Dylan and Maggie were shocked to discover each other's connection to Jessica. Dylan suggested to Maggie that they tell Jessica the truth, but Maggie didn't want to hurt her daughter. Dylan told Maggie that he loved her. Maggie refused to see Dylan, but he wouldn't accept that and convinced her to go away with him for a few days. They realized how much in love they really were and decided to come clean with Jessica.

Just before Dylan was about to tell Jessica the truth about his romance with Maggie, Jessica fainted. Later, she was diagnosed with diabetes, which was treatable through medication and diet.

Stephanie deduced that Dylan and Maggie were dating and, out of concern for Jessica, criticized both of them. Michael offered Dylan a solution to spare Jessica's feelings: she'd pose as his girlfriend. Maggie broke off her relationship with Dylan for Jessica's sake. Later, Dylan responded to a kiss from Michael.

Dylan sent Jessica a breakup letter with some flowers. Believing that Dylan was still involved with Maggie, Stephanie became livid. Later, Maggie refused Stephanie's request that she leave town. Instead, she reinvented herself to show Stephanie how well she could fit in. Meanwhile, Michael told Jessica that she was the other woman in Dylan's life. Maggie was relieved that Jessica thought the girl in Dylan's life was Michael—but Maggie also felt a twinge of regret because she realized things were finished between her and Dylan.

Sly caught Dylan off guard when he revealed that he'd seen Dylan and Maggie kissing. Soon after, Sly and Jessica began dating again. Meanwhile, Sly promised Maggie that he'd never hurt Jess. But after Sly's boss at the Bikini Bar berated him in front of his friends, Sly devised a get-rich plan. Sly proposed to Jessica. She agreed to wear his ring while she made up her mind about his proposal.

After Ridge told Maria, Stephanie's housekeeper, she could visit her ill aunt, Jessica suggested that Maggie take over in Maria's absence. Unable to find work, Maggie agreed and gave Stephanie cooking tips so that she could snare Eric. Later, Jessica gave Maggie an angel pin for Christmas for watching over her.

BROOKE/RIDGE/TAYLOR/OMAR

Taylor was stunned to discover that Omar's biographer, Brewster MacKensay, was her former mentor, James Warwick. Taylor tried to convince James that she loved her new life as Princess Laila of Morocco and almost succeeded when she performed a sensual snake dance for Omar in James's presence. She finally confessed that she was staying in Morocco because Ridge loved Brooke now and she didn't want to complicate his life.

Unable to change Taylor's mind, James returned to the U.S. and swore Connor to secrecy that Taylor was alive. Connor feared for Brooke's future, since she was considering returning their company stock to the Forresters now that she was married to Ridge. Meanwhile, Stephanie tried her best to befriend Brooke so that Brooke would return their stock.

Taylor's dad, Jack, suffered a heart attack after visiting Taylor's "grave." James phoned Taylor in Morocco and informed her of Jack's condition. Taylor

BELOW: *Taylor does a Moroccan-style snake dance.*

BELOW RIGHT: *When Taylor returned to America to check on her ailing dad, she arranged a makeover with Gladys, a beautician (played by Phyllis Diller). The disguise was so convincing that Taylor was able to be in the same room with Brooke and Ridge—and not be recognized!*

returned home to visit her dad. But a heavily medicated Jack thought he'd seen an angel. Meanwhile, Taylor hired a beautician named Gladys to give her a disguise so that Taylor could roam about Los Angeles and not be recognized. On a subsequent visit to the hospital, Taylor revealed to Jack that she was still alive but asked that he keep the news to himself. Meanwhile, Omar flew to Los Angeles with the intention of bringing Taylor back to Morocco.

Overjoyed to discover that his daughter was still alive, Jack recuperated quickly. A disguised Taylor spied on Ridge and Brooke as they con-

ducted a seminar. Jessica gave Taylor a tour of Forrester, not knowing that her new friend was Ridge's "deceased" wife.

Meanwhile, Ridge was blinded in a laboratory accident. Taylor visited Ridge in the hospital but didn't reveal her identity to him. Jack urged Taylor to fight for Ridge.

Brooke presented the Forresters with a preliminary agreement to return their stock. But when Taylor revealed her presence to Brooke, she retracted her offer. Stephanie was furious.

Ridge underwent surgery to restore his eyesight. While he recovered, Brooke let Taylor care for Ridge so that she could see how happy he was. Later, Taylor revealed herself to Stephanie. Taylor told Stephanie about her ordeal and subsequent marriage to Prince Omar. Stephanie called Taylor a bigamist and ordered her to stay away from Ridge. Taylor considered returning to Morocco.

Ridge's final bandages were removed and his vision was restored. He opened his front door and found Taylor standing before him. Ridge was both

Ridge sees Taylor for the first time since her "death."

stunned and overjoyed to discover that Taylor was alive.

But Ridge felt betrayed by Taylor when Omar informed him that Taylor was Princess Laila—his wife.

Taylor explained that she had wed Omar after she saw how happy Ridge and Brooke were from behind a one-way mirror. Dismayed that Taylor had moved on so quickly, Ridge walked away.

The Forresters held a press conference to announce Taylor's return.

Stephanie apologized to Taylor for initially having been less than thrilled by her return and once again welcomed her into their family.

At the hearing to determine who Ridge was legally married to, the judge asked Ridge which wife he loved. Ridge said that he loved both women.

The judge ruled that Taylor and Ridge were still legally married and that Ridge and Brooke's union was invalid. Ridge went to the Forrester cabin to contemplate which woman he wanted to spend the rest of his life with. Despite Stephanie's campaigning for Taylor, Ridge selected Brooke. Taylor was devastated, Brooke ecstatic. After Taylor rejected Omar, the prince returned to Morocco.

Sheila tries to drown Lauren in a hot tub.

SHEILA/JAMES

Upon his return from Morocco, James resumed his counseling sessions with Sheila. James assured Sheila that any discussion they had would be held in confidence unless Sheila confessed to a crime.

Eric confided to Lauren that Sheila no longer made him happy. Sheila stalled Lauren from telling Eric about their past by reminding her about Scott's dying wish. When that no longer worked, Sheila tried to drown Lauren, but Lauren hit her on the head and escaped. Lauren then revealed Sheila's shady past to James.

Confident that James would fill Eric in on his nasty wife, Lauren returned to Genoa City. Before James could tell Eric anything, Sheila and Mike kidnapped him and locked him in a secret dungeon located beneath Sheila and Eric's house. Sheila had plenty of contraptions to bind James. After all, the house had once been owned by Harry Houdini.

Sheila forced James to phone Eric and Stephanie and say he was leaving town indefinitely. Eric handed Sheila a divorce petition and moved out, then fired her from Forrester. James offered Sheila some words of comfort. She rewarded James with food and care after he became sick.

James realized the only way Sheila would ever release him would be to convince her he was in love with her. Mike became jealous when he came upon James and Sheila kissing. Mike taunted Sheila and

LAUREN FENMORE

Tracey Bregman enjoyed making several crossover appearances from *The Young and the Restless* over the years, so when the decision was made to permanently move the character to *The Bold and the Beautiful* in 1995, Tracey was already familiar with the cast, producers, and crew. "I had been doing the show for the last three years, I had established relationships, so it was safe," she told *Soap Opera Digest*.

"I'm thankful that Lauren's sexual side has been brought back on *The Bold and the Beautiful*," says Tracey. "It's a big part of who she is." Of course, showing Lauren's sexy side, also meant being dressed in more revealing clothing, such as swimwear. One of Tracey's first scenes on *The Bold and the Beautiful* involved a fantasy scene with Ronn Moss at a swimming pool. "I knew Ronn, but not very well,"

Traceey Bregman

Tracey says. "I thought, Well, we're going to get to know each other today. He couldn't have been more of a gentleman." Tracey was also impressed by director Susan Flannery's sensitivity toward her fellow actors. "Susan was really conscientious about the angle at which my body looked the best and turned off the monitors in the whole building. I came home and said to my husband, Ron Recht, 'It was really okay.'"

Since Lauren's arrival in Los Angeles, she's had plenty of opportunity to stir up trouble, such as flirting with Ridge, despite his obvious interest in Brooke and Taylor. She's also been busy working on a business project with Eric Forrester. "Lauren's still very powerful and interesting," observes Tracey. "And spicy. I've always loved the spicy part of her personality."

said James was only romancing her to win his freedom, but Sheila was already falling in love with James. James made love to Sheila.

Stephanie overheard Mike talking about a psychiatrist. Knowing that Mike and Sheila were pals and concerned about James's disappearance, Stephanie barged into Sheila's house and asked her about James. Having heard the doorbell ring, James banged on a metal pipe for help but later lied to Sheila that he did it because he thought she was in danger. Sheila didn't believe him and realized James had betrayed her.

Sheila came at James with a knife, but he managed to overpower her and locked Sheila in the dungeon that had kept him prisoner. James left to get the police, but upon his return he found that Sheila had escaped. Per Stephanie's request, Lauren finally told Eric everything about Sheila, including how she once kidnapped her son, Scotty.

Sheila holds the Forresters and Lauren Fenmore at gunpoint.

Sheila summoned Lauren, Eric, Stephanie, James, Ridge, and Brooke for a showdown. Sheila held the group at gunpoint and threatened to kill Stephanie. After Brooke and Ridge offered to take a bullet first, Sheila swallowed a bottle of poison and appeared to die. But later, Lt. Burke told everyone that Sheila had survived and was in a hospital for the criminally insane.

Lauren moved to Los Angeles and into the Forrester guest house. She and James bonded over their ordeals with Sheila.

BRIAN/SHEILA/SARAH

Eric needed Sheila to sign their final divorce papers, so he and Stephanie went to visit Sheila in prison. Eric and Stephanie were surprised that Sheila so willingly signed the divorce decree. Dr. Brian Carey, Sheila's doctor, was impressed with Sheila's progress.

Sheila's unstable roommate Sarah went berserk and tried to kill Stephanie. Sheila saved Stephanie's life. Still, thanks to a letter from Stephanie and

RIGHT: *Sheila testified before the parole board and asked for a second chance.*

BELOW: *Sheila's most credible supporter was Dr. Brian Carey, her psychiatrist, who felt that his star patient deserved to be paroled.*

Lauren, Sheila's parole was denied. Later, Sheila and Sarah were assaulted by Geri and Ulma, two inmates. Sheila refused to name her attackers.

At a second hearing, the Forresters, James, and Lauren testified that Sheila should remain in jail. Meanwhile, Brian, Nurse Croft, and Sarah were in Sheila's corner. The parole board announced that Sheila would be released—provided she continued to receive treatment from James. Brian helped Sheila settle into her new home in West Hollywood.

Sheila met with Brooke and thanked her for always being her pal. When Brooke received a rose sent by Sheila, Stephanie thought it came from a lover and assumed that Brooke was cheating on Ridge. Concerned about the Forresters' reaction to Sheila, as well as her earlier behavior, Brooke informed Sheila that she and Brooke couldn't be friends anymore. Sheila was devastated. Mike lifted an invitation to Ridge and Brooke's wedding from Brooke's assistant Megan's desk and gave it to Sheila so that she could crash Ridge and Brooke's ceremony.

ERIC/TAYLOR/RIDGE/BROOKE/ERIC JR./C.J.

Stephanie helped Taylor find a new home by the beach and urged her to fight for Ridge.

Eric Jr.'s sudden unruly behavior caused stress for Brooke and Ridge. They were shocked to see that Eric Jr. was starting fights with Sally's son, C.J. (also known as Clarke Jr.). The young Spectra boy bullied Eric Jr. because his half-brother was also his stepdad. The problem escalated to the point where Macy and Thorne's wedding was marred when Eric Jr. and C.J. engaged in a brutal fistfight. Stephanie advised that Eric Jr. get counseling from Taylor.

Later, Ridge saved Taylor from a masked attacker in her home. Since Ridge fell asleep on Taylor's sofa, Brooke accused Taylor of inventing the prowler, until Ridge confirmed his existence.

Eric Jr., who started going by the name Rick, told Taylor that he wished that she and Ridge were still married so that his parents could be together. Eric confessed to Taylor his wish for a reunion with Brooke. Meanwhile, Brooke reminded Eric that their love affair was over.

Rick asked Ridge to move out until after he wed Brooke. Naturally, Brooke and Ridge refused. Rick checked with Connor to see what his legal rights were in case he wanted to live with Eric.

Eric started to fantasize about Taylor. When a Forrester employee complained of stress, Eric hired Taylor to act as an in-house therapist. Brooke disapproved of Eric's choice. Eric visited Taylor often at her new home, and one night he kissed her. Taylor gently informed Eric that there was no way she could ever get involved with him because she wouldn't want to hurt Stephanie.

Ridge and Brooke agreed to throw a party for Eric so that he could meet some women. Among the invited guests were Stephanie and Lauren. Eric gave Taylor a gown from his new collection and invited her to be his date at the party. Not wanting to hurt Stephanie, Taylor sent Forrester model Samantha in her place. Samantha handed Eric an apology note from Taylor, who had gone to Palm Springs. Eric was devastated and sought solace in Stephanie.

In an effort to get Taylor and Ridge back together, Stephanie arranged for them to be trapped

Although Rick didn't live with his dad, Eric, they shared a close father and son relationship.

Mr. Blackwell with Stephanie and Sally at a party for Eric that Ridge and Brooke arranged so Eric could meet women.

in an elevator. Unaware that Taylor was claustrophobic, Ridge comforted Taylor but remained committed to Brooke.

Lauren told Maggie that she was going to pursue Ridge because he wasn't officially married to Brooke yet. Lauren flirted with Ridge in the steam room, but Brooke caught them and ordered Lauren to back off. Later, Ridge had Taylor sign their divorce papers. Taylor refused Ridge's invitation to attend his wedding and Rick turned down Ridge's offer to be his best man.

THORNE/MACY/ANTHONY/IVANA

Macy's doctor told her that her cancer operation was a success, but he doubted that she'd ever be able to sing again. Anthony and Ivana secretly wished that Macy wouldn't recover her voice so that she and Thorne would have one less reason to be together.

Thorne asked Macy to remarry him and she joyfully said yes. Later, at a lavish party, Anthony proposed to Macy. She said no. Ivana and Anthony both felt that Thorne was responsible for their unhappiness.

Macy sadly announced to Decadent record executives that she wouldn't be able to sing for them anymore because of her cancer. Meanwhile, Thorne's engagement did nothing to deter Ivana's interest. Anthony was furious to learn that Sally would accept Thorne as her son-in-law again.

Anxious to have Thorne for herself, Ivana locked the two of them in his office and began undressing. Thorne ordered her out. Eric's secretary, Trish, witnessed the encounter but assumed Thorne wanted Ivana.

Next, Ivana wrote a cruel "fan" letter to Macy and signed it "Irv." Darla read the nasty note. Macy couldn't believe that someone would want her to suffer. Anthony suggested to Ivana that they double-date with Thorne and Macy. The foursome enjoyed a nice evening, but Ivana was perplexed by Macy's news that she'd received a second threatening letter. Ivana knew she had only sent one. After getting a third note, Macy involved the police. Ivana was crushed when Anthony said he didn't believe Ivana wrote only one letter. Meanwhile, Macy found roses in her home from Irv.

Thorne realized that the initials of Ivana's full name—Ivana Richards Vanderveld—spelled out I.R.V., so he called the police. Meanwhile, Ivana accused Anthony of sending the letters. He calmed her by proposing marriage. Ivana accepted but was later a suspect when her fingerprints were found on one of Macy's "fan" letters.

Anthony stole a letter opener from Thorne that contained Thorne's fingerprints. Later, Ivana caught Thorne searching for evidence in her apartment. An angry Thorne warned Ivana to stay away from Macy. Ivana called the police for help, but Thorne quickly departed. Anthony arrived and revealed to Ivana that he was Macy's secret letter writer. Then Anthony murdered Ivana with Thorne's letter opener just before the police arrived.

As Thorne and Macy stood at the altar about to exchange vows, the police arrested Thorne for Ivana's murder. Lt. Burke reminded Thorne that he had once shot Ridge, even though Burke was never able to prove it. While Thorne was held without bail, Anthony's grieving boyfriend act won sympathy from Macy. Macy feared that a depressed Anthony would commit suicide, so she asked him to move in with her so she could keep an eye on him. Anthony asked Macy to go to Mexico with him so they could fully concentrate on who killed Ivana and framed Thorne. Macy reluctantly agreed.

Thorne's cellmate, Slash, told Thorne that he was planning a prison break. Once in Mexico smooth-operating Anthony put the moves on Macy, claiming she reminded him of Ivana. Meanwhile, Dylan found the same stationery used for Macy's evil fan letters in Anthony's office and told Thorne. Slash and Thorne escaped by hiding in laundry carts. Thorne learned from Dylan that Macy was in Mexico with Anthony and raced to confront him. Macy overheard Anthony confess to Thorne that he, Anthony, had indeed murdered Ivana. Macy formulated a plan and pretended to believe that Anthony was innocent and that Thorne was guilty. Devastated, Thorne took off but was recaptured. Macy and Anthony returned to Los Angeles. Macy visited Thorne in jail, and Macy revealed to him that she knew Anthony was the killer.

Macy lied to Anthony about what a turn-on it was that Thorne killed Ivana. Hoping that Anthony would confess his crime to her, Macy tape-recorded their next several discussions. Finally, Anthony confessed murdering Ivana to Macy, who recorded his tale on tape. But Macy learned that the tape was inaudible because the batteries on the recorder were low, and then she inadvertently dropped the cassette.

Anthony murdered Ivana and framed Thorne for the crime. Here, Macy holds Anthony at gunpoint after getting him to confess to his plan.

Anthony found the audiotape and deduced that Macy was setting him up. Sally snuck into Macy's apartment to warn her about Anthony, but he had already pulled a gun on Macy. Sally was shot by Anthony instead of Macy. As Sally lay bleeding, Anthony planned on raping and then killing Macy. Just then, the police, including Lt. Burke, burst into the room. Anthony was arrested as Sally was rushed to the hospital.

A mother's love: Sally took the bullet that Anthony had intended to put into Macy. Macy comforted her mother just before the police burst in and rescued them.

Thorne was released from prison. Sally recovered but found her hospital roommate, Jasmine, an aspiring designer, annoying. Jasmine had interviewed for an internship at Spectra Fashions, but she and Sally took an immediate dislike to each other. In fact, Jasmine was in the hospital recovering from injuries she sustained when the faulty Spectra elevator plunged three floors. George, a lawyer, tried to get Jasmine to sue, but Jasmine's friend Michael told her that she shouldn't because she wasn't seriously hurt.

Jasmine overheard Sally complain about Spectra's lack of new gowns now that they were without a designer. So she snuck one of her own sketches into Sally's pile of work. Unaware that Jasmine was the designer, Sally put her design into production.

Stephanie informed Macy that she was welcome in the Forrester family. Macy and Thorne wed on the beach outside the Bikini Bar. Miraculously, Macy's singing voice returned and she sang a song to Thorne at the reception.

Sally hired an unsuspecting Jasmine to redesign sketches for gowns stolen from Forrester Creations. But fearing that stealing from Forrester would jeopardize Thorne and Macy's marriage, Sally put her plan on hold. Until, that is, Rick Forrester dumped chocolate mousse on her son C.J.'s head. Sally then instructed Saul to hire ex–Forrester security head Mike Guthrie. In a meeting with Mike, Sally ordered him to steal designs from Forrester for her. Desperate for money, Mike accepted the job.

Mike got his spot at Forrester back by "rescuing" Eric from muggers. Eric was so grateful that he didn't realize that Mike had arranged for Eric to be attacked. Once inside Forrester, Mike photographed several Forrester sketches. Sally had the sketches copied and then gave the sketches to an innocent Jasmine, who was asked to modify each sketch.

Michael sensed something was wrong and quizzed Ridge about design security. Darla spotted Ridge explaining to Michael that Forrester sketches have identifying marks on them that make them unique. Since Sally's sketches still had the Forrester mark on them, she feared that her plan would be

Mike, here posing as a homeless man, arranged for Eric to be mugged so that Mike could save him and win Eric's gratitude. It was all part of Mike's scheme to get back into Forrester Creations so that he could steal designs for his new boss, Sally Spectra.

exposed and offered Michael a modeling gig to buy her silence. Michael said no thanks. Meanwhile, Mike wanted payment from Sally, but she didn't have the cash.

Eric trusted Macy with a sneak preview of his newest collection, unaware that Spectra Fashions had already seen it. Michael informed Eric that Sally was ripping him off. Eric planned to romance Sally so she'd feel too guilty to steal from him. Stephanie was devastated when she spied Eric flirting with Sally. Eric confided his scheme to Lauren.

ABOVE: *Eric wooed Sally so she'd abandon her scheme to steal his designs. His plan worked, but Sally couldn't stay mad at Eric forever.*

RIGHT: *Los Angeles's most eligible bachelor was Eric Forrester. Even Sally's secretary, Darla, fantasized about being the special woman in Eric's life.*

After Sally had a few more dates with Eric, Darla pointed out that her pal Sally would have to choose between Eric and his designs. Eric proposed marriage to Sally after a Forrester fashion show and gave her an engagement ring. Sally said yes. She then ordered Saul to pull Eric's designs from her showing, which was being held at the same time.

Eric told a heartbroken Stephanie why he had proposed to Sally. The Forrester matriarch barged into Sally's office, explaining why Eric had proposed to her. She smashed Sally's "diamond" ring into glass pieces. Sally was devastated. Eric gently admitted to Sally that he had to save his collection. Sally told Eric that she still loved him.

Later, Mike and Jasmine quit. Jasmine took a waitressing job at the Bikini Bar and flirted with Sly. Stephanie took pity on Sally and invited her and C.J. to spend Christmas with Macy, Thorne, and the rest of the Forrester family.

The Bold and the Beautiful *marked its two-thousandth episode with producers and cast cutting the cake. They included, front row, left to right: Katherine Kelly Lang (Brooke), Ronn Moss (Ridge), Bradley Bell (executive producer and head writer), Susan Flannery (Stephanie), Maitland Ward (Jessica), co-creator Lee Phillip Bell, Jeff Trachta (Thorne), creator William J. Bell, and associate producer Rhonda Friedman.*

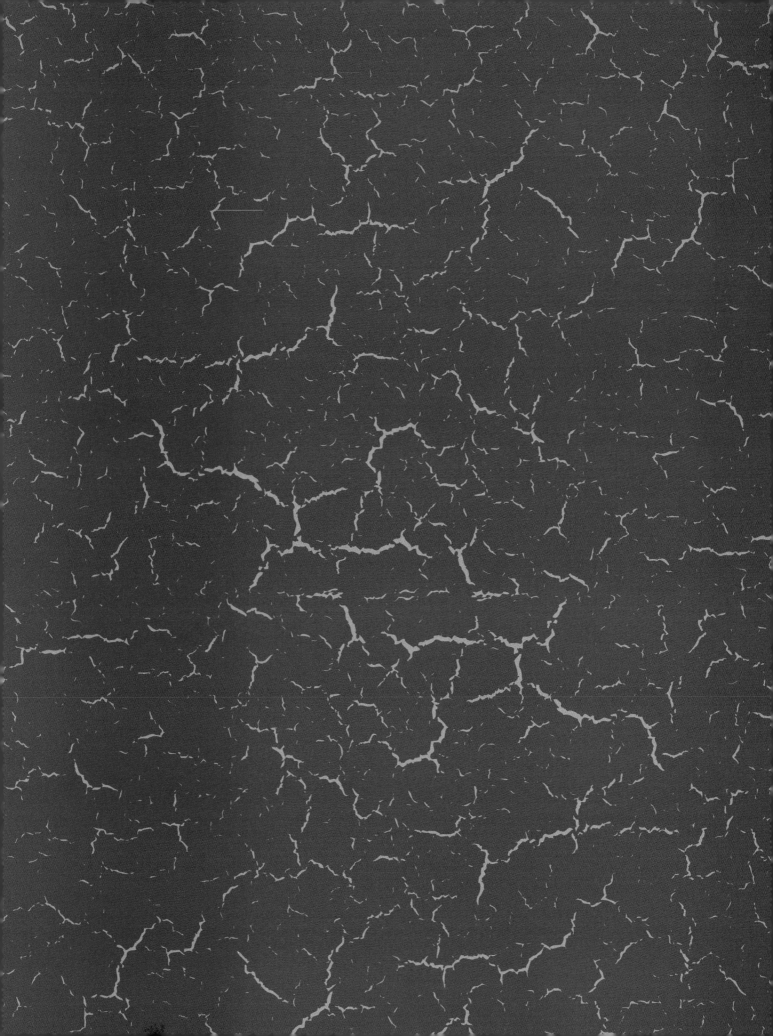

SEASON TEN

TAYLOR/RIDGE/BROOKE/BRIDGET/ERIC/SHEILA/MIKE

Taylor reprimanded Stephanie for trapping her in the elevator with Ridge. Stephanie apologized and said she hadn't known that Taylor was claustrophobic. Meanwhile, Brooke visited Sheila and ordered her not to attend her wedding. Mike was livid that Brooke was so mean to Sheila. Stephanie chastised Brooke for seeing Sheila. Unfortunately, Ridge agreed with his mother and said it was best for everyone if Sheila stayed out of their lives.

Sheila warned James that Mike could harm Brooke. At the same time, Mike confronted Brooke for not befriending Sheila. Sensing she was in danger, Brooke attempted to call for help, but Mike yanked her phone out of the wall. As Mike drew a gun on Brooke, security officials entered and threw Mike out of the building. Ridge was relieved that Brooke was unharmed. Later, Mike hit Sally up for some money, but she refused.

Sheila and Maggie met at Insomnia, a coffeehouse, but Maggie didn't know that this was the same woman who was married to Eric. When Maggie discovered Sheila's identity, she had doubts about continuing their friendship. Eventually, Maggie changed her mind and befriended Sheila.

Beth returned home to help Brooke prepare for the wedding. Meanwhile, after Ridge took Rick on a helicopter ride, Ridge asked Rick to be his best man and he agreed. Bridget was excited to be appointed flower girl.

Later, Ridge, who was feeling very contented with his life, took out a favorite book from his bookcase. When Ridge opened the book, an old letter fell out. The letter was addressed to Brooke, from Dr. Tracy Peters, who had performed Bridget's paternity test several years earlier. In the note, Dr. Peters

With Ridge having divorced Taylor, Ridge and Brooke made plans for their upcoming marriage. A surprising turn of events developed, however, that postponed the ceremony.

acknowledged that she would agree to Brooke's request that Ridge be revealed as the father—whether he was or not—in exchange for $1 million. Ridge confronted Brooke with the note and she denied any involvement. Brooke accused Stephanie of sending the note, but the Forrester matriarch charged that the letter was probably authentic.

Ridge and Brooke discovered that Dr. Peters would be unable to verify the letter since she'd been killed in a recent mugging. After examining a sample of Dr. Peters's writing, Brooke and Ridge were stunned to discover that the signatures matched. Ridge accused Sheila of being behind the scam, but she claimed innocence. Meanwhile, Stephanie informed Eric of the letter. Eric was visibly shaken and insisted they run another paternity test. In an emotional confrontation with Brooke, a furious Eric asked her how she could have robbed him of his daughter's early years. Although Brooke understood Eric's reaction, she maintained that the letter was a fraud and refused to take a new set of blood tests. But Stephanie finally persuaded Brooke to change her mind when she promised to accept Brooke into the Forrester family if the test proved Ridge to be Bridget's father.

While the paternity test results were being determined, Ridge and Brooke went to the Forrester cabin, where they contemplated leaving Los Angeles and never coming back.

When Brooke came home, she found Stephanie searching for proof that Brooke had paid off Dr. Peters. Stephanie suggested to Eric that if he turned out to be Bridget's father, they should have both Rick and Bridget taken away from Brooke.

Mike suspected that Sheila had written the letter from Dr. Peters. Feeling that Mike was a loose cannon, Sheila lured him to her home. With her tape recorder running, she got Mike to describe how he would have planted the letter in Brooke's house and how he would have killed Dr. Peters so she couldn't testify against him. Sheila played back Mike's "confession" and blackmailed him into leaving town.

Dr. Benson announced to Eric, Stephanie, Ridge, and Brooke that Bridget's biological father was Eric. The news was a crushing blow to Brooke and Ridge, but Stephanie was thrilled. Eric was eager to build a relationship with Bridget and became more involved in her life, but a decision was made not to immediately break the news to Bridget.

Lauren visited Sheila and accused her longtime nemesis of causing the paternity mixup. Sheila said she'd never hurt her best friend Brooke.

As a result of the paternity results, Ridge was not emotionally ready to marry Brooke, which devastated her. Ridge, too, was devastated by the loss of the daughter whom he loved so much. He was also unconvinced that Brooke had not participated in what Dr. Peters's letter accused her of. Brooke was deeply hurt by Ridge's lack of faith in her.

Meanwhile, Sheila paid a visit to a despondent Brooke and suggested that the Forresters had never really cared about Brooke; they were only interested in her children.

In an effort to give Brooke the benefit of the doubt, Stephanie suggested they have the letter authenticated. Brooke stated that the letter had mysteriously vanished. Sensing Brooke's vulnerability and concerned for the welfare of her own family, Stephanie badgered Brooke into going back to Paris with her mother. Feeling defeated, Brooke agreed to go for a short while. Stephanie then arranged for Eric, Rick, and Bridget to stay at her mansion while Brooke was away. After observing Eric with his children, Stephanie suggested he seek full custody of Rick and Bridget.

Ridge informed Taylor that he wanted to work things out with Brooke. While Brooke was out of the country, Ridge spent time with Taylor, who drew on her skills as a therapist to help Ridge prepare Bridget for the news that Eric was actually her father.

After learning from Maggie that Stephanie was caring for Brooke's children, Sheila devised a plan to help her absent pal. Sheila did some research about poisons that could cause mental instability but were nearly impossible to detect in the human body. Later, while visiting Maggie at the Forrester home, Sheila snuck into Stephanie's medicine cabinet and replaced her calcium supplements with mercury pills.

The Forresters didn't understand why Brooke had stopped making daily phone calls to her children from Europe. When Jessica overheard Eric and Stephanie discussing the possibility of Eric seeking custody of the children in Brooke's absence, she warned Ridge to locate Brooke. Later, Beth was surprised when Ridge called her in Paris looking for Brooke, because she had already left for America. Ridge and Lauren, who had a mad crush on Ridge and saw this as an opportunity to spend some time alone with him, began their search for Brooke. Ridge also hired a private eye to help find Brooke. Ridge and Lauren's first stop was Paris. Finding that to be a dead end, they followed a lead to Miami. Having no luck there, the private eye sent them to Barbados based on information he had received.

Lauren accompanied Ridge to Barbados to help him search for Brooke. Ms. Fenmore always had a crush on Ridge, but she knew his heart belonged to Brooke.

Back in the States, James and Taylor deduced that Brooke was suffering from a condition called "brief reactive psychosis," brought on by the stress of the paternity test results. Indeed, Brooke was in a dazed state on Barbados and had stolen two dolls that she thought were Rick and Bridget. A young island girl named Abigail befriended Brooke. After Lauren headed back to L.A., Ridge found Brooke and promised never to hurt her again. She and Ridge enjoyed a romantic reunion in Barbados and returned home.

Meanwhile, Eric, aided by Stephanie and his lawyer, Jonathan Young, sued for custody of Rick and Bridget. Sheila tried to testify on Brooke's behalf, but the judge awarded custody to Eric. Stephanie's behavior was becoming erratic as a result of her mercury poisoning. Outside the courtroom, she physically lashed out at Sheila but was pulled away by Jonathan before she inflicted serious harm.

Fearing that she had lost Ridge, Brooke left the country and ended up in Barbados, where she suffered from a "brief reactive psychosis." When Ridge finally found her, she clung to two dolls, believing they were her children, Rick and Bridget.

Ridge phoned Stephanie from Barbados and announced he was returning with Brooke. Concerned for the children's safety, Stephanie convinced Eric to take Rick and Bridget to the Forrester cabin in Big Bear until they could assess Brooke's mental stability. When Ridge and Brooke returned, they were furious to discover that Stephanie had sent Rick and Bridget away, making it impossible for Brooke to see her children. Meanwhile, Taylor followed Eric to the Big Bear cabin and implored him to return to L.A. so that Brooke could be reunited with her children. Eric agreed.

Brooke finally enjoyed a joyful reunion with her children. Unfortunately, it was short-lived because Stephanie continued her efforts to keep Brooke away from them. Determined to win them back, Brooke agreed to seek therapy. But when Stephanie still resisted turning the children over to her, Brooke violated the custody agreement by running off to Big Bear with Rick and

Bridget. Ridge followed Brooke to Big Bear, and for a brief respite, they once again felt like a family. But when Stephanie learned of the children's whereabouts, she told the police, who arrested Brooke for child abduction.

Back in Los Angeles, Ridge visited Brooke in jail and tried to lift her spirits by displaying the engagement ring he had bought for her. Fearing for her safety in jail, Brooke pleaded with a conflicted Eric to post her bond and free her. At Brooke's hearing, Eric spoke on her behalf and the judge agreed to release Brooke.

Ridge proposed marriage, but Brooke said their happiness would have to wait until after their problems were resolved. Soon after, Brooke returned to work at Forrester Creations.

Meanwhile, Stephanie's physical and mental condition continued to deteriorate to the point where her unexplained illness forced her to be committed to a psychiatric hospital. Sheila taunted Stephanie in her hospital room. Stephanie fell into a deep depression and lost her will to live. Eric and Ridge tried to convince a nearly catatonic Stephanie to fight back but were unable to get through to her. Brooke came to see Stephanie and begged her to fight this illness because Rick and Bridget loved her and desperately needed her in their lives. Brooke's plea aroused something in Stephanie and she slowly began to recover.

JASMINE/SLY/JESSICA/DYLAN/MICHAEL

Although Sly was attracted to Jasmine, he launched a scheme to get Jessica pregnant, marry her, and live off the Forresters' millions. Meanwhile, Dylan and Michael warned Jessica to be leery of Sly. When Jasmine revealed to Jessica that Sly planned to get her pregnant by getting her drunk and poking a hole in a condom, Jessica decided to turn the tables on Sly and teach him a lesson. At a beach party with Jessica, Sly got so drunk he awakened the next morning unable to remember what had happened the previous night. Jessica used it to her advantage and told Sly they had made love. Later, Jessica announced she was pregnant. Sly proposed marriage, but Jessica told him he needed to prove to her that he was ready to take on the responsibility of being a father. Meanwhile, Jessica confided to Stephanie her plan to teach Sly a lesson.

Dylan began a romantic relationship with Michael but ended it so that he could resume dating Jessica. Since Dylan knew about Jessica's plan with Sly, Dylan agreed to keep quiet about their romance.

Jessica also enlisted James, who was dating her mother, Maggie, in her efforts to make Sly aware of the responsibilities of parenthood. James provided Sly with a computerized baby doll that randomly cried and wouldn't stop until Sly determined what the doll needed. Sly didn't take the assignment

Sly wanted Jessica to wed and Jasmine to bed. But Jessica turned the tables on Sly and showed him that impending fatherhood wasn't going to be a free ride. Jasmine also found herself fed up with Sly's unethical ways.

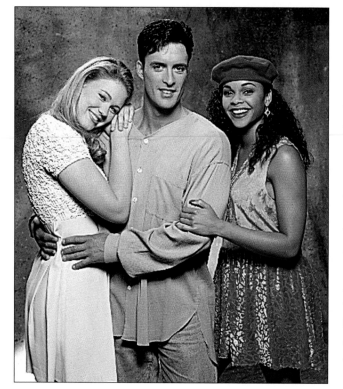

seriously and threw the doll around like a toy. Jessica threatened to end her relationship with Sly after she saw him abuse the doll. Meanwhile, Sly continued to see Jasmine.

Sly was dumbfounded when Jessica announced that the Forresters refused to provide financial assistance for their baby. She also presented Sly with an estimate of how much it was going to cost them to raise the baby on their own. With the walls closing in on him, Sly began to silently question what he had gotten himself into with Jessica.

THORNE/MACY

Thorne landed the lead role of Danny Zuko in the Broadway production of *Grease* and temporarily left Los Angeles. Meanwhile, Macy stayed behind to help rescue her mother Sally's failing business. Taking a more active interest in Spectra Fashions, Macy offered an exclusive designing deal to Lauren, who owned a chain of department stores. But, out of loyalty to Eric, Lauren graciously declined the lucrative offer.

After several months of performing on Broadway, Thorne returned home to Macy.

Thorne and Macy survived a four-month separation while Thorne did a stint on Broadway in Grease. *During his absence, Macy honed her business acumen by bringing Clarke Garrison back into the Spectra fold.*

JESSICA/DYLAN/LAUREN

Dylan had trouble paying his credit-card bills and making the rent after he was laid off from Spectra, so he took a job as a waiter at a male strip club called the Beverly Hills Hideaway. Knowing that Jessica would disapprove of it, he opted not to tell her where he was working.

Vince, the club's owner, informed Dylan that he could make a lot more money if he started stripping. Meanwhile, with Eric's help, Dylan applied and was accepted to the prestigious Design Academy. In order to pay the $20,000 tuition, however, Dylan realized he needed to make big bucks in a hurry and accepted Vince's offer to train him to become a male stripper. With Vince's help, Dylan became a smashing success, but he was still $10,000 short of his goal.

Soon after, a savvy woman named Brenda offered Dylan an opportunity to make a lot of money by performing at her private parties. Once Dylan clarified that he wouldn't have to perform any sexual acts, he agreed to the gig. But as luck would have it, Lauren, a guest at the party, arrived just as Dylan was performing his routine!

Dylan explained his financial dilemma to Lauren and begged her not to tell the Forresters. Lauren agreed to keep quiet and also offered to pay Dylan's tuition, provided he become her personal sex slave. Knowing that the next day was the deadline for paying his tuition, he accepted Lauren's offer but ultimately realized that he couldn't betray Jessica—or himself. Dylan tore up the check and left.

The next day Roberta, from the Design Academy, confirmed to Dylan that his tuition had been paid by Lauren Fenmore. Dylan stormed into her office and told Lauren he wouldn't be repaying her in her bedroom. Lauren explained to Dylan that she never intended to have sex with him. She just wanted to test him to make sure he would never hurt Jessica. Dylan was shocked to find out that by doing the right thing, he finally got his chance to attend the design school.

SALLY/CLARKE/C.J.

With Spectra on the verge of bankruptcy and Saul at home recuperating from an illness, Macy made a last-ditch effort to save the company by attempting to contact Sally's ex-husband, Clarke Garrison, and rehire him as Spectra's designer. Meanwhile, Sally asked her pal Eric to buy out Spectra Fashions, but he told her his company just didn't have the available resources to do it.

C.J. set aside his bullying ways and became friends with Rick. In their conversations C.J. told Rick how lucky he was to have Eric as a dad since C.J.'s pop, Clarke, had walked out on him when he was a baby.

Just as Sally, Macy, and Darla were about to close up Spectra Fashions forever, Clarke stepped off the elevator. An incredulous Sally ordered Clarke out the door. But Clarke insisted on seeing his son.

Sally finally agreed to let Clarke see C.J., but the young boy initially felt resentment toward Clarke for abandoning him and said he didn't want anything to do with him. But Clarke, who was determined to build a relationship with C.J., eventually began to make inroads.

Meanwhile, Clarke met with Sally's business managers and agreed to return to Spectra as top designer. Sally conceded to Clarke's wish to come back to work after getting C.J.'s approval. Her creditors gave Sally an extension on shutting down Spectra Fashions.

Clarke claimed he had turned down an offer to work for Antonio Giovanni, a world-famous designer, just to be with C.J. But Macy and Darla learned that Antonio had never even met Clarke. Sally kept this news from C.J. so he wouldn't be hurt.

C.J. tried to impress his school pals by taking them to his dad's penthouse hotel suite. As they approached his door, C.J. overheard Clarke tell Michael, whom he had met at the Bikini Bar and was now dating, that he didn't even want C.J. when Sally revealed she was pregnant. But C.J. bolted before he heard Clarke add that his son was now the most important person in his life.

Clarke cleared the air with C.J. after dropping by to take him to a baseball game. Saul returned to work at Spectra and was less than thrilled to find out that Clarke was back. Clarke confronted Saul after he overheard him tell Sally that he didn't trust her ex-husband. Saul remained firm in his dislike of Clarke.

RIDGE/TAYLOR/GRANT/MICHAEL/CLARKE

Grateful to Michael for tipping him off that Sally was stealing his designs, Eric gave her a marketing position at Forrester Creations.

While Ridge was in Barbados searching for Brooke, Eric hired designer Grant Chambers. When Eric introduced Grant and Taylor to each other, they

GRANT CHAMBERS

Charles Grant initially auditioned for the role of Clarke Garrison, a character who was returning to *The Bold and the Beautiful* after being chased out of town by his ex-wife, Sally Spectra, several years earlier. Ultimately, the producers decided to bring back Dan McVicar, who originated the role. But they were so impressed by Charles's screen test that Bradley Bell hired Charles and proceeded to work on developing a character for him. Bradley says, "I knew it was going to take a little time before I was ready to bring on his character. So I thought, Why don't I hire him now, deal with the groundwork, introduce him to the cast, and when the story I want him involved in is ready, Charles will be ready, too."

"It's been a humbling experience for me," Charles told *Soap Opera Weekly*'s David Johnson. "I understand the com-

Charles Grant

plexity, responsibility, and importance of being given such an opportunity." Previously, Charles appeared as Preacher Emerson on *The Edge of Night*, Evan Frame on *Another World,* and Connor McCabe on *Santa Barbara*.

Prior to beginning his new role as Grant Chambers, Bradley Bell invited Charles to visit his office and discuss the character. It was an opportunity Charles welcomed. "Bradley was very open to all of my suggestions," he told David Johnson. "I'm having a great time. They've given me that canvas to paint on." Describing Grant, Charles said, "Chambers graduated at the top of his class. He's traveled the world and worked for all the top designers. But he doesn't have attitude. He has deep feelings for Taylor. She's like his first love."

acted as if it was the first time they had met, but once alone, the old friends were delighted to see each other and locked in an embrace.

Grant dropped in on his new neighbor Sheila, unaware of her connection to the Forresters. Sheila tried several times to seduce him, but each time circumstances stopped her from being successful.

Stephanie accused Grant of standing in the way of a Taylor/Ridge reunion. Later, Grant decked Clarke after seeing him in Michael's office. Grant informed Michael that Clarke had mistreated his sister and advised her to stay away from Clarke.

Grant also urged Taylor to forget about Ridge, since he wasn't interested in her. Michael pointed out to Grant that he was exhibiting similar behavior in his pursuit of Taylor. Eventually, Michael and Grant acknowledged their mutual attraction and agreed to pursue a romance. Later, Michael informed Clarke that she didn't want to date him anymore because of Grant. With Michael out of the picture, Clarke put the moves on a lonely Darla.

Concerned for Taylor, Grant confronted Ridge and advised him to stop turning to his ex-wife for help, particularly when it came to his relationship with Brooke, because it was tearing Taylor apart emotionally. Later, Grant asked Taylor to consider a relationship with him, but Taylor said she wasn't over Ridge. After asking Grant to sublet her beach house, Taylor left town, unable to cope with living so close to Ridge.

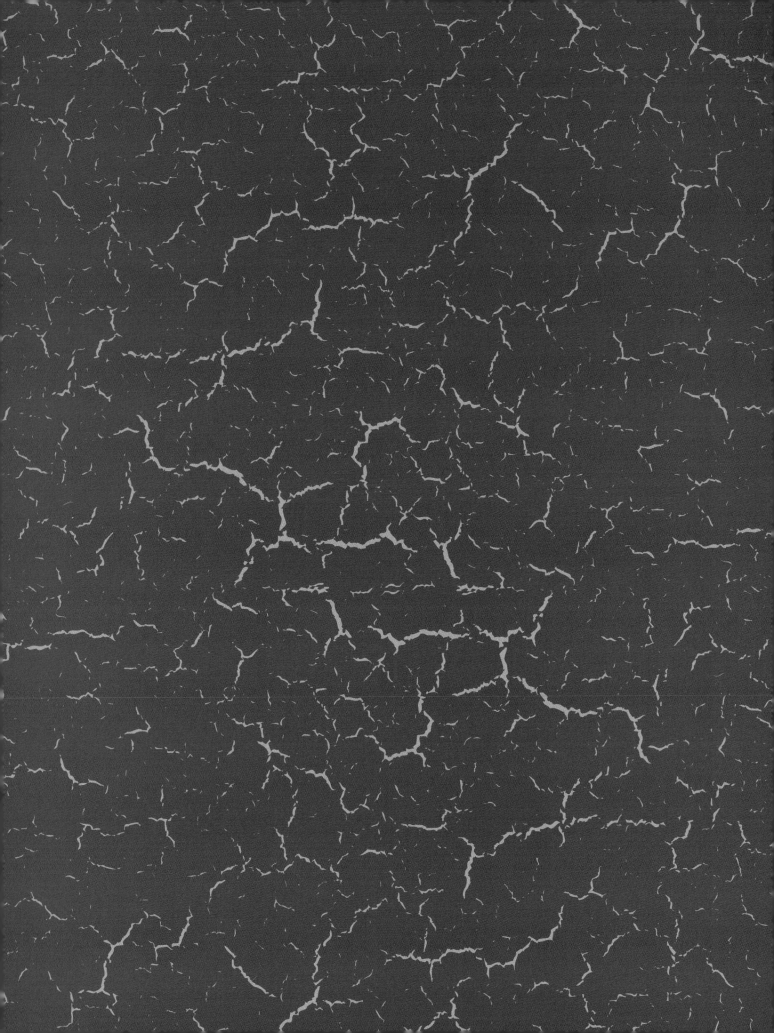

Part II

Bold and Beautiful Events

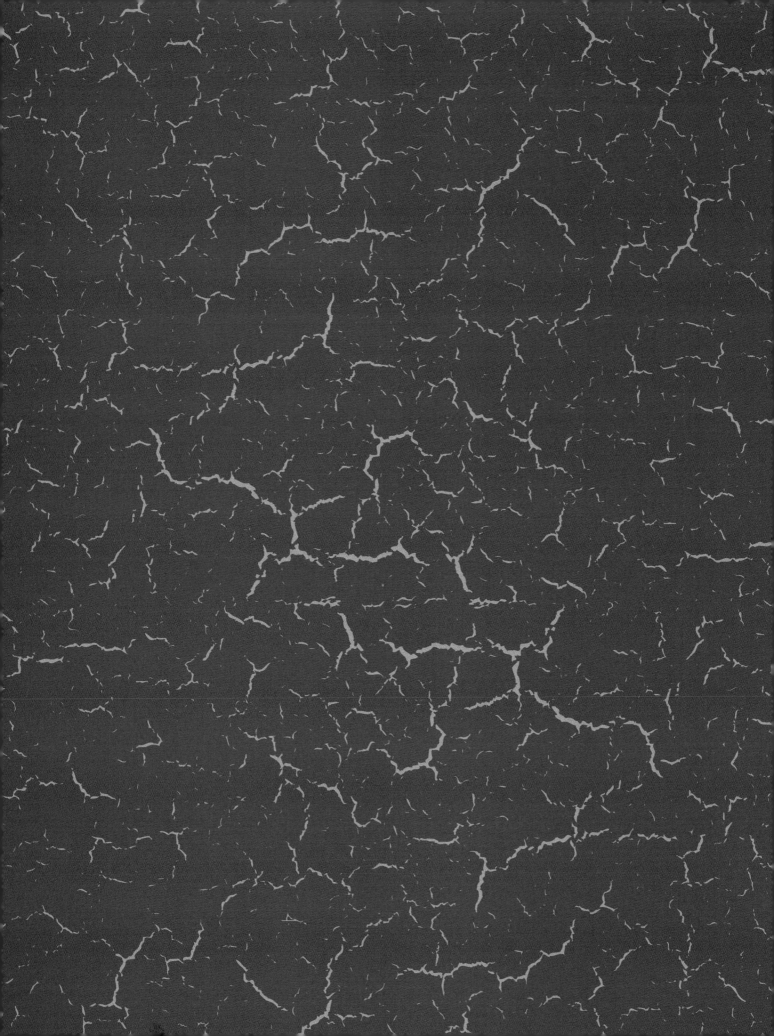

Romance and Weddings

"Romance is what best sets us apart from the other shows," says Bradley Bell. "We tend not to have supercouples or spies and adventure stories. I like to think of it as a human drama. We do have our excitement, but it all revolves around romance."

"Romance and Weddings" includes the memorable weddings, near weddings, and quickie ceremonies that have been featured on *The Bold and the Beautiful*, starting with its first season, as well as the show's most romantic adventures, which took place in such picturesque places as Barbados and St. Thomas. Behind-the-scenes anecdotes are also included.

RIDGE AND CAROLINE'S FIRST WEDDING
1987

Ridge and Caroline's aborted wedding.

Ridge and Caroline's first wedding was in jeopardy before it even began. Caroline's father, Bill, who opposed the marriage, tried to blackmail Ridge into calling it off with incriminating photos of him in bed with another woman. As the ceremony was about to begin, the guests gathered, including Thorne, who acted as Ridge's best man, and Kristen, who served as Caroline's maid of honor. Moments before she walked down the aisle, Bill revealed the truth to Caroline about Ridge's infidelity. Before Caroline reached the altar, she fainted and was rushed to the hospital. Meanwhile, the wedding was postponed indefinitely. A few months later Caroline confided to Ridge that the postponement was the best thing that could have happened to her. Caroline explained that she was so in love with the idea of becoming Mrs. Ridge Forrester, and so caught up in the fantasy of marriage, that she lost sight of herself. Now that she had time apart from Ridge, she was able to develop a clearer sense of her own identity.

Caroline in her wedding gown.

Caroline's wedding gown was designed by *The Bold and the Beautiful's* first costume designer, David Dangle.

THORNE AND CAROLINE'S WEDDING
1987

Thorne and Caroline's wedding (Brooke, Caroline, the minister, Thorne, and Ridge).

Caroline married Thorne while on the rebound from Ridge. She had become more independent, but her life took a tragic turn when she became the victim of an acquaintance rape. Thorne comforted Caroline and Ridge wrote her a letter professing his love for her. The letter was intercepted by Brooke Logan, Caroline's friend, who had also developed feelings for Ridge. Brooke maintained that she kept the letter from Caroline because she honestly believed Caroline would be better off without Ridge.

CLARKE AND KRISTEN
1988

An impulsive Clarke and Kristen flew to Vegas for a quickie wedding that was presided over by a justice of the peace. When the Forresters discovered the marriage, they were aghast, because they knew Clarke was a devious man. Nevertheless, Eric struggled to accept the marriage and eventually offered Clarke a position as a designer at Forrester Creations. Since Clarke and Kristen eloped, the bride didn't have time to buy a wedding gown. But Eric made up for it when he designed a showstopper gown in his next fashion show that was modeled by Kristen.

Clarke and Kristen

Margo in her wedding gown.

MARGO AND BILL
1989

Margo and Bill were married at an outdoor chapel nestled on a hill overlooking the Pacific Ocean. Until the day of her wedding to Bill, Margo held out hope that Clarke would leave Kristen and declare his love for her, particularly because they shared a child, Mark. Moments before the ceremony began, Caroline inspected the fresh flowers that adorned the chapel. She also took time out for a few private words with her mother, who had died several years earlier, to express her feelings about her father's plans to marry Margo, a woman Caroline suspected didn't really love him. "I just want him to be happy," she told her mother.

Caroline was pleased that Ridge respected her

Margo and Bill

wishes and arrived without Brooke. Other guests included Stephanie and Kristen, who was deeply relieved to see Margo actually walk down the aisle. Perhaps now, Kristen thought to herself, her marriage to Clarke had a real chance to survive. However, even after Margo's marriage to Bill, she continued to believe that she and Clarke would ultimately be together.

Sandra Bojin-Sedlik, *The Bold and the Beautiful*'s costume designer, describes the gown Margo wore. "The dress had flowers around the bottom and was made of silk shantung. The veil she wore really framed her face nicely."

CAROLINE AND RIDGE
1990

Caroline and Ridge

Three years after their first wedding was canceled, Caroline and Ridge finally made it down the aisle in a breathtaking ceremony that included a mariachi band and soaring doves. Originally the wedding was supposed to be filmed at the mission in San Juan Capistrano. But at the eleventh hour, representatives from the mission decided against loaning their grounds for a television shoot. Hope Harmel Smith and John Zak, who produced the wedding together, hustled to find another location. Eventually they found it right near the CBS lot where *B&B* is taped at the Gilmore estate, which includes a traditional hacienda and beautifully landscaped grounds. "It's gorgeous to begin with, but we really enhanced it and made it a fairy-tale wedding for Ridge and Caroline," says Hope. Additions to the setting included a charming gazebo built by CBS's shop department. Although proximity to CBS simplified the shoot, Hope and John were still saddled with a logistical challenge. Time was of the essence because they were shooting the wedding ceremony on the shortest day of the year, in December, and everything had to be shot before nightfall.

The story, meanwhile, was fraught with a different tension. Brooke, who was opposed to the wedding because she desperately loved Ridge, arrived and tried to stop it. She was stopped, however, by Stephanie, who made it absolutely clear that nothing was going to prevent Ridge and Caroline from marrying.

Devastated, Brooke found comfort in sharing her sorrow with Thorne, Caroline's ex-husband, who was also despondent about the marriage.

With Brooke out of the way, the ceremony took place without any further incident. After exchanging wedding vows, Ridge tenderly lifted Caroline's veil and the couple kissed. The camera swirled overhead, creating a blissful effect, which was further enhanced by several white doves flying gracefully past Ridge and Caroline in slow motion. Tragically, soon after the wedding, Caroline learned that she was fatally ill, which she chose to keep from Ridge.

"I designed Caroline's wedding dress," says Sandra. "I had the bodice hand-beaded. It was the most interesting part. The rest of it was simple. It wasn't a true white. It was more of a champagne color. We wanted something that would have a fairy-tale, princess-type feel to it. Joanna made a pretty bride."

Ridge and Caroline's wedding was originally supposed to be in San Juan Capistrano, but when plans fell through, a peaceful setting adjacent to CBS Television City was utilized.

BROOKE AND ERIC
1991

Brooke and Eric's wedding and honeymoon were shot over two days in Palm Springs, California. "We wanted to do something that had a Southern California flavor to it," says John Zak, who arranged the location through a friend of his, Chuck Murowski, a former art director who was on the city council of Palm Springs. "When we approached him, he opened the doors to us," adds John.

Brooke and Eric's wedding (Ridge, Donna, Brooke, Eric, and Katie).

The first part of the honeymoon sequence was shot at 6:00 A.M., before the wedding, with John McCook and Katherine Kelly Lang, who were dressed in casual clothes for horseback riding, because it involved a ride in a hot air balloon. "It had to be early in the morning because there's no wind at that time," explains John McCook. "Brooke and Ridge take off in the hot air balloon," continues John Zak, "and they land in the middle of the desert, where they take off on horseback to a private oasis that Eric has created for his new bride. In order to make this pay off, we had to shoot in a remote area." With his friend's help, John and *The Bold and the Beautiful* arranged to shoot on Native American tribal land in a canyon near Palm Springs.

John recalls, "It was only supposed to be Brooke and Eric in the hot air balloon, but we also had a cameraman, Teddy Morales, and the pilot." There was also a second camera crew flying over the hot air balloon in a helicopter for aerial shots. "We had a big canvas drop to throw over Teddy and the pilot whenever the other crew was shooting us. Teddy would shoot us in the balloon, then the other crew would have their chance. I think we went up about eight hundred feet into the air."

"The balloons don't normally go that high," Katherine Kelly Lang points out. "But we had to do it because of the crew on the helicopter. Neither John nor I had ever been on a hot air balloon before. It was incredible. When you're going with the wind, you don't hear anything and it becomes very quiet. It was weird looking over the basket, though, because it felt like you would fall over the edge. I also started thinking, What if the bottom just fell out?"

The sequences had to be finished by 9:00 A.M. because a local ordinance prohibited later hot air balloon flights. Soon after, Katherine and Eric changed into their wedding costumes for the ceremony. Katherine wore a white taffeta gown designed by Sandra, and John dressed in a classic double-breasted tuxedo by Armani. Sandra says, "When we were designing the dress, we weren't sure if she'd be riding a horse. So I designed a shorter skirt."

Taping the wedding ceremony lasted longer than the crew expected because a local radio station announced that *The Bold and the Beautiful* was shooting in the area. Consequently, a stream of cars drove by to observe the proceedings. Whenever a car came into view, the cameras had to stop rolling.

The scenes were finally finished by 8:30 P.M. Katherine Kelly Lang told *Soap Opera Weekly*, "This was one of the hardest days I've ever had. My own wedding day was a snap compared to this."

The second day of shooting involved scenes of Brooke and Eric horseback riding, which was anything but a snap for John. "We rode very fast. Katherine rides horses, so she knows

TOP LEFT: *After their wedding ceremony, Eric surprised Brooke with a romantic ride in a hot air balloon.*

ABOVE: *Brooke in her wedding gown.*

LEFT: *Eric and Brooke on horses at their wedding.*

how to do it. But I'm not particularly comfortable going practically ninety miles an hour on a horse, especially when next to us is a truck with a camera on it! But once we got through that sequence, I enjoyed the rest of the day getting shots of us riding through different areas."

Eric knew the honeymoon was over when it became painfully apparent that his bride hadn't gotten over her feelings for Ridge—he caught them kissing.

SALLY AND CLARKE
1991

Sally and Clarke

Sally and Clarke's union was more of a business merger than a wedding. She agreed to share ownership of Spectra Fashions with Clarke provided he marry her. Meanwhile, as Sally's wedding neared, she realized that people were speculating that, considering their age difference, the marriage was one of convenience. To silence the gossip, a shrewd Sally arranged a wedding ceremony that combined a touch of romance with a flair for the offbeat. The ceremony was held in Sally's high-rise apartment. Sally wore a full-length, cotton-candy-colored chiffon gown, complete with a train and a colorful concoction of shimmering iridescent organza. Her headpiece, also pink, was teardrop-shaped, with netting, beading, and floral ornaments. Sally's bridal gown was accented with pink diamond earrings and pink satin shoes with lace rosettes and rhinestones. "This was a fun gown to design," says Sandra. "I call it the 'cotton candy' gown. It was all pink. Everything we did was very big."

"I think the dress was spectacular," Darlene Conley, who participated in the design plans, told *Soap Opera Weekly.* "Sally had planned this to be a big open wedding with press in attendance. In order to keep anyone from saying, 'Oh, this is ridiculous, she's too old for him,' she deliberately made a sideshow of it. She put on this spectacular pink dress, which makes her look like Glinda the good witch with cleavage. That gown said everything."

Macy and Thorne's Weddings
1991, 1995

Macy and Thorne's first wedding threatened to erupt into a feud. Just before the wedding, Eric had Sally arrested for stealing designs when he discovered her in his office dressed as a man. Sally actually donned the disguise to gain entry to Forrester Creations so that she could persuade Thorne to put aside a misunderstanding between him and Macy and proceed with the wedding. Sally, who was determined to make her daughter's wedding day beautiful, also persuaded Clarke Garrison to design Macy's wedding gown. Finally, Thorne persuaded Ridge to be his best man. Unfortunately, the tensions between the Forresters and the Spectras continued after the wedding and Macy and Thorne eventually divorced. Several years later the couple realized they had never fallen out of love and arranged a second wedding ceremony. But just as they were about to exchange vows, Thorne was arrested for the murder of Ivana, a top model at Forrester Creations who supposedly had been sending threatening letters to Macy. Thorne, who had been briefly involved with Ivana, had a fight with her on the day she was murdered, which made him the prime suspect in her death. However, Macy was able to prove that the real culprit was Anthony Armando, a Spectra Fashions designer who wanted Thorne out of the way so that he could have Macy for himself. Soon after Anthony's arrest, Macy and Thorne were finally wed in a ceremony held at the Bikini Bar. The happy occasion was nearly marred by a fight between the young Forrester and Spectra. Sally's son, C.J., spent the entire day bullying Rick Jr., Eric and Brooke's son. Rick finally got fed up with the abuse and defended himself. Fortunately, the boys were separated and the festivities continued. But the trauma wasn't quite over. Jessica

Macy and Thorne

suddenly fainted and was rushed to the hospital, where she was diagnosed with diabetes.

Recalling Macy's first wedding gown, Sandra says, "It was a favorite among viewers. I got so many letters from viewers wanting copies of the design." In fact, one of the admirers included Bobbie Eakes, who wore a copy of the gown in her real-life wedding to David Steen. "It was a perfect gown for her," offers Sandra. "It had a beaded lace bodice. There was a full skirt, a long train, and a long veil. It was a classic and romantic look."

LEFT: Thorne and Macy's aborted wedding (Anthony, Thorne, C.J., Macy, and Jessica).

BELOW: Thorne and Macy's Bikini Bar wedding (Jessica, Macy, the minister, Thorne, and Dylan).

RIDGE AND TAYLOR'S ST. THOMAS INTERLUDE
1992

St. Thomas provided an idyllic setting for Ridge and Taylor's romance. Taylor wanted a peaceful retreat from Ridge and his ongoing involvement with Brooke. When Ridge discovered Taylor's destination, he launched a passionate pursuit to win her back.

Ridge had only one week to romance Taylor in the Virgin Islands and convince her to marry him. Taylor feared that Ridge only wanted to make himself unavailable so that Brooke would resume her marriage to Eric.

Initially, there was talk of shooting in Venice, Italy. But the proposed shooting schedule coincided with Holy Week, making it logistically impossible to tape scenes. Another idea was to develop a storyline shot on location, where Karen was introduced. Ridge spots her and thinks his late wife Caroline is alive. Ultimately, the show decided on Ridge and Taylor's tropical romance.

A series of scenes involved a playful Ridge sending Taylor on a *Treasure Island*–type scavenger hunt on a small island located miles away from St. Thomas. "Michael Stich, who directed the scenes, wanted viewers to have the feeling that Ridge and Taylor really were on a tiny, remote island," says John Zak, who joined the director on a search for an appropriately sized island. Eventually they found a small piece of land, roughly the size of a gymnasium, situated between St. John and St. Thomas, where they decided one portion, the climax, of the scavenger hunt would be shot. Meanwhile, the bulk of the hunt was shot on St. Thomas, with cleverly arranged camera angles that made it look like a small island. Taylor neared the end of her search when she came upon a lavish dinner setting, complete with a steel band, all of which had been arranged by Ridge. As the band played, Ridge would take Taylor into his arms for an intimate dance. This was the sequence John and Michael wanted to shoot on the tiny island. "We wanted an aerial shot of the romantic setting situated on this little palm-lined atoll," John explains.

Logistically, the shoot quickly became a nightmare because the island was so small they couldn't easily land the boat carrying the equipment. "We literally had to beach an inflatable raft, put a metal picnic table out on the island, and dress it to match exactly what we were shooting on St. Thomas," says John, who landed on the island first with production designer Sy Tomashoff, set decorator Jay Garvin, and two prop men. They were scheduled to be followed shortly by Ronn Moss, Hunter Tylo, the band, and, finally, Michael and a cameraman, who would fly over the island in a helicopter at a designated time for an aerial shot. With time racing against them, John and company frantically tried to dress the table. "But we didn't plan that it might be windy that day, so the tablecloth kept blowing off," reveals John. "Meanwhile, the clock is ticking, and Ronn and Hunter are on their way over, with the band, followed closely by the helicopter. Everything had to run on a precise schedule or we'd lose the shot because the helicopter could only stay aloft for a specific amount of time." They solved their flapping tablecloth problem by attaching double-sided tape. "Then Jay, who was always one to have a beautiful table setting, started taking out all these elegant pieces of silverware and crystal-ware and carefully arranging them on the table, along with a huge lobster, which he stuck on a plate garnished with flowers," says John. Meanwhile, everyone had to make space on the cramped island for Ronn, Hunter, and the steel band. "When the helicopter arrived, anyone who wasn't in the shot had to stay out of sight," John says. "But the only place to hide was in the under-brush, where we were attacked by sand crabs!"

Meanwhile, as the shoot stretched on, the crew was losing daylight. "The culmination of the hunt was Taylor finding the treasure box with the ring inside," explains John. "After which, Ridge proposed and Taylor accepted. But it kept getting darker and darker. Finally we put Ronn and Hunter on the sand and lit it for daylight. So the whole final sequence, which to the audience appeared to be shot in bright, beautiful sunlight, was actually done in pitch darkness."

RIDGE AND TAYLOR'S WEDDING
1992

Taylor in her wedding gown.

The night before Ridge wed Taylor, he shared an intimate dance with Brooke. On the day of the wedding, Brooke discovered she was pregnant. Convinced the baby was Ridge's, even though she had also made love with Eric, Brooke rushed to the chapel to announce the news. But Brooke was too late. She arrived at the chapel after the couple had already exchanged vows.

Taylor's gown was designed by Sandra. "I designed the gown to emphasize Hunter's beautiful figure," says Sandra. "She made a smashing bride."

Ridge and Taylor's wedding took place against a dire backdrop of Los Angeles lit by flames. The ceremony was shot on the campus of Pepperdine University in Malibu over the course of two days. The first day of shooting coincided with the announcement of the not-guilty verdict in the trial of the policemen who were charged with beating Rodney King. In the hours after the verdict, outrage led to rioting in the streets of the showbiz mecca and that day fires had broken out all over the city.

Hope Smith, who produced Ridge and Taylor's wedding, recalls, "I had gone to bed very late the night before, watching the news reports on television of the riot that was growing by the minute."

Meanwhile, Hope wanted to arrive at the shoot to meet with the crew. "Our call time wasn't until six A.M., but I wanted to get there early since I was producing and I wanted to see how the crew, which had arrived at four, was doing. I remember getting up at three-thirty, usually everything's quiet at that time and very still. But I could smell the acrid smoke floating up, even into the hills where I lived, and thought I was kind of immune from all the burning." Hope remembers the drive to Malibu, in the dark, with the smell of smoke thick in the air, as surreal. "Looking back in my rearview mirror, I could see areas of the city from the freeway that were aglow from the fires. Even at night you could see the black smoke filling the sky. I felt like I was driving through a war zone. I was on my way to produce a wedding, with Los Angeles burning." To Hope's amazement, not one person out of the nearly one hundred scheduled to work on the shoot was absent. "Talk about commitment," she says.

Hope says, "From the bluff we were on, high in the Malibu hills, you could see smoke rising from Santa Monica. People were very anxious to get back to their families, to see what was going on in their own neighborhoods." Adding to their anxiety was a lack of news because at the location site there was no access to television or radio. Telephone lines were also jammed by people all over the country calling to check on loved ones who lived in Los Angeles, which made it difficult for people at the site to use the few cellular phones that were available. "We had to keep everybody calm," adds Hope.

Meanwhile, it was imperative that they complete shooting that day. Ronn Moss was scheduled to leave for Italy the next day for several weeks to film a movie. Like Hope, Ronn also felt uneasy seeing smoke billowing along the coastline. "It was a very eerie feeling," he says.

The possibility of moving the wedding back to the CBS studio where *The Bold and the Beautiful* tapes was also considered, but the producers ultimately decided against it. "We were hearing reports about all of the burning going on in the Fairfax district, where CBS Television City is located. We didn't know what state the studio was in," says Hope. In fact, a camera store located on the same street as CBS and less than a mile away, was burned to the ground. "We knew it wasn't going to be a safe situation to bring everybody in to tape the next day," adds Hope. "We also heard that a citywide curfew was being issued for nightfall. So we tried to shoot as much as we possibly could complete."

When the shooting finally wrapped, it was still daylight, and people literally ran to their cars, bracing themselves for the potentially perilous drive home. Meanwhile, a decision had to be made on the spot about how to handle the footage, which needed to be delivered to CBS for editing. Ultimately, the responsibility fell on the shoulders of associate director Cathy Sedwick, who had been with the show from the beginning. "We couldn't entrust just anybody from the show with the remote tapes," says Hope. "Hundreds of thousands of dollars had just been spent to shoot on location and now there was a question of, Who's going to transport the tapes back to the studio to put them in a vault for safekeeping? Cathy put them in her car, drove with her head down low, and got the tapes safely back to CBS."

Taylor and Ridge

Fortunately, everyone from the shoot made it home without incident. By Monday, the city had returned to relative calm and *The Bold and the Beautiful* resumed taping. A few weeks later, viewers would watch Ridge and Taylor marry in an exquisite, sun-drenched setting that showed no traces of the bleak real-life drama that transpired as the wedding ceremony was being shot.

SHEILA AND ERIC
1993

Sheila and Eric

The night before her wedding, Sheila was embroiled in an explosive fight with Lauren. The bride-to-be, fearful that Lauren would expose her sordid past to the Forresters, had been keeping Lauren at bay with incriminating photos of the young woman in bed with a man other than her husband. The fight ended with Sheila's wedding gown in shreds and Lauren feeling triumphant because she believed the last bit of evidence regarding her infidelity had been destroyed. However, the next morning Lauren discovered that Sheila still had copies of the tawdry photographs.

Later that day Sheila arrived at the church, wearing the gown she had modeled in a nightmare. Moments before the ceremony Lauren pulled her aside and vowed there'd be serious trouble if the marriage took place. Meanwhile, Sheila was disappointed to see the Forresters, in an obvious protest, dressed in dark colors. Unable to deal with the tension, Sheila fled the church. But soon after she met privately with Eric and told him she felt awkward being wed surrounded by people who didn't support the marriage. Afterward, Eric and Sheila proceeded with their wedding, minus the hostile guests.

Sheila's dress, which was designed by costume designer Sandra Bojin-Sedlik, was of white silk taffeta, featuring a sweetheart neckline adorned with white satin roses and a bell-shaped skirt, also adorned with roses.

SHEILA AND ERIC ENCOUNTER
LAUREN AND SCOTT ON CATALINA
1993

Soon after Sheila and Eric wed, their marriage was mired in serious trouble, partly because Sheila took a job with Brooke Logan, who had gained controlling interest of Forrester Creations. In an effort to revive their romance, Sheila persuaded Eric to join her for a getaway to Catalina Island. Unknown to Sheila,

Eric and Sheila enjoy a bicycle ride on Catalina Island. Wide shots helped disguise Kimberlin Brown's pregnancy. Director Deveney Marking said, "John would lean in and give Kimberlin a hug at just the right moment, which also kept her pregnancy disguised."

Lauren Fenmore and her husband, Dr. Scott Grainger, who was suffering from a terminal illness, were also on the island. The sequences were produced by Hope Harmel Smith and directed by Michael Stich. "Catalina offered a beautiful vista," says Hope. "It was also fun to do because of the near-misses between the two couples."

Eventually, Sheila and Eric did encounter Lauren and Scott. Later, Sheila visited Scott in his hotel room. Meanwhile, Lauren was preparing to expose Sheila's past to Eric. But as Scott's condition took a turn for the worse, Lauren interrupted her meeting with Eric to be by her husband's bedside. With his final breaths, Scott pleaded with Lauren to give Sheila another chance. Before Scott died, Lauren tearfully agreed.

RIDGE AND BROOKE
1994

Brooke and Ridge

When Brooke and Ridge finally married after a seven-year on-again, off-again relationship, *The Bold and the Beautiful* designed an enchanting wedding with a Camelot theme that was shot on Point Dume Beach in Malibu. The scenic setting included a turreted sandcastle, medieval-costumed trumpeters, and the bride arriving by horseback. Hope Harmel Smith, who produced the wedding sequences, says, "We did it over two and a half days. The night before the wedding ceremony was shot, the tide was getting too high. So we had to build a wall of sand to make sure nothing was washed out to the ocean."

Many guests attended the ceremony, including Brooke's mother, Beth, two sisters, Donna and Katie, and her older brother, Storm (with Ethan Wayne returning in the role), who was Ridge's best man, while Kristen acted as Brooke's bridesmaid. Brooke's wedding gown was designed by Sandra Bojin-Sedlik's assistant, Michelle Wright. "It was a full-length gown that was tied with little bows at the sleeves," says Sandra.

BROOKE AND RIDGE'S HONEYMOON
1994

After the wedding, Brooke and Ridge departed for the Canary Islands. Their honeymoon included a boat ride, which proved to be an uncomfortable journey for several of the *Bold and the Beautiful* staff. John Zak, who produced the honeymoon sequences, laughs at the recollection and says, "I had the experience of working on a boat shoot at *General Hospital*, so I knew what the logistics would be. The reality is, whenever you shoot on board a boat, you have to plan that it will take five times longer than when you're shooting on land because the swaying and rocking forces you to constantly reset the lights, as the boat's always drifting into different positions. You're always working in a very confined space. The swells were so rough that people started getting seasick."

Ronn Moss says, "I think Katherine and I were the only two who weren't affected. We'd be in the middle of a scene, I'd turn around, and all of a sudden, one of the prop guys was handling the camera. At one point, John directed for Michael Stich, who was momentarily unavailable. Everybody had different jobs because they were covering for each other, depending on who was hit by seasickness."

"Ronn and Katherine were real troupers," says John. "They continued to perform the scenes without missing a beat."

RIDGE AND BROOKE IN BARBADOS
1996

In season ten, Brooke left the country to clear her head when new paternity tests revealed that Eric, and not Ridge, was the father of her daughter, Bridget. The truth was discovered when Ridge stumbled upon a letter to Brooke, supposedly written by Dr. Tracey Peters, the doctor who performed Bridget's original paternity test, in which Dr. Peters agreed to falsify the results in return for the $1 million Brooke had offered. After leaving Los Angeles, Brooke was so traumatized by the prospect of losing Ridge and her children that she had a "brief reactive psychosis," which resulted in the temporary memory loss. She ended up in Barbados wandering aimlessly. Ridge followed her to Barbados in the hope of saving their relationship and returning Brooke to her children. The story climaxed with Ridge spotting Brooke. He followed Brooke to a dark cave, where he gently tried to coax her into regaining her memory. After a hectic chase

through a sugarcane field, Ridge succeeded and they made plans to return home together.

Ridge and Brooke in the animal flower cave in Barbados, with cameraman and stagehand.

Hope Smith, who produced the Barbados sequences, said, "It was an incredible shoot. We shot one hundred and twelve pages in five days. The story included action, adventure, and romance. Brooke, who had been in Barbados for several weeks, was stealing food to survive. The one thing that remained constant was her tender, loving, nurturing instincts toward her children, which was evident in her behavior toward two dolls that represented Rick and Bridget to her. Michael Stich did a fabulous job of directing. It was a very physical remote for Katherine and Ronn because they were running through sugarcane fields. We did aerial shots with helicopters and had great chase scenes."

Crowds gathered when The Bold and the Beautiful *shot several episodes on location.*

As with all location shoots, *The Bold and the Beautiful* conducted a survey of Barbados, to brainstorm exciting ways to use the backdrop. Ron Weaver says, "It was our second location shoot out of the country. Bradley went with us and it was the first time he had scouted locations. Bradley had researched the country and discovered that one of the traditions on the island had to do with what they call chattel houses, which are essentially little cottages that are moveable. They were originally made that way because many years ago, some

FILMING IS IN PROGRESS IN THIS AREA FOR THE BOLD AND THE BEAUTIFUL YOUR PRESENCE IN THIS AREA AUTHORIZES THE PRODUCERS TO USE YOUR LIKENESS IN EPISODES OF THE SERIES

people couldn't own land. So if you had a house and there was some reason you had to get off the land, you were able to take your home with you. Brad had a germ of an idea about Brooke finding a chattel house and taking up residence in it. The first day we were in Barbados, the tourism authority provided a bus for us, and a couple of their people to drive us around to see the sights. We did this over three days, and we were particularly on the lookout for a chattel house, but nothing that we saw seemed quite right for our needs. Finally, we were driving along this beautiful rocky coast and there was this little house sitting on a rock. Everyone spotted the house at the same time and called out, 'Stop the bus!' It turned out be a small house with plumbing, for taking baths. The tourism board thought we had lost our minds because we were so excited about the house. But it was perched on a rock, right at the water's edge, with huge boulders and rocks in the water. It was just an extraordinarily visual location. So Sy Tomashoff made a chattel house out of it. He put wood trim around it, added a door and a tin roof, and later he built a set to match which we used in Los Angeles for interior scenes when we returned from Barbados. We made something really special out of it."

TOP: B&B's production designer Sy Tomashoff transformed this abandoned bathhouse in Barbados into a "chattel" house (before).

ABOVE: "Chattel" house (after).

TAYLOR ("LAILA") AND OMAR
1994

Taylor, who was believed dead, resigned herself to the fact that Ridge had built a new life with Brooke, and she agreed to marry Prince Omar. He had fallen in love with Taylor several months earlier, after rescuing her from a hospital where she was suffering from amnesia caused by a beating she took when thieves knocked her unconscious and stole her belongings and airline ticket. Recalling Taylor and Omar's wedding, Sandra Bojin-Sedlik says, "In my research I found out that they wore very elaborate caftans in Morocco. So I took the theme of the caftan shape and ran with it. I wanted to create a very royal look. We sprayed it gold and put jewels on the clothing. There was also a tiara for Taylor. I wanted

Taylor/"Laila" and Omar

to make everything look as rich as possible because Taylor was marrying into royalty."

The traditional Moroccan-style wedding ceremony took place in Prince Omar's palace to the music of an authentic Moroccan band. The palace was filled with fresh orchids, candles encrusted with gold beads on long bronze stands, and a variety of floral arrangements especially designed for the wedding. Taylor's marriage to Omar, however, proved to be invalid and was annulled, after Taylor returned to Los Angeles and revealed to Ridge that she was still alive.

RHONDA FRIEDMAN AND JOHN CASTELLANOS (JEFF TALON)
1992

While *The Bold and the Beautiful* has created several magnificent weddings, it also played a role in the real-life wedding of associate producer Rhonda Friedman to John Castellanos, who played Jeff Talon on the show and currently appears as John Silva on *The Young and the Restless.*

John joined *The Bold and the Beautiful* in its first season. Although Rhonda was romantically involved with another man at the time, she and John immediately clicked and became friends. But, as is too often the case in the entertainment business, they rarely saw each other after John's part on the show ended. A year later John landed his role on *The Young and the Rest-less* and they discovered that, for the first time since they'd known each other, they were both romantically uninvolved. Rhonda explains, "As a single woman, I ate out frequently and knew the restaurants in the area. John, being fairly new to Los Angeles, said, 'Since you know all the restaurants in town, and I don't, why don't you introduce me to them.' So we started having lunches together and always had so much fun. John has a wonderful sense of humor and he'd have me laughing all through lunch. After a month or so, he asked me out on a 'night' date. I was hesitant because a night date was completely different than a 'lunch' date. I really valued our friendship and didn't want to jeopardize it. But after all those wonderful lunch dates, I couldn't deny that this was something worth pursuing." Finally, Rhonda and John attended a New Year's Eve party together and acknowledged their burgeoning feelings for each other. "From that day on, we've been together," says Rhonda.

Rhonda and John were married in Florence, Italy, on December 23, 1992.

Rhonda Friedman and John Castellanos (Jeff Talon) at their real-life wedding ceremony.

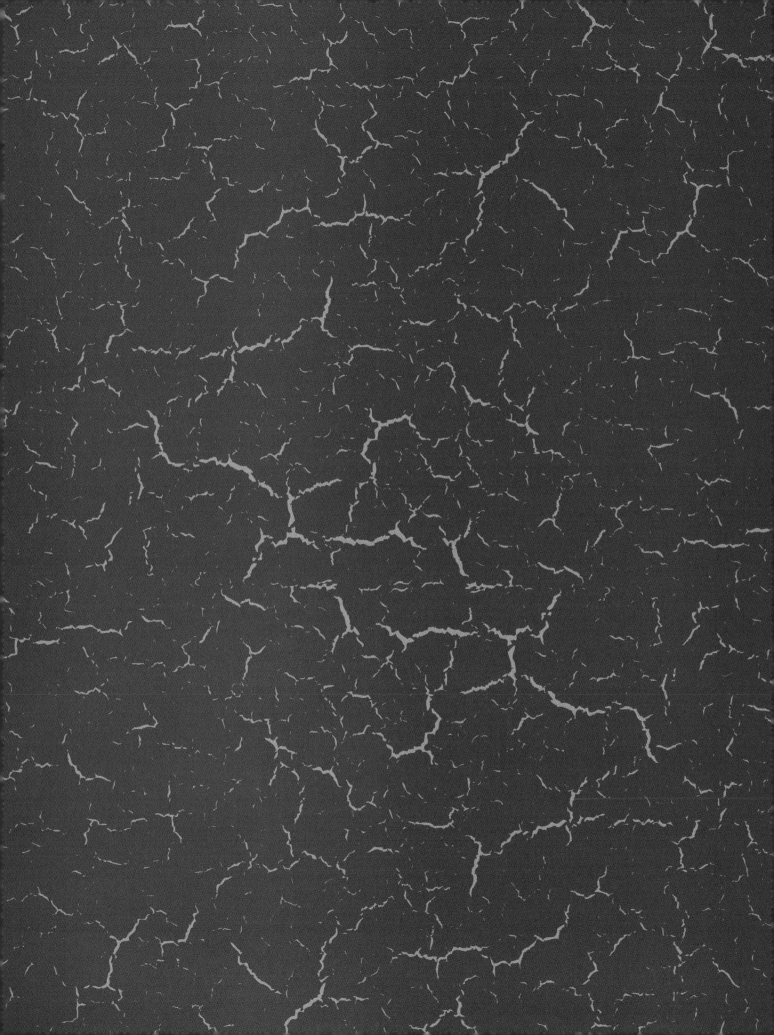

Fashion Shows

Whether it's Sally Spectra, the proverbial underdog, battling the Forresters in a crafty game of one-upmanship, or a designer on the rise, such as the ambitious Clarke Garrison, looking to make a name for himself, *The Bold and the Beautiful*'s fashion shows propel the various storylines while providing viewers with a sneak peek of the clothing lines they can look forward to seeing in the months ahead. From its premiere episode, the show has successfully used its fashion industry backdrop to present exhilarating fashion shows that offer a fascinating and informed behind-the-scenes look at the logistics of unveiling a new collection. *The Bold and the Beautiful*'s writers and producers infuse their fashion shows with an impressive touch of authenticity by keeping abreast of what's actually happening in the fashion industry. "We have to be on top of things," explains producer Hope Harmel Smith, "so I've gone from casually reading *Bazaar* and *Vogue* to reading *W*, a well-written periodical of the fashion industry, and *In Style*. I also watch TV reports of Milan and Paris fashion shows."

Soap Opera Digest cited *The Bold and the Beautiful*'s elaborate and innovative fashions shows as the Best Special Event in daytime soaps. "When *B&B* premieres Forrester Creations' latest collection, they don't mess around," the magazine enthused. "Modeled on the fashion extravaganzas in such famed fashion industry capitals as New York, Los Angeles, Paris and Milan, *B&B* uses elaborate sets, gorgeous runway models, sophisticated lighting techniques, stunning choreography and exquisite garments to create the illusion of a real fashion show."

Creating a new fashion show begins at a production meeting, where the show's writers, producers, and key members of the production staff gather around a large conference table and discuss upcoming storyline developments. John Zak explains how a typical fashion show is born. "Often, we've had situations where we've been building to a certain story point and Brad, or Bill Bell in the show's early days, will say, 'We need a fashion show. What can we create as a venue to add glamour and excitement to the fashion show.' Each of us on the producing team has come up with suggestions, pitched them, and done an actual selling job. If Brad, or Bill in the earlier days, likes the feel of it, then we go with it. What they're looking at, above and beyond everything else, is: Does this service the story, how is it going to enhance the story, is it going to move the story forward, and will it bring a certain juxtaposition of characters into play that will allow the writing staff to pay it off? If the fashion show fulfills those needs, and gives a dose of glamour at the same time, then you're in business."

Once the theme has been approved, *The Bold and the Beautiful*'s production staff starts laying the groundwork for everything that will be needed to bring the show to dazzling life. Depending on how much time is available in the planning stages, *The Bold and the Beautiful*'s costume designer, Lori Robinson, creates the designs herself or supplements her collection by diligently scouring the California Mart, Los Angeles's trade fashion center, for eye-catching new designs that will appropriately fit the proposed fashion show's theme.

Meanwhile, production designer Sy Tomashoff is busy working with Jack Forrestel, the art director, drawing sketches for potential sets and backdrops. Despite the air of authenticity that permeates *B&B*'s fashion shows, Sy stresses that the shows aren't a literal reenactment of actual fashion shows. "The fashion shows have always been a big challenge for us," he notes. "Everyone knows what fashion shows are in real life. It's a big white wall in the back, the models come out from behind another wall and walk down a runway. Why should we do a fashion show that way? It's not really interesting to do that on television because it's not provocative and it won't hold your attention. So for each fashion show, we've always tried to do something different. The backdrop of one Forrester fashion show was Impressionist paintings, which appeared on a rear projection screen behind the models. The paintings changed for each of the different fashion groups that came down the runway. The backgrounds went from Van Gogh to Matisse to Monet."

After the sets are approved, *The Bold and the Beautiful*'s construction department, which is also located in the CBS building in Los Angeles where the show is taped, begins building them. Lee Moore Jr. and Joseph A. Armetta, *The Bold and the Beautiful*'s set decorators, have also been called into action to make a tour of the Los Angeles–area furniture stores, as well as CBS's extensive prop department, for pieces that will enhance the set.

As this frenzy of activity mounts, *B&B*'s casting director, Christy Dooley, and her able assistant, Jennifer Hodill, are situated on another floor of the CBS building, arranging casting sessions for the models and actors who will appear in the fashion show sequences.

Working in conjunction throughout the entire process is executive producer/head writer Bradley Bell, producer Hope H. Smith, producer/director John Zak, coordinating producer Ron Weaver, associate producer Rhonda Freidman, and the director, either John, Mike Stich, or Deveney Marking Kelly, who's assigned to direct the proposed fashion show.

On the days that the fashion show episodes are taped, *The Bold and the Beautiful* often stretches its schedule into the late hours of the night. It's not uncommon for the day to begin at 6:00 A.M. and end as late as 2:00 A.M. the next day. With the dozens of added performers and technicians, as well as new sets, there's also a heightened charge of energy in the air. Everyone also has to be prepared for the unexpected, such as a costume ripping. "We've had zippers break in the middle of a fast change and we'll just sew the model in as fast as we can," Sandra Bojin-Sedlik, *The Bold and the Beautiful*'s former costume designer, told *Soap Opera Magazine*. "During one change, we had to lift a model off the ground to get her in a dress which was very tight. It worked out, but she couldn't breathe. She ran back to me and said, 'I can't feel my thighs!'"

While taping one of the elaborately produced shows, John Zak confided to *Soap Opera Digest* that he found himself wondering "if this is how Ralph Lauren or Valentino feels when a fashion show is about to go? We have that same adrenaline high and the same sense of not being one-hundred-percent certain that it's all going to come off. And then there's a sense of relief afterward."

THE FIRST FASHION SHOW
1987

The Bold and the Beautiful's first fashion show, seen in the show's first episode, was actually a behind-the-scenes glimpse at the excitement going on backstage in the Forrester fitting room as Forrester Creations unveiled its fall/winter collection. Ridge Forrester was seen taking a private moment in his office, thumbing through sketches of various designs used in the fashion show, while his father, Eric, stood in the thick of things in the fitting room, making last-minute adjustments to the models' accessories. As Eric gave each model a quick once-over before she headed out onto the runway, he also tried to keep an eye on the fashion show as it unfolded on a nearby television monitor in his direction. At Eric's side was his personal assistant, Margo Lynley. Eric was jubilant because this particular fashion show marked twenty years of running his own fashion empire.

In the midst of the well choreographed chaos, Thorne, Eric's second son, entered and enthusiastically announced to his big brother, Ridge, that the audience was responding positively to the collection. "That's the press. They're all in the trade," a pessimistic Ridge flatly responded. "The bottom line is the public; the people, will they buy it? We won't know that until August." As a loyal Thorne defended his father's taste and skill, a preoccupied Ridge surveyed a rack of clothes and said, "Something's missing. . . . The line is flat. It doesn't turn me on. It needs more sex, more sensuality."

Sensing that Ridge was trying to lay the blame on their dad, Thorne pointed out, "You're the vice president, big brother. If you have problems with the fall/winter collection, this is a hell of a time to bring it up."

Tossing their father a disparaging look, Ridge asked, "Has Dad ever listened?"

"Has he ever been wrong?" challenged Thorne.

"Yeah, he's been wrong," Ridge answered. "He could be wrong again."

Fed up with skirting around what Ridge was really trying to say, questioning their father's judgment and indirectly implying that he could do a better job, Thorne looked his brother squarely in the eye and said accusingly, "You're just waiting, aren't you?"

Ridge, however, had grown tired of their discussion and, instead, changed the subject. Observing his father and Margo in a playful exchange, as Eric ran his fingers along the brooch Margo was wearing, Ridge asked aloud, "I wonder if they've ever made it together."

Choosing not to speculate on whether or not their father was engaged in an illicit affair with Margo, Thorne silently walked away. Moments later, he approached Eric, who was still busy examining the models. "Well, son, what do you think?" he asked Thorne with a confident air of exuberance.

"I think it's your best collection ever!" Thorne offered.

"That's just what I was telling your father," Margo chimed in.

"And your big brother," asked Eric as he quietly continued to quiz his youngest son. "What's Ridge's reaction?"

With an obvious hesitation, Thorne answered unconvincingly, "He thinks you've got another winner, too."

In a single episode, creators William J. Bell and his wife, Lee Phillip Bell, along with their son, Bradley, who at the time was a member of *The Bold and the Beautiful*'s writing staff, as well as John F. Smith, skillfully established the relationships between the Forrester men. Eric was the confident but even-tempered head of Forrester Creations, whose affection for his children, and interest in them, was obvious. Ridge was the oldest son, anxious to make his mark in the world, but his judgment was marred by a troublesome display of rebellion. Thorne was deeply loyal to his father and actively sought his approval, partly because of his painful awareness that Ridge was the "heir apparent," destined to one day assume leadership of Forrester Creations. There was also a foreshadowing of underlying tensions in Eric's marriage to Stephanie, as illustrated by Ridge's speculation that Eric might be having an affair with Margo. Stephanie's conspicuous absence at the Forrester fashion show helped to underscore that Eric's marriage could be on shaky ground.

KRISTEN'S BETRAYAL
1988

The centerpiece of the Forrester fashion show in season two was a stunning dress that Eric believed his daughter, Kristen, had designed. But Clarke Garrison, who worked for Spectra, a knockoff fashion company, had actually designed it. In the final hours before the show, Kristen desperately pleaded with her father not to feature the dress in the grand finale, claiming she wasn't comfortable with the attention, particularly because she'd be the model. But a proud Eric stood by his plans. In an effort to protect her daughter, as well as the Forrester reputation, Stephanie, who was wise to the truth, warned Clarke he'd face serious trouble if he revealed himself as the true designer.

Meanwhile, problems were also escalating in other branches of the Forrester family. Caroline, recently married to Thorne, attended the show as a member of the press. Ridge ignored Caroline's marital status and flirted shamelessly with his brother's bride. Later, Thorne and Ridge fought over Ridge's determination to mass-market Forrester Creations' designs. Thorne believed it would tarnish Forrester Creations' image, but Ridge was convinced that mass-marketing their designs would skyrocket the company to a new level in the fashion industry. In the Forrester fitting room, Eric stayed busy solving the usual assortment of minor problems that cropped up at every fashion show. With a bemused smile, he turned to Stephanie and commented, "Some things never change." For Stephanie, who clearly understood that everything was changing in the Forrester family, particularly in her relationship with Eric, the irony of Eric's words hung in the air.

With the show in progress, Clarke shielded himself behind a curtain and watched as Kristen was introduced onstage, wearing his dress. While Kristen modeled the dress, Margo described its unique design, which made it possible to adopt three different looks by adjusting the hemline. With the thundering

FORRESTER

Kristen in a wedding gown designed by Eric Forrester.

applause of the audience echoing, Kristen was joined onstage by the other models and a beaming Eric. Meanwhile, Clarke, for the moment, had to be satisfied with a private victory. Even though he had finally accomplished his long-standing goal of seeing one of his designs praised by the Forresters and the fashion community, the applause and kudos were going to Eric Forrester and his daughter.

FORRESTER CREATIONS' FALL/WINTER COLLECTION
1989

There were significant changes afoot at Forrester Creations as the company's fall/winter collection was unveiled. For starters, Stephanie chose not to attend the show. Meanwhile, Clarke, who had married Kristen in a quickie Vegas wedding ceremony, was now a Forrester Creations designer, but his career tottered perilously on the brink of disaster, thanks to Sally Spectra, who was under the mistaken impression that Clarke had slipped her designs for several of the clothes that were featured in the Forrester fashion show. On another front, Kristen pressed Eric to show her the gown she'd model in the finale. But he chose to keep his daughter in suspense.

A restless Sally was so anxious to see "her designs" featured in the Forresters' show that she decided to attend the show incognita and directed her ditzy assistant, Darla, to get her "a dark wig, and something conservative to wear, a suit, navy blue." When Darla questioned why Sally didn't want one of her usual vibrantly colored outfits, the Spectra maven shot back, "You can't get lost in a crowd wearing a bold print!" Sally, dressed in her clever disguise and speaking with a German accent, succeeded in slipping past a Forrester security checkpoint and inadvertently took Caroline's seat, where she waited for the fun to begin. But as the show built to its final moments, Sally's exuberant mood vanished, thanks to the conspicuous absence of the designs Clarke had passed on to her.

In the Forrester fitting room, Kristen stood by her father's side as Thorne unveiled the spectacular wedding gown, designed by Eric, that she'd wear in the finale. As an awestruck Kristen marveled at the beauty of the gown, Eric quietly told her, "I never had a chance to walk down the aisle with you. And I never had a chance to see a very special dress that I might have designed for a very special occasion. This is something I've dreamed of since you were a little girl and, finally, we get to have that moment together, you and I."

Moments later, the lights dimmed, and Kristen made a stunning entrance, accompanied by a recording of Frank Sinatra singing "Our Love Is Here to Stay." The enchanting impression Kristen made was strikingly enhanced by lighting, which silhouetted her figure in shadow as the gown literally glowed. Eric took his place onstage and lifted the veil and they walked down the runway, arm in arm. While the audience applauded enthusiastically, Sally scurried out of her seat and confronted Clarke, who was standing at the back of the house. "I paid for some Forrester originals, Bucky, and I haven't gotten them. Now it's all over for you!" she spat at him. As Sally stormed out of the building, a nervous Clarke chased after her.

Behind the scenes, Sandra Bojin-Sedlik, *The Bold and the Beautiful*'s costume designer at the time, marked a milestone. "It was the first fashion show I designed," she reveals. Recalling the bridal gown Kristen wore, Sandra says, "Teri Ann Linn had such a wonderful body that it was so easy to do anything on her. This was a very body-conscious gown. The fabric was very clingy. She couldn't wear anything under it." But Sandra wasn't the only one who basked in the glory of the fashion show's success. *The Bold and the Beautiful*'s creative team was also proud of the exciting new techniques they had implemented, such as the superb lighting effect for Kristen's bridal gown and featuring all of the fashions on a fully built runway.

THE QUEEN MARY
1989

Three models walk down the runway at the first combination Forrester/Spectra fashion show, held on the Queen Mary *in Long Beach, California.*

The Bold and the Beautiful's company stretched its creative talents even further with the lavishly produced Forrester/Spectra fashion show held aboard the *Queen Mary*. It was the first time Forrester Creations and Spectra Fashions joined forces to stage a joint fashion show, thanks to Sally, who deftly sweet-talked Stephanie into pooling their efforts, ostensibly to benefit the Children's Medical Center, a facility championed by the Forrester matron. John Zak produced the episodes and Michael Stich directed. "These were two of the men who were in on the creation of Spectra," notes Darlene Conley. "They had the right kind of humor and approach to staging the show, the right sense of theatricality."

John and Michael welcomed the chance to maximize the *Queen Mary*'s extraordinary setting and do something remarkably different. The first step was visiting the *Queen Mary*, which is referred to as "surveying the location." Ultimately, they made six different surveys, accompanied by various members of *The Bold and the Beautiful*'s creative team. "The surveys are probably the most exciting part of the whole experience because they're usually an on-location brainstorming session," explains John. "The vision starts out very cloudy, but as you survey the location and share ideas, you start seeing sparks and imagining the possibilities."

One of the first challenges facing John and Michael was finding the perfect area to shoot the fashion show. "The obvious choice was not the one we made in the end," reveals John. Initially, a large area on the deck toward the tail of the ship was considered. "From the stern of the ship you could look out to Los Angeles in the distance," says John. "But as we poked around the ship, we kept saying, 'What is it we want to accomplish here?'" In their discussions they talked about a fashion show that harkened back to the thirties and evoked Cole Porter and the Broadway musical *Anything Goes*. "So we went to the bow of the ship, which was closed to all tourists," says John. "As we got to the very bow of the ship, Michael and I turned around, looked back toward the ship, and there it was, much like the big 'W' in *It's a Mad, Mad, Mad, Mad World*, an area that just revealed itself to us. There was no other choice but to shoot on the bow of the *Queen Mary*, because you saw the entire ship, including the bridge, the upper decks, and all the flags flying; this was something you could never create in the studio."

Meanwhile, Darlene Conley, who went with John and Michael on one survey, found herself caught up in the excitement of brainstorming. "We went crazy on that boat," says Darlene, laughing at the recollection. "Whatever idea I had, I discussed with them and they'd go for it. We planned shots of Sally up on the bow of the ship, or walking down the runway and grabbing Eric Forrester's hand at the end of the show, savoring the victory with him. It was a collaboration in the truest sense of the word. You could talk things over and make suggestions."

Once the area where the fashion show would tape was agreed on, other members of *The Bold and the Beautiful* team, including Sy Tomashoff and Jack Forrestel, went to work figuring out a way to build a stage on the bow. Their plans also included hanging a five-foot-by-seventy-foot banner on the upper deck that read, THE *QUEEN MARY* WELCOMES FORRESTER CREATIONS AND SPECTRA FASHIONS. Sy and Jack also designed replicas of the *Queen Mary*'s staterooms, which would be shot back at the studio and edited into the *Queen Mary* location segments. Jack happened to discuss the shoot with Hub, art director of the prime-time series *Murder She Wrote*. Hub Braden revealed that *Murder She Wrote* had filmed an episode on the *Queen Mary* a few weeks earlier and also created replicas of the staterooms, including murals that hung on the walls. "He offered to loan us the murals, and we immediately took him up on his offer," says Jack.

In the meantime, Sandra Bojin-Sedlik was busy designing costumes for the show. "I had three weeks to put the show together and there were at least sixty costumes," she reveals, "because we did both Forrester and Spectra, which we took with us to the *Queen Mary* on location. I did swimsuit cover-ups for the show and accessory pieces because the fashions featured were holiday cruisewear. In the showstopper, Kristen and Donna wore the same outfits. They were done on different fabrics. Kristen wore black polka dots and Donna's was brown and gold."

Although John and Michael were excited about the remote, they eventually discovered that it was harder to shoot on the bow of the ship rather than the rear deck. "While it looked very spacious on camera, it was actually a very tight area," John explains. "But it paid off big-time because it was really interesting visually and it created the whole design theme of the remote."

For Michael, the most difficult part of the shoot was offering a view of the fashion show in progress. "The best way to show we were on the *Queen Mary* was to have an overhead helicopter shot," says Michael. "If the cameras were only on the deck, the audience wouldn't be able to see how massive the *Queen Mary* is. So we shot everything on the boat itself and then we brought in a helicopter and used the same models walking down the runway again. We had to strike all the equipment that was on the boat, the lights, the cameras, everything had to be taken off the boat, packed away on trucks, and driven away. Then the helicopters came in to shoot and we hid. I hid behind one of the tables. Then we had to bring everything back in again."

The shoot stretched over a four-day period. For two of the nights cast members who appeared in the fashion show scenes slept in the staterooms on the *Queen Mary*. Jeff Trachta, who stepped in as Thorne Forrester two weeks before the *Queen Mary* shoot, says, "It was a great thing for me because I got to spend quality time with everybody. I had a new job and I was happy to be with the cast, who were becoming my friends."

Clarke's Triumph
1990

Clarke, with models, appears triumphant as he finally receives full recognition after the fashion show that exclusively featured his orginal designs.

Spectra Fashions went high-tech with a show that finally enabled designer Clarke Garrison to reap the success and recognition he'd been clamoring for his entire career. The set included sixteen television monitors mounted together. "It could be played so that there were different images on each screen or one whole image on the entire bank of monitors," explains Sy Tomashoff. Despite the sleek, futuristic look of the backdrop, the fashions were influenced by mod sixties-style designs. "While the models came down the runway, we had different camera angles on them that were fed into the monitor walls," reveals John Zak. In the story, Clarke's mistress, Julie, was bent on seeking revenge against him because he had mistreated her. "This was a show where we built to one very powerful image at the conclusion," says John. "What we wanted was Clarke, basking in his glory, and yet there was a question of how long it would be before someone knocked him down again. An image that we talked about, and succeeded in achieving, was a shot of Clarke standing at the foot of the runway, taking thunderous applause for his designs. Behind him, on the screen, was a hugely magnified close-up of his grinning face, bigger than life. It was reminiscent of the film *Citizen Kane*, with Kane standing before a crowd as his campaign photo towers behind him. It was such a powerful image. You saw this man, who was on top of the world, and yet you were interested to see whether he was going to topple, and how it might happen."

FELICIA'S HIP-HOP FASHION SHOW
1992

When Sally Spectra made Felicia Forrester a lucrative offer to design clothes for her company, the young designer quickly accepted. Unfortunately, the ink was barely dry on Felicia's contract with Spectra Fashions before she discovered that her father was about to make her a comparable offer at Forrester Creations. When Sally refused to release Felicia from her contract, she plotted her freedom by deliberately designing a line of clothes she thought were so atrocious that they were doomed to fail. To further aggravate Sally, Felicia also staged the fashion show on a backlot and substituted dancers for models. "At that time, I was taking street-jam classes," says Sandra. "I thought, Wouldn't it be fun if Felicia did a dance-inspired fashion show?" Since no one was supposed to like the clothes, Sandra bought several inexpensive pieces to include in the show. "It was completely different from any other fashion show we have done," Colleen Dion, who played Felicia Forrester, told *Soap Opera Weekly*. "Formerly, we've had more traditional-type shows, where the models walked down the runways. This time we had seven dancers as models who did hip-hop dancing down the runway."

Ironically, Felicia's show was a hit and she was forced to continue at Spectra.

ENVIRONMENTAL FASHION SHOW
1992

Production designer Sy Tomashoff, art director Jack Forrestel, and costume designer Sandra Bojin-Sedlik worked in conjunction to create a cohesive design for Spectra's environmental fashion show. In the story, an environmentally conscious Felicia Forrester created a collection of fashions that also drew attention to endangered species.

In keeping with the show's environmental theme, Sandra used synthetic materials, rather than real fur, for the costumes. "I built everything from scratch, because it was so specific, with the animal theme," says Sandra. "There were eighteen different outfits. I made a leopard coat for Darlene and she had an amazing black feather hat. In fact, the whole outfit was inspired by the hat, which I had found for Sally. So I decided to make a zebra-type coat."

The set Sy and Jack designed was also a departure from previous fashion shows. "The stage and runway were camouflaged to look like natural environments, even though they were supposed to be in a showroom. We had a bridge going from the stage crossing into a downstage platform area, where there were jungle plants. Under the bridge there was a pond. Behind the models we had a rearview projection with jungle scenes that featured endangered species, such as peacocks, leopards, and jaguars, in their natural habitats. At the end of the show, there was a rainfall."

Although the fashion show was a treat for viewers, Felicia didn't fare as well with Sally Spectra, who quickly pulled the young designer's endangered species collection because of lackluster sales.

SHEILA'S WORST NIGHTMARE
1993

In this suspense-filled fashion show, viewers thought the day of reckoning had finally arrived for Sheila Forrester. The show climaxed with Lauren Fenmore threatening to expose Sheila's criminal past to the entire Forrester family.

For the fashion show, Sy and Jack designed six classical columns with a rear projection behind the runway. "The columns were in semi-ruined state," says Sy. "The shop did a marvelous job of chipping off and cracking the columns to make them look ancient." As the models came down the

runway, wearing various pieces of the new Forrester collection, the rear projection displayed a different monumental image for each outfit, including Egyptian pyramids, the Paris Opera House, the Eiffel Tower, and Mt. Olympus. For the showstopper, Sheila, who was engaged to marry Eric Forrester, wore a bridal gown that he designed. "We had an autumnal landscape as the background," says Sy. Meanwhile, Sandra designed the bridal gown Sheila wore in three days. "It was one of my favorite wedding dresses," she says, "with the way the netting came around the hat and the length of the bell skirt, which had roses around it."

At a Forrester fantasy show, Sheila wears the wedding gown Eric designed.

As Sheila modeled the gown, Lauren Fenmore suddenly rushed to the stage and tore the veil from her face, and the episode suddenly ended, leaving viewers in shock. "The audience was left thinking, 'This is it. Lauren's going to get her,'" says Michael Stich, who directed the episode. In the following episode, Lauren Fenmore exposed Sheila's criminal past to a horrified audience that included the Forresters. The police joined Lauren onstage and dragged Sheila away. People were convinced Sheila had finally been caught. But later, it was revealed that the fashion show existed only in the mind of Sheila Carter, who lived in fear of her nemesis Lauren Fenmore's close ties to the Forresters and subsequent arrival in Los Angeles for Forrester Creations' upcoming fashion show. "The next time we saw Sheila," says Michael, "she was waking up in a hospital bed."

Meanwhile, Michael found the fashion show fascinating to shoot because, besides himself, only three people, head writer Bradley Bell, producer John Zak, who produced the episode, and associate producer Rhonda Friedman knew it was all a fantasy. "We shot the scene of Sheila in the hospital room two days before it actually aired," reveals Michael. "I needed to know it was going to be a fantasy so that we could shoot other things and come out of the fantasy in the right way."

Later, when Sheila married Eric Forrester, in a private ceremony that didn't include any Forresters as guests, she wore the bridal gown featured in her nightmare.

Recalling the storyline, Kimberlin Brown says, "People were upset that the fashion show was a dream, but they were also very excited. If the dream had been real, it would've meant the end for Sheila. As much as people love to toy with the idea of Sheila being caught, I think the majority of them don't really want to see it happen."

Eric, AFI director Jean Firstenberg, and Anthony are surrounded by models from the "Salute to Hollywood" fashion show.

SALUTE TO HOLLYWOOD
1993

The Bold and the Beautiful took a short trip to the studio next door, where *The Price Is Right* is taped, to shoot its "Salute to Hollywood" fashion show. In the story, Stephanie Forrester arranged a fashion show with film actor Charlton Heston and Jean Firstenberg, the president of the American Film Institute, to benefit film preservation. When Sally got wind of Stephanie's plans, she forced herself onto a soundstage where Charlton Heston was working and charmed him into making the fashion show a joint venture between Forrester Creations and Spectra Fashions.

"The challenge in doing all of these fashion shows and special events is always, 'How do we top ourselves?'" says John Zak. "For this particular fashion show we wanted something that was appro-

priate to Hollywood—very grand and glamorous. So we chose to shoot on the stage next door, which is where Carol Burnett did her variety show for CBS. It's one of the only full-audience stages in Hollywood."

As a production designer, Sy especially appreciated a feature that made the studio particularly unique: the stage was elevated above the audience, which meant

The Bold and the Beautiful's costume designer, Lori Robinson, seen with the models from the Forrester "Romance" fashion show.

A *lavishly designed stage was the setting for the spectacular Forrester/Spectra "Salute to Hollywood" fashion show.*

the shop department wouldn't have to create an illusion of height for the fashion show by building a runway that stood thirty inches high. "We got the additional three or four feet in the height of our stage and we created a proscenium with a large-scale replica of unraveled film strip surrounding it. In the center, above the stage, we had the MGM lion medallion hanging. However, instead of the lion, it had the Forrester logo in the center of the medallion. At the end of the Forresters' section of the fashion show, Sally sprung a surprise on them. At the moment her portion of the show began, the medallion flipped over and revealed an image of Sally. It was a gag I had done on a drawing, not thinking it would be used," he adds. "But Bradley saw it and said yes, to include it."

Sandra, who was eight months pregnant with her first child, remembers designing the fashions, which in an unusual move also included men's clothing, in two days. "I'm fond of the 'Salute to Hollywood' show because Spectra and Forrester were both in it," she says. "It was a nice juxtaposition to see the different styles. Spectra had to look good, but still have its own style."

Meanwhile, the show originally had plans to include classic clips from vintage movies but discovered that the cost to clear the clips was prohibitively expensive. Instead, John says, "we came up with the idea of the rear-screen projection and we picked various film personalities as a basis for modeling each fashion sequence." The personalities included Mae West, Audrey Hepburn, Elizabeth Taylor as Cleopatra, and, for the swimsuit line, a salute to *The Blue Lagoon*. Meanwhile, the studio audience was filled with extras and fans who volunteered to spend the day as spectators at the fashion show. "We filled the audience," says John, "and it looked like a full-blown show."

SALLY AND ANTHONY'S GRAND DIVA COLLECTION
1994

Sally and Anthony bask in their smashing success with models from the "Diva" fashion show.

Sally enjoyed critical acclaim with her show featuring fashions for plus-sized women that were created by her new designer, Anthony Armando. Accompanying Sally at the show was the L.A. Dodgers' Mike Piazza.

The designs in the show were created by an L.A. designer and supplemented with accessories designed by Sandra.

Sy and Jack created a set that included large letters spelling DIVA that lit up. "Originally, we wanted to run the lighting inside the letters," reveals Sy, "but the cost was prohibitive. So we designed the letters so that lights were rigged on the outside of the letters."

Models walk down the runway at the Spectra "Diva" fashion show for plus-size women.

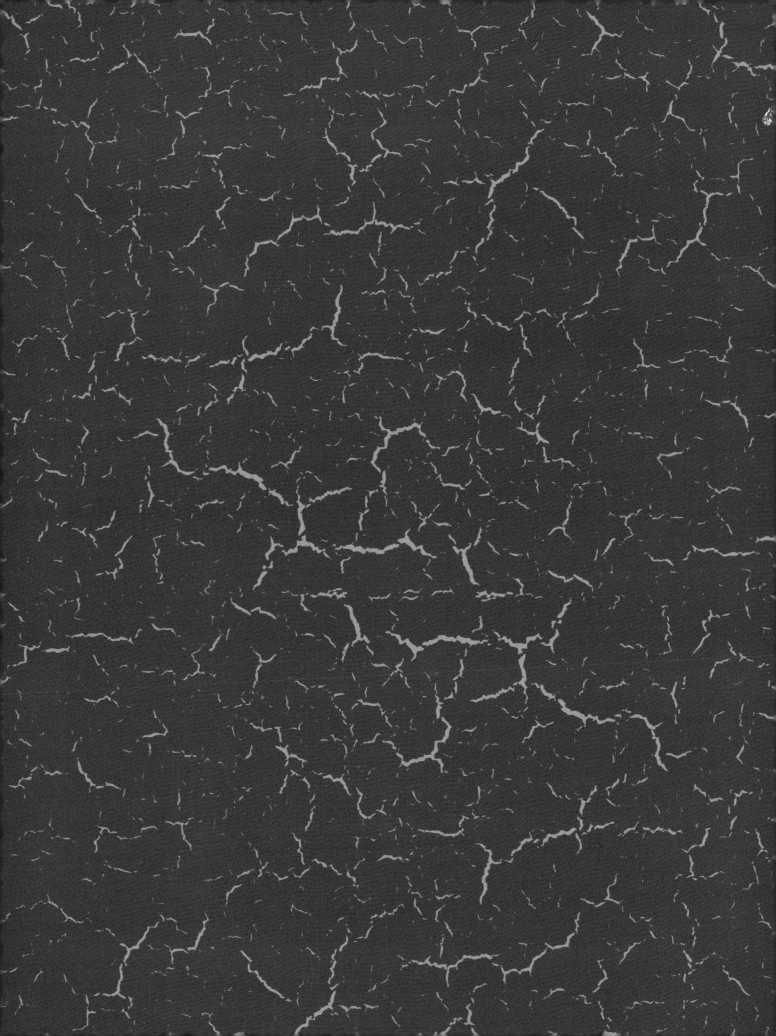

Part III

The Bold and the Beautiful
Phenomenon

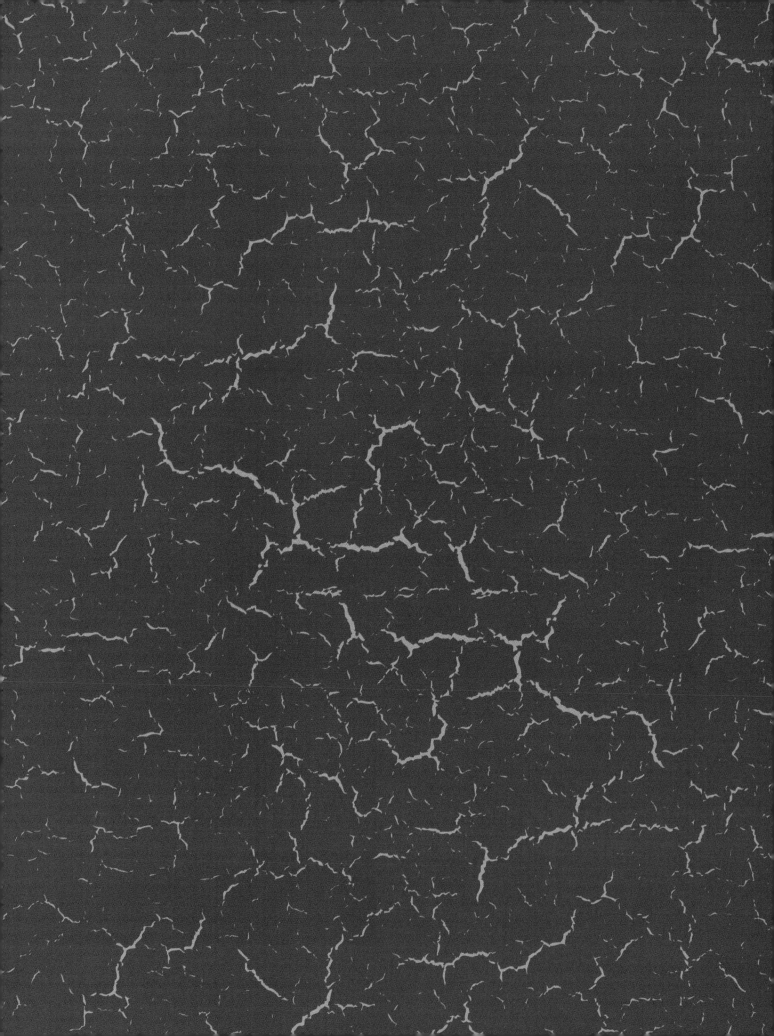

International Appeal

A sudden spurt of fan letters written in Greek was the first inkling in 1988 of *The Bold and the Beautiful*'s growing worldwide appeal. "We had been hearing stories of the show's popularity abroad," says Ron Weaver. "Then we started getting fan mail from Greece, which was one of the first countries to start airing the show." The volume of Greek mail addressed to the show and cast became so large that "we hired someone on the staff whose mother spoke and wrote Greek to respond," Ron reveals.

Soon after, the show received a call from a Greek reporter asking if he could visit the set. His request was obliged and he spent two weeks watching the show tape, interviewing the actors, and taking photographs. After his first set-side feature was published, *The Bold and the Beautiful*'s production office was besieged with calls from other European journalists requesting visits to the studio.

But the strongest indication of the surge in international popularity erupted after Ronn Moss and Joanna Johnson accepted an invitation to visit Greece, where they were scheduled to appear on a television talk show and make personal appearances at department stores. They were accompanied by Ronn's wife, Shari Shattuck, who plays Ashley on *The Young and the Restless*. Meanwhile, John Zak and Rhonda Friedman took a later flight to help coordinate their visit. "We got off the plane and there were still thousands of people at the airport, though Ronn and Shari had arrived hours before," reports John.

"It was like a madhouse," Ronn Moss continues. "When I was getting off the plane, I thought there was somebody on board that they were waiting for, maybe the president of Greece had arrived."

While John and Rhonda waited for transportation to the hotel, John approached an airport newspaper stand and was amazed by what he saw. "Every magazine had a cover photo of characters from the show," he says. "At the snack bar, they had cheese puffs and potato chips with the faces of our actors on the bags." With a laugh, he adds, "I thought, I've never actually known anybody whose face was on a potato chip bag before; this must be pretty big stuff."

Arriving at Thessaloniki airport created a logistical nightmare, and at one point John was separated from Ronn and Shari. "I came within about two inches of being shoved into a plate-glass window by the crowd trying to get near Ronn," John reveals. "Finally somebody saw me and waved at the security guard to let me in. We went into a waiting room, where we sat until everything calmed down and we could go to the hotel."

Days after, Ronn and his wife were en route to an autographing at a department store in downtown Athens. They were followed in a second car by John and Rhonda. "At one point, as we reached downtown Athens, the traffic became so snarled that there was no more room for car traffic. There were just thousands of people in the streets," says John. "I thought it was a political insurrection. I didn't know what was going on."

The car carrying Ronn and Shari inched its way through the crowd, and as the car drove inside the building, Ronn began to feel as if he were in a James Bond movie. "We were still in the car and it was going up an elevator, with the walls moving past us, and several security guards standing around the car. I couldn't really see where I was or what was happening."

Meanwhile, John and Rhonda's driver lost sight of Ronn and Shari and unceremoniously deposited the producers in the swarming crowd. "The driver turned to us and said, 'Get out. You go to the department store. It's down to the left.' So Rhonda and I poked our way through a sea of faces, trying to get into the department store." It was a sweltering summer day, with the temperature hitting 100 degrees, so the crowd wasn't in the best of moods, as scores of anxious people tried unsuccessfully to enter the store. Eventually, John and Rhonda made their way to the back of the store, and after receiving clearance from security, got inside the building, where they reconnected with Ronn and Shari on the seventh floor. Ronn took a seat at a table, with a single-file line in front of him that snaked far out of view, and began signing autographs.

After ten minutes, it became apparent that with all the commotion inside and outside the department store, not everyone was going to receive an autograph. As Ronn continued to sign, a representative from the department store asked if he could step away from the table and address the crowds outside, who had been told no more people would be allowed inside the store. "I walked out on a catwalk and climbed through a tiny door that was about three feet tall," says Ronn. Stepping out into the sunlight, he viewed an amazing spectacle. "As far as I could see, in all directions, there were people." At first, Ronn assumed there was a carnival in progress. "But all of a sudden they looked up and started screaming. It was absolutely phenomenal. I was just stunned. My system shut down because I didn't know how to react. Every time I waved, the crowd would surge. The police were telling me, 'Don't wave, don't wave!,' because they thought, with the crowd surging, people might get hurt. I walked around the edge of the building so everybody could see. It was something I'll never forget."

"You would have thought it was a papal audience," says John. "It was incredible, all of the people out there, trying to see Ronn. It was as if he were the biggest rock star in the world."

In Piraeus, a nearby city, 37,000 more people awaited Ronn's arrival for a second appearance at another department store. But Ronn couldn't get out of Athens, where government officials declared a state of emergency as the police struggled to disperse the crowds.

Just as with the airport adventure, there was a long wait while arrangements were made to get Ronn and the others out of the building safely. Eventually Greece's National Guard was summoned to help them exit. "I felt bad that all of a sudden I was out of touch with everybody that had come," says Ronn. "We literally stayed in that department store for four or five hours, while the crowd dissipated." Soon after, the Greek media offered a variety of conflicting explanations for the canceled autographings.

To clear up the confusion, Ronn wrote a letter to the newspapers, which was published, that set the record straight by pointing out that everyone concerned was unprepared for the level of interest the signings would generate.

Joanna Johnson, who faced similar pandemonium in another Greek city, says, "I think the worldwide success took all of us by surprise. In America, if you're on a soap, you're not going to become really, really famous. Generally, unless you're Susan Lucci, you're not as famous as actors on a prime-time show. It gives you a certain anonymity. . . . But on *The Bold and the Beautiful*, we were thought of as celebrities internationally. In several of the countries, we were also seen in prime time."

John McCook, Darlene Conley, Bobbie Eakes, and Jeff Trachta experienced a level of attention that's usually reserved for rock stars. In 1994 and 1995 they traveled to Holland, where they performed a series of concerts in Rotterdam. The first concerts, held in 1994, were videotaped by a Dutch production company and subsequently incorporated into the show's storyline. So, while the people attending the concert in Rotterdam saw the stars of *The Bold and the Beautiful*, viewers who later watched the concerts within the context of the soap essentially saw the characters performing in Europe.

Ron Weaver, who helped organize this mixture of fiction and fact, says, "It was a once-in-a-lifetime experience that I'll never forget, watching nine thousand people in a sports arena who are going absolutely crazy over not only the fact that they're watching their stars from their favorite soap, but they're also seeing a real world-class concert. Bobbie and Jeff and John and Darlene did quite an amazing job in that concert. In that hall, there was this wave of love, and everybody kind of got on and rode it, including the performers, and everybody sort of fed off each other. It was an astonishing experience."

"It was so magical the way everything fell into place," Bobbie Eakes concurs. "So many things could've gone wrong. We didn't know the band. They had charts of our music. But we had never rehearsed with them until we got there, which was the day before. We also didn't know how the people were going to respond, if they'd be responsive or judgmental, either of which would've affected the performance. But as it turned out, everything went off without a hitch. The band was great and the audience totally loved everything."

"We didn't all do the same material, either," says Darlene Conley. "Bobbie and Jeff performed their music, which they're known for in Europe, and John sang several sophisticated songs that originated in Broadway plays. Basically, I did Marlene Dietrich for them and they went nuts."

The cast performed two sellout concerts. "It seemed surreal," offers Jeff Trachta. "You have all of these people enjoying what you're doing and when you walk off the stage and go to your dressing room, it's quiet. So you go through the whole screaming and yelling, to the quietness of your hotel room." Coincidentally, one of the concerts was on Jeff's birthday. "Nine thousand people sang 'Happy Birthday,' and a cake was wheeled onstage," he says. "There were banners that read, 'Happy Birthday, Jeff!,' gifts that people gave me, such as stuffed animals and flowers."

Concert in Rotterdam.

Concert footage was flown back to America, where it was later edited into the show, as if Thorne, Macy, Sally, and Eric had performed in Rotterdam. Meanwhile, several sets were also built on the *Bold and the Beautiful* soundstage, including a backstage area, green room, corridors, and a dressing room to continue the ongoing storyline, which revolved around Macy potentially losing her voice because she was possibly suffering from throat cancer. "We matched the sets with the concert footage," says Ron. "They watched the tape to match the lighting colors." Recalling the episodes, Bobbie Eakes adds,

"They did a great job of making it look like we were backstage and then stepping onto the stage in Rotterdam."

Later, people in the television industry who saw the concert episodes found the matches so realistic that they asked Ron how *The Bold and the Beautiful* was able to shoot on such a spectacular scale, even including nine thousand extras!

"It was believable because they are such great performers that we were able to build a believable story about them being successful performers in Europe. You literally saw them on-stage making the crowd go crazy."

In fact, *The Bold and the Beautiful*, which is broadcast in nearly 100 countries, is the most watched television series in the world. It's the number one–rated American soap in Italy, Belgium, Germany, Denmark, Sweden, Greece, The Netherlands, Finland, South Africa, Switzerland, France, Egypt, and India. *The Bold and the Beautiful* has also won numerous awards worldwide for performance, writing, art direction, costume design, lighting, editing, and camera work.

Jeff Trachta and Bobbie Eakes in Rotterdam.

There are several reasons for *The Bold and the Beautiful*'s unprecedented success. One is the Los Angeles backdrop, both because it conjures up mythical images of sun, sand, and celebration and because it is a real, recognizable place. "The international audiences enjoy the references to the Pacific Ocean, Beverly Hills, and Rodeo Drive, places that they've heard about all their lives," says Rhonda. "It gives people something to dream about because it's so different from their own culture," adds Teri Ann Linn, who played Kristen Forrester. Meanwhile, Dan McVicar, who plays Clarke Garrison, believes that the show's unassuming attitude toward itself plays a significant role in its worldwide success. "*The Bold and the Beautiful* is a soap opera that doesn't apologize for being a soap opera. It's primarily entertainment and romantic fantasy. It's a show that people can enjoy for a half hour, get away for a while from the routine of their lives, and go then back into their daily lives."

Ultimately, what makes *The Bold and the Beautiful* such a success worldwide is the universality of its themes. "When I've traveled to other countries," observes John, who grew up traveling around the world because his father was in the airline business, "I found that the problems and issues that we portray on the show are the same worldwide, whether it's Ridge confronting his mother because she's interfering in his relationship with Brooke or Sally battling her ex-husband Clarke. *The Bold and the Beautiful* presents situations that transcend all cultural boundaries because in some form, they exist throughout the human condition. I think *The Bold and the Beautiful*'s glamour is only one facet of its success worldwide. I think the 'heartbeat' and the soul elements of the stories are the most profound draw for audiences all over the world. The writers create stories that are truthful and compelling, and they give the actors material that enables them to really dig beneath the surface of the characters they play. From that comes something universal that touches audiences everywhere, whether they're in South Africa, or Finland, or Italy, or China."

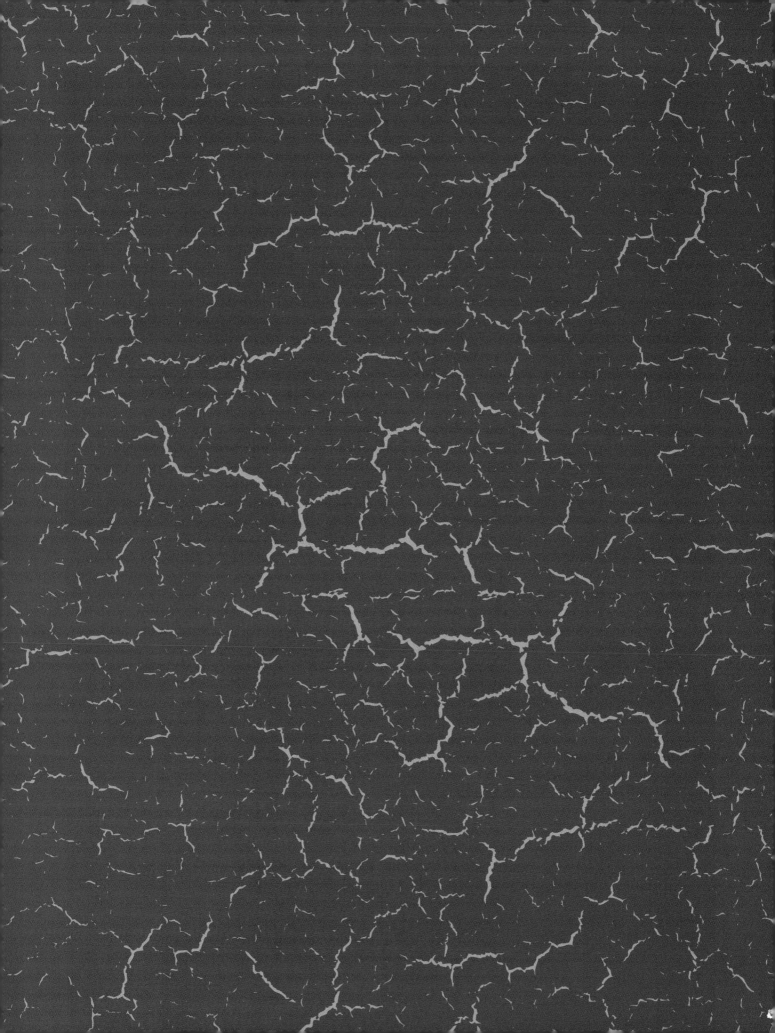

Real-World Issues

Over the course of ten years, *The Bold and the Beautiful* has tackled a number of significant subjects that have heightened the public's awareness about such issues as homelessness, alcoholism, sexual abuse, and teenage pregnancy. Reports of acquaintance rape were creeping into the newspapers in 1987 when *The Bold and the Beautiful* chose to heighten the viewing public's awareness of the heinous crime by dramatizing the damaging emotional effects sexual abuse can have on a woman, particularly when the vicious act is committed by someone the woman trusted. Caroline, the show's virginal heroine, encountered a handsome stranger at a restaurant. They enjoyed a brief but friendly conversation and the stranger introduced himself as Ron Deacon. When they continued to run into each other at the restaurant, Caroline eventually agreed to have dinner with Ron. Later he forced his way into Caroline's apartment and savagely raped her. "This was an issue that needed to be addressed and to get people talking about," says Hope Harmel Smith. "Here you have this virginal character who has very little experience with men, other than casual dates. She lost her mother early in life and was raised by an overbearing, overly protective father. She's a beautiful, innocent girl who meets a good-looking stranger in a restaurant, who appears to be a clean-cut, preppy guy. But once they're alone in her apartment, he sexually attacks her. We wanted the public to be aware that you can know your attacker. There were news accounts in the papers. Usually the young women didn't report the crimes to the police because they felt ashamed or responsible because they didn't say no soon enough. We wanted to get the message across that once you say no, it means no. Just because Caroline agreed to have dinner with Ron, which he paid for, didn't mean she agreed to be brutally raped by him. He forced himself on her. We wanted to get that message out, so that if it happened to other women, it would dawn on them, trigger something that would help them to realize that they weren't in the wrong. We were also speaking to young men, trying to educate them that there is a line that has to be drawn and that they are accountable for their actions."

In the storyline, Caroline was ultimately persuaded to press charges against Ron and he was brought to trial. Lee Phillip Bell says, "Many times women don't want to go to court. We tried to encourage women to go to court and stand up and to also have their friends help them." The courtroom scenes, which were researched by Lee and the show's writing staff with the assistance of a legal consultant, Sherman Magidson, provided an accurate depiction of the process women could expect to encounter if they chose to bring the case to trial. With the help of Caroline's friends, particularly Ridge, who testified on her behalf, Ron was ultimately convicted of rape and sentenced to a long prison term.

"Bill Bell has always talked about the responsibility we have to our audience with this half hour of television that we use five days a week, a responsibility not to condescend to the audience, to keep them aware and informed, to tell a truthful story, which is our biggest responsibility. When we tell a story that deals with a theme, such as acquaintance rape, we get facts and figures to back it up," says Hope Harmel Smith.

Often a social issue is inspired by an article one of the show's writers reads in the morning newspaper. Referring to Stephanie's experience with homelessness in season five, Maria Arena, a former *Bold and the Beautiful* scriptwriter, told *Soap Opera Weekly*, "We were spurred by an article in the *Los Angeles Times* about the hidden homeless—women who are middle or upper class, and through divorce or unrealistic career expectations are living in their cars—they are not necessarily people who are mentally ill." To vividly bring the message home to viewers, *The Bold and the Beautiful* purposely selected Stephanie, who, because of her wealth, status, and ties to the community, was an unlikely candidate to suddenly find herself out on the street without support from her friends or family. But when Stephanie suffered from a pin stroke, which caused the Forrester matriarch to temporarily lose her memory, she was forced into a situation that millions of people find themselves in every day on the streets of America: she no longer had a place to call home. "We played the horror and the nightmare of being on the street," says Hope. "We also played the humanity and the compassion people on the streets have for each other. It was really interesting to see the matriarch of one of the wealthier families in Los Angeles go through this complete transition. Financially and socially, she was on the streets. We really got to know the core of Stephanie, how strong she was to be able to survive that experience."

Stephanie homeless.

Joanna Johnson and Keith Jones on the set of The Bold and the Beautiful.

When *The Bold and the Beautiful* presented a storyline depicting Macy's battle with alcoholism, Bobbie Eakes says the storyline had a personal impact on her life. "It was very interesting because at that point in my life, I had been going through a real emotional time with someone very close to me, who I felt had a problem. There were so many questions, such as Do you intervene? I learned through this story how to deal with the situations in my life where, if someone I knew had a problem, such as drinking, how it affected me and how to deal with it. One of the things that was so enlightening for me and, hopefully, the audience was that alcoholism can happen to anybody, and it doesn't mean you're a bad person. Yet there is a way to overcome it, and it's not the end of the world. The show touched on all of those aspects."

"Macy was an interesting character, not only for herself but for the characters that surrounded her," Darlene Conley concurs. "Even the elements that came into play, when it was decided that Sally and the other people in Macy's life needed to do an intervention, it was directed by Keith, who had firsthand experience with twelve-step programs. So here you had this young black man who was trying to help this young white woman. Even in the subtext, and the unspoken, there was a bit of the racial aspect explored."

"It was a truthful story," offers John Zak. "And there's so much power in that because it's very likely that, in this day and age, a person may have to participate in an intervention when one of their friends or relatives is involved in an addictive behavior, whether it's alcohol or drugs."

In season four, *The Bold and the Beautiful* offered a compelling story on a subject that had never been explored before on a daytime soap, the unique damage that's inflicted on a young man's psyche when he's sexually abused by an older, and trusted, male figure. The story was told through Margo's younger brother, Jake, who found himself unable to have a fulfilling relationship with a woman because he hadn't yet come to terms with the horrors of his childhood. "The person that's been abused has to face the abuser and let out their anger," Lee Phillip Bell told *Soap Opera Weekly*. "If they can do that over a period of time, then they'll be healed, or will have adjusted to it. Jake eventually figured out he wasn't to blame for what happened to him."

One storyline that proved to be particularly controversial to viewers was Sally's midlife pregnancy. "People didn't want to believe it was possible," explains Darlene Conley. "But we made it very clear, had this been her first child, it would not have necessarily been a good idea."

"One of the things that was unique about that story was that it didn't concentrate on the jeopardy that the baby may have been in because of a midlife pregnancy," offers John Zak. "Sally had a healthy delivery. What the story stressed was the emotional dilemma of a woman alone, who had already had her first family. This is a very common situation with women who have children late in life, many of whom have already raised children now in their teens, and who are starting over again with a new baby. There's an inherent dilemma when a woman who soon expects to be a grandmother finds herself to be the single mother of a young child. Sally was a wonderful choice for this story because she's a person who walks a fine line between being very strong and also being a bit vulnerable and even needy on occasion."

"One of the things I enjoyed most," says Darlene Conley, "was Sally's reaction when it became clear Clarke wasn't interested in helping her raise their child. She decided, 'All right; I'll do it myself then.' It really showed her strength and her ability to confront a tough situation and deal with it. I can't think of any other older woman character in daytime that would have been as logical as Sally."

In season ten, *The Bold and the Beautiful* explored another fascinating angle of the same story when Clarke Garrison suddenly reappeared in Sally's and their son C.J.'s lives after an absence of several years. "This is an example where the writers have taken an issue that's prevalent in modern life, such as 'absentee fathers,' and have made it an integral part of the story," says John. "That's the best way to tell an issue-oriented storyline, because you already know the characters and you care about them. Everyone knows how Sally felt raising her son alone, and they also know the effect it had on C.J., not having a father in his life. But they weren't sure how Clarke felt. They didn't know if Clarke was going to pass muster or not. So they're curious to see whether he's going to reform and actually become a father to C.J."

Sly planned to get Jessica drunk so he could seduce her, but she proved too clever for him.

The Bold and the Beautiful is also the first daytime soap to cast a mentally disabled actor. In 1993, eighteen-year-old Keith Jones joined the show as Kevin Anderson, an employee at the Bikini Bar. Keith, who attended the ERAS School in Santa Monica, California, was discovered through the Best Buddies Program, a national nonprofit organization that provides an opportunity for college students and persons with mild to moderate mental disabilities to become friends. Anthony Kennedy Shriver, founder of Best Buddies and a consultant for *The Bold and the*

Beautiful's innovative storyline, told *Soap Opera Weekly*, "I think it's important for us to be involved in a show like this because it will be showing millions of people what people like Keith Jones are capable of doing."

By adding Keith to the cast, headwriter Brad Bell hoped to dispel the misconception that all mentally disabled people require a great deal of care. Kevin was, as Keith is, a highly functioning, capable person. Bobbie Eakes, who performed in several scenes with Keith, especially during Macy's struggle with alcoholism, recalls the young actor with affection. "He was always very prepared, professional, and affectionate. He was very happy to be there." With a smile she adds, "It was funny. If you'd forget to give him a hug sometimes, after the end of the day he'd say, 'I need my hug.' He was very charming."

John says, "It was a very rewarding era for us on the show because we got to work very closely with this young man. Almost immediately, Keith fit in beautifully to the cast. He really became a part of the team, which was wonderful because here we were telling a story that's a 'life lesson' and we were also living a story that was a 'life lesson.'"

In 1996, *The Bold and the Beautiful* has tackled a subject that is familiar on daytime soaps, teenage pregnancy. However, the writers have approached it from an interesting angle, to help teenagers, both male and female, truly understand the long-term responsibilities that becoming a parent entails.

In the story, Sly, who was anxious to gain access to the Forrester fortune, deduced that the best way to achieve his goal was to impregnate Jessica and, subsequently, trap her into marriage. But Jessica caught on to Sly's plan and turned the tables by teaching him a lesson on what it really means to be a parent. Thanks to a well-crafted plan, Jessica convinced Sly that she was pregnant (even though they hadn't slept together, Sly, who passed out on the evening in question, believed they had been intimate).

As Jessica's "pregnancy" progressed, she persuaded Sly to participate in a child-rearing workshop led by Dr. James Warwick. For a period, Jessica and Sly were given a doll to carry around with them that, in every significant way, acted like an actual baby. "The name of the doll said it all, 'Baby Think It Over,'" says John with a laugh. The doll contained a computer chip programmed to simulate crying. In the back of the doll, there was a key the "parents" turned, to indicate if they attended to the baby's need, such as feeding it or changing its diapers. The doll also weighs approximately the same as a newborn infant. "It's a brilliant concept," enthuses John, "that is being used in teenage-parenting classes throughout the country to give kids a chance to really see what it's like to take care of a child."

Bradley Bell was inspired to create the storyline after he saw research from a soap summit sponsored by the Population Communications International Group. During the summit, the organization presented statistics that demonstrated to American television producers how soaps in foreign countries have served as an influence in reducing population growth. Since *The Bold and the Beautiful* enjoys worldwide popularity, Bradley Bell realized that creating the storyline would have an impact both in America and abroad. He told *Soap*

Opera Update, "We're still writing shows with the U.S. audience as our primary focus, but we also wanted to reach and affect people in India and some of the other countries where we're popular."

"We feel you can deal with any issue," says Lee Phillip Bell, "if you approach it with great respect and accuracy. You must be honest."

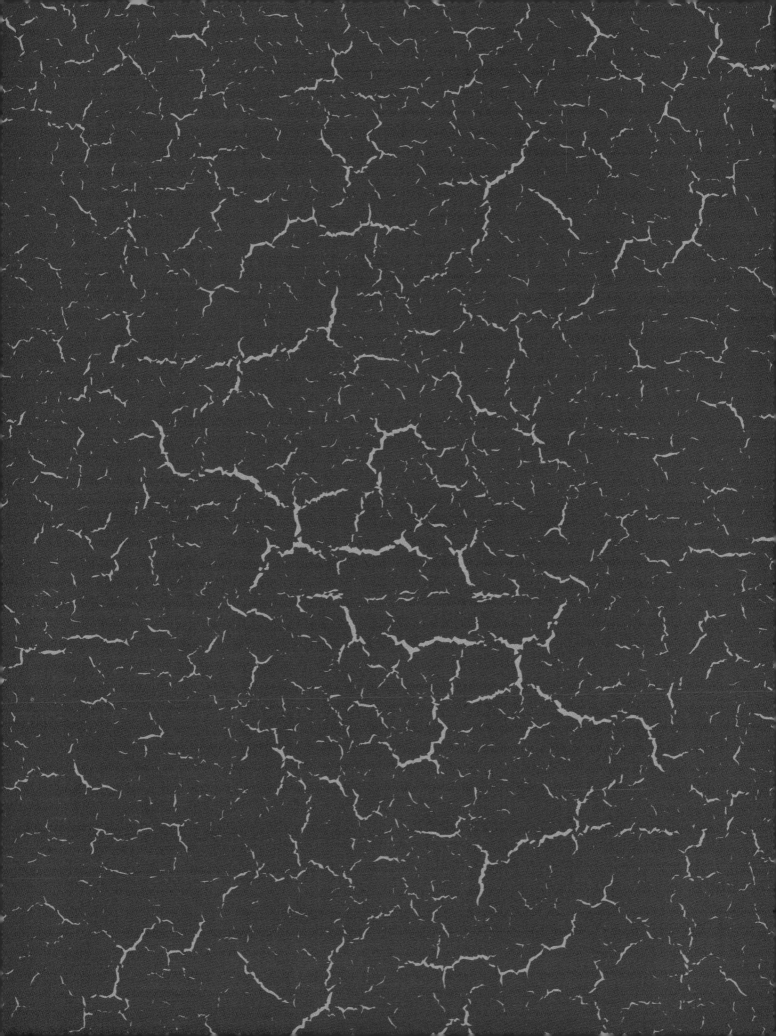

PART IV

Bold and Beautiful People

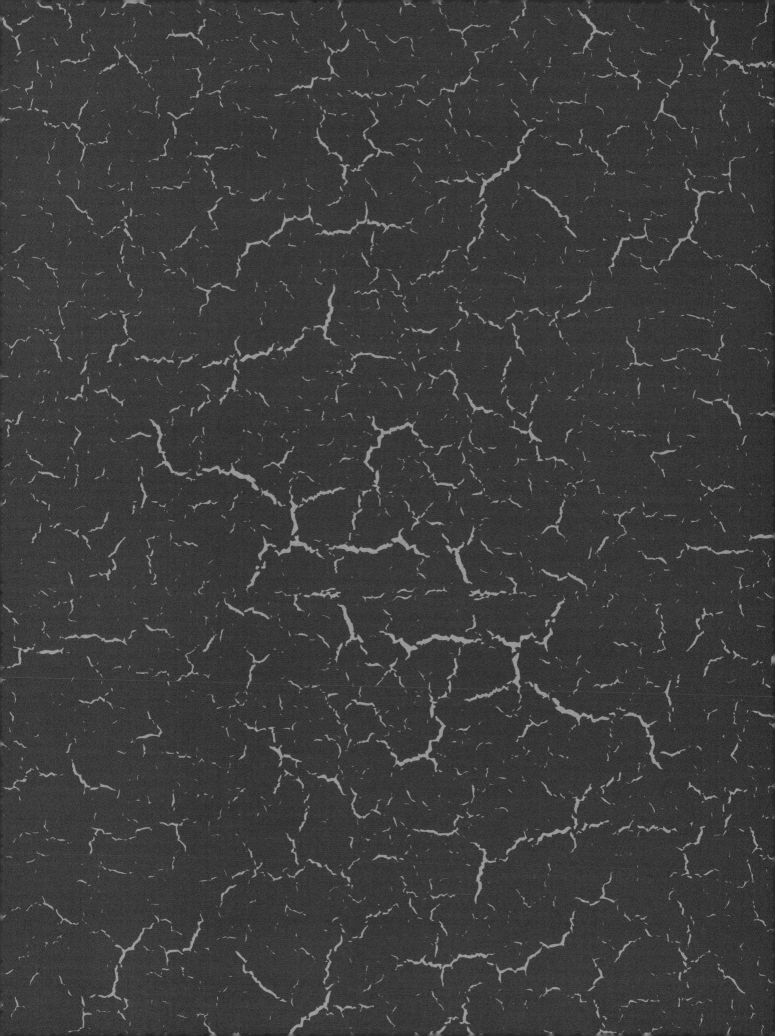

Characters and Actors

THE FORRESTERS

Eric Forrester

The proud patriarch of the Forrester family, Eric is the founder and head designer of Forrester Creations, a prestigious fashion house based in Los Angeles. Eric is personable, kind-hearted, and loyal to his family and friends. His artistic eye, combined with his astute business sense, have enabled him to reach an enviable level of success in the glamorous, yet often cutthroat, fashion industry.

Eric has four children, Ridge, Thorne, Kristen, and Felicia, with first wife, Stephanie. He also has two children, Rick and Bridget, with his second wife, Brooke Logan, and is divorced from his third wife, Sheila Carter.

John McCook

Discovered by legendary movie mogul Jack Warner while starring as Tony in the New York City Center revival of *West Side Story*, John was one of the last products of Hollywood's famed studio system and talent development program. He was later signed by Universal Studios as a contract player before being drafted by the U.S. Army for a two-year stint.

California-born and raised, John attended Long Beach State College long enough to appear in a production of *Tea and Sympathy* and land a job at Disneyland. He made his professional debut at the San Diego Circle Arts Theatre and then appeared at Melodyland in *Guys and Dolls* with Hugh O'Brian and Betty Grable, *Firefly* with Anna Maria Alberghetti, and *Flower Drum Song* with Pat Suzuki.

John then starred in the national tour of *Barefoot in the Park* with Virginia Mayo and in the Los Angeles and Las Vegas productions of *Mame* opposite movie and stage legend Ann Miller, prior to being cast as the passionate Lance Prentiss on the drama *The Young and the Restless*. John's potent interpretation of the sensual role of Lance catapulted him to national prominence. His television exposure provided John with the opportunity to return to the musical theatre with starring roles in *Oklahoma!*, *The Pirates of Penzance*, *They're Playing Our Song*, *Seven Brides for Seven Brothers*, *Fiddler on the Roof*, *Peter Pan*, and *Man of La Mancha*. At the Long Beach Civic Light Opera, John starred in *Man of La Mancha*, *42nd Street*, and opposite Carol Burnett in *From the Top*.

John was a series regular on *Codename: Foxfire* and has made dozens of guest-star appearances on such series as *L.A. Law*, *Murder, She Wrote*, *Moonlighting*, *Newhart*, *WKRP in Cincinnati*, *Amazing Stories*, *Too Close for Comfort*, *Alice*, and *Three's Company*, among many others.

John is a recipient of the MVP Award from *Soap Opera Update* magazine for his portrayal of Eric Forrester.

He is married to former television actress Laurette Spang, and they have three children, Jake, Becky, and Molly. John also has a son, Seth, from a previous marriage.

Stephanie Forrester

The strong-willed matriarch of the Forrester family, Stephanie doesn't suffer fools kindly and believes she's an excellent judge of character. First impressions matter to this woman, just ask Brooke Logan Forrester! Since their first encounter ten years ago, Stephanie has continued to believe Brooke's interest in the Forrester men is based strictly on their wealth and powerful position in the fashion world. In the beginning, Stephanie helped to finance Eric's career and was a driving force behind his success. She initially fought his divorce efforts and continues to hope she'll win him back someday. She loves her family very much and will do anything to protect them and keep them together.

Susan Flannery

Susan Flannery, a Golden Globe and Emmy Award–winning motion picture and television actress, is New York born and raised. She received her BFA in theater at Stevens College in Missouri and attended graduate school at Arizona State before arriving in Hollywood. Discovered by producer Irwin Allen, Susan made her television debut in *Voyage to the Bottom of the Sea* and shortly thereafter was offered the role of Dr. Laura Horton on *Days of Our Lives*, a role that won her an Emmy Award during her eight-year stint.

She was cast as Robert Wagner's secretary and lover in Allen's epic disaster film *The Towering Inferno*, a role that won her a Golden Globe Award for Outstanding Acting Debut in a Motion Picture.

Susan received an Emmy nomination for her starring role in the NBC miniseries *The Money-changers*, opposite Kirk Douglas, and appeared in the television movies *Woman in White* and *Anatomy of a Seduction*. In 1981, she did a ten-week stint as a devious, high-powered public relations consultant in conflict with J. R. Ewing on *Dallas*.

Off-screen, Susan produced the cable soap opera *New Day in Eden* with Michael Jaffe. She resides in Santa Barbara and is a licensed pilot and a gourmet cook.

Besides starring on *The Bold and the Beautiful*, Susan also serves as a regular director on the series, and in 1995 was nominated for a Directors Guild Award for a *Bold and the Beautiful* episode she directed.

Ridge Forrester

The charismatic oldest child of Eric and Stephanie, Ridge lived the life of a playboy until two women, Caroline Spencer and Brooke Logan, captured his heart. Ridge married Caroline but lost her to an incurable disease. Convinced that Ridge's love was unattainable because he had married Caroline, Brooke fell in love with and married his father, Eric. After Caroline's death Ridge chose not to pursue his father's wife, Brooke, and fell in love with Taylor Hayes. Believing Taylor perished in a plane crash, Ridge and Brooke were finally married, a union that was declared legally invalid by the court. Ridge and Brooke's star-crossed love has involved them— and the people around them—in many adventures.

Ronn Moss

A native of Los Angeles, Ronn was originally attracted to the rock-and-roll music field. At eleven, he started learning drums, electric bass, and guitar. Ronn was a recognized talent on the Los Angeles music scene before he was old enough to drink in the establishments he performed in.

In 1976, Ronn joined three fellow musicians to form the musical group Player. Music impresario Robert Stigwood signed them to his RSO Records, where they produced the albums *Player* and *Danger Zone*. Later, with the Casablanca Records label, they produced the album *Room with a View*. Following the release of these albums, the group toured with such groups as Gino Vanelli, Boz Scaggs, Eric Clapton, Heart, and the Little River Band. In the first three weeks of 1978, their single "Baby Come Back" occupied the number one position on the national pop charts and Player was voted to *Billboard*'s honor roll of best new singles artists of 1978.

After leaving Player in 1981, Ronn pursued his interest in acting, studying with Charles Conrad, Chris O'Brien, Kathleen King, and Peggy Feury. He was subsequently spotted by an ABC talent scout and signed to a two-year contract.

Various feature films followed prior to his originating the character of Ridge on *The Bold and the Beautiful*.

Ronn now lives in the Hollywood Hills and is married to actress Shari Shattuck, who recently appeared in the Steven Seagal film *On Deadly Ground* and is now starring on the CBS daytime drama *The Young and the Restless*. They have one daughter, Creason Carbo. When not in the television studio, Ronn can be found in the music studio working on the next Player album with original band member Peter Beckett.

Thorne Forrester

The youngest son of Eric and Stephanie, Thorne married Caroline, but it ended in divorce. He then married Macy, Sally Spectra's daughter. Their romance was initially a source of tension in the Forrester family because Sally's company, Spectra Fashions, had a nasty habit of ripping off Forrester designs. Thorne sometimes feels trapped in the middle of the two families. While growing up, Thorne felt overshadowed by his older brother, Ridge. But Thorne has come into his own as an adult and now enjoys a loving relationship with every member of his family. Thorne is a talented singer who has a successful recording career with his wife, Macy. He has also performed on Broadway in Grease.

Jeff Trachta

Jeff Trachta is familiar to daytime audiences for his starring roles as Hunter Belden on *Loving* and Boyce McDonald on *One Life to Live*.

Born on Staten Island, New York, Jeff attended St. John's University, where he received a degree in psychology and theater arts. After attending the prestigious American Academy of Dramatic Arts,

Jeff went on to appear in the feature films *Do It Up* and *Catch Your Future* and the HBO special *Robert Klein on Broadway*.

Jeff's extensive stage experience includes starring as Prince Charming in the Los Angeles Civic Light Opera's production of *Cinderella*, which co-starred his on-screen wife, Bobbie Eakes, from *The Bold and the Beautiful*, as well as television legends Jayne Meadows, Steve Allen, and Rose Marie. Jeff also appeared opposite Bobbie Eakes in the West Coast production of *Love Letters*.

He also played the mad dentist in *Little Shop of Horrors* at the Burt Reynolds Jupiter Theater, and appeared in the Richard Foreman/Stanley Silverman production of *Africanis Instructis* at the Lenox Arts Center. He has also had lead roles in *Cabaret*, *Equus*, *Grease*, *Media Messiah*, and *Bleacher Bums* at theaters around the country. Most recently, Jeff has starred on Broadway, playing Danny Zuko in the popular Tommy Tune production of *Grease*.

Jeff is an accomplished trained singer and standup comedian. He has made appearances in nightclub acts opposite Bobbie Eakes in Las Vegas, Los Angeles, and Toronto. As a soloist, he has opened for Bob Hope at the Beverly Hills Hilton. He frequently donates his musical talents at various charity functions around the country and has contributed to the album *With Love from the Soaps*.

Last year Jeff appeared in *Agency*, a one-man play, in the Los Angeles area, receiving rave reviews. Jeff, with his co-star Bobbie Eakes, also released a double-platinum, chart-topping album throughout Europe titled *Bold and Beautiful Duets*. Their followup to this album was released in Europe in the fall of 1995.

Other recent projects include a lead role in the direct-to-video release of *Night Eyes 4* with Paula Barbieri. Jeff also appeared as Brent Jekyl in *The Munster Movie* for Fox TV, which aired on Halloween 1995.

Brooke Logan Forrester

A Valley girl who made it big, partly because of her association with the Forresters, but also because of her talent as a chemist, Brooke helped to develop the miraculous BeLieF antiwrinkle formula for Forrester Creations. Because Forrester Creations neglected to obtain a legal release from Brooke for the BeLieF patent, Brooke was able to wrest controlling interest in the company away from the Forrester clan. Although romantically involved with Ridge Forrester, she married his father, Eric, founder of Forrester Creations. Later, she resumed her relationship with Ridge. She's a fantastic mom to her children, Rick and Bridget, who were fathered by Eric. Brooke has an impulsive side, which often gets her into trouble. But she's also a fiercely determined woman who usually manages to overcome any obstacle that gets in her way.

Katherine Kelly Lang

Katherine Kelly Lang is one of three children in a show business family. Her parents are Keith Wegeman, an Olympic long-jump skier who went on to play television's "Jolly Green Giant," and Judith Lang, a film, television, and commercial actress. Her grandfather was Charles Lang, a famed motion picture cinematographer.

Katherine graduated from Beverly Hills High School, where she was more excited about the prospect of becoming a jockey or being in the Olympics than studying to be an actress. Although she had taken a few drama classes in school, fate for the most part guided her into her acting career. She was on the set of *Skate Town USA* when the producers took one look at Katherine and cast her as the lead's girlfriend. She signed with an agent and soon she was doing guest spots on *Happy Days*, *Masquerade*, *Magnum, P.I.*, and several *Last Precinct* shows. She also appeared in the Showtime miniseries *Training Camp . . . First and Ten*.

Her first taste of daytime television came when she played Gretchen on *The Young and the Restless*. She was also seen in *Discovery Bay*, produced by former daytimer Ellen Wheeler and co-starring Tom Eplin. Not one to leave any genre untried, Katherine also starred in a horror film, *The Nightstalker*, that received very favorable reviews. Katherine has been featured in the Disney film *Mr. Boogedy*, which aired on the Disney Channel, in the feature film *Til the End of the Night*, and in all of the Beach Boys' music videos, epitomizing her as the modern California girl! Katherine recently guest-starred in a few episodes of the syndicated series *Lonesome Dove*, where she played a tough gunslinger determined to avenge her brother's murder. Katherine also appeared in the original Showtime movie *Flashframe*, co-starring Ian Ziering.

Katherine received a nomination in 1990 for Outstanding Heroine for the Soap Opera Digest Awards and has received two consecutive MVP Awards, given annually by *Soap Opera Update* magazine.

Katherine has two sons, Jeremy and Julian.

Rick Forrester

Eric's son with Brooke Logan, Rick had difficulty accepting Ridge as the father figure in his life, but, for the moment, they share a strong relationship. At school, Rick is classmates with Sally Spectra and Clarke Garrison's son, C.J. Rick is extremely protective of his kid sister, Bridget.

Steven Hartman

Although new to daytime audiences, Steven has a long list of credits already under his belt. He has been featured in the films *Candyman II*, *Speechless*, and *North* and has also guest-starred in episodes of *Baywatch*, *Later with Greg Kinnear*, and *Melrose Place*, where he played Jake as a child in flashback segments. Steven has also appeared on several national commercials, from Pringles chips to Kellogg's Apple Jacks Cereal, and in various voice-overs and industrial commercials. For the past two years, Steven has been the voice of Charlie Brown in all of the Metropolitan Insurance commercials.

Steven has had extensive training in gymnastics and ballet and plays several sports, his favorites being football, swimming, Rollerblading, baseball, and soccer.

Steven, who was born in Westlake, California, now lives in Newbury Park, California, with his parents, two sisters, three dogs, nine cats, and two chinchillas, which he explains are hamsters with a lot of hair.

Bridget Forrester

Eric's daughter with Brooke Logan, Bridget, a wide-eyed, innocent, has grown up believing that Ridge is her dad, thanks to a mixup involving blood samples from a paternity test. Eric, Brooke, and Ridge have recently revealed to Bridget that Eric is her real father.

Landry Allbright

Bridget Forrester is Landry's first continuing role in a series. Previously, she guest-starred on the Fox TV series *VR5*. Landry has also appeared in several commercials, including McDonald's and MCI. Landry enjoys reading, math, dancing, singing, and playing dress-up. She has an older sister, Kayla, who is also an actress, and two goldfish, Jimmy and Ellis.

Maggie Forrester

Jessica's mother from Iowa, who was previously married to John Forrester, Eric's brother, Maggie married at a young age, which caused her to grow up fast. Maggie's trusting nature occasionally allows manipulators to take advantage of her. Shortly after moving to L.A. to reestablish a relationship with her daughter, Maggie unknowingly became romantically involved with her daughter's boyfriend, Dylan Shaw. Needing a job, Maggie agreed to work in the Forrester mansion as a maid.

Barbara Crampton

Barbara was born in Levittown, New York, and was raised in Vermont. She spent summers while growing up traveling the country with a carnival.

Barbara studied acting in high school and received a Bachelor of Arts degree in theater arts from Castleton State College in Vermont, where

she developed her acting talents with starring roles in *The Crucible, The Importance of Being Earnest,* and *Cabaret.* After graduation, Barbara made a brief stop in New York, where she appeared as Cordelia in *King Lear* for the American Theater of Actors.

From New York, Barbara moved to Los Angeles, where she went on to star in the cult suspense features *Reanimator* and *From Beyond.* She also had feature roles in the films *Puppetmaster* and *Fraternity Vacation.*

Barbara made her television debut on the daytime drama *Days of Our Lives,* where she played the lighthearted role of Tricia Evans for one year. She went on to play Leanna Love on *The Young and the Restless* as well as Melinda Lewis on *The Guiding Light* before joining *The Bold and the Beautiful.* She has guest-starred on *Rituals, Hotel, The Insiders,* and *Hollywood Wives.*

Barbara will soon be seen in the feature film *Space Truckers,* alongside Dennis Hopper.

Jessica Forrester

Eric's niece, Jessica was unexpectedly dropped off by her parents on the Forresters' doorstep. Her middle-America upbringing initially made it hard for her to adapt to life in metropolitan Los Angeles. She developed feelings for Dylan Shaw but did not have the approval of her guardians, Eric and Stephanie, who attempted to have Dylan convicted of statutory rape. A year after Jessica arrived in L.A., her mom, Maggie, now divorced from Eric's brother, showed up on the Forresters' doorstep with the intention of taking her daughter back to Iowa. Instead, Maggie remained in L.A. Jessica is a trusting soul, but her time in L.A. has made her aware that trust is something that has to be earned.

Maitland Ward

Maitland Ward joined the cast at the age of seventeen while still attending high school as a junior, where her curriculum centered around the craft of acting. She graduated in June 1995 and is now attending college at a Los Angeles–area university.

Maitland has wanted to act all her life and appeared in many community theater and school productions, but she waited until her teens to actively pursue an acting career. The audition that landed Maitland her role on *The Bold and the Beautiful* was only her second major audition.

THE SPECTRA GROUP

Sally Spectra

A ruthless businesswoman with one thing on her mind, recognition from the Forresters, Sally had been copying Forrester gowns for years before getting Eric's top designer, Clarke Garrison, to work for her. She got Clarke to marry her and father her son, C.J. The rivalry between Spectra and Forrester has made life difficult for Sally's daughter, Macy, who is married to Thorne Forrester. That rivalry was heightened when Jack Hamilton entered Sally's and Stephanie's lives. Sally was engaged to marry Jack, but thanks to Stephanie's interference, the marriage was called off. Sally has spent her entire life building Spectra Fashions. But the cost has been high. It nearly destroyed her relationship with Macy and has contributed to the destruction of most of her romantic relationships.

Darlene Conley

Film, stage, and television actress Darlene Conley has received Emmy nominations for Outstanding Supporting Actress in 1991 and 1992 for her portrayal of Sally Spectra. Additionally, she received a *Soap Opera Digest* nomination for Outstanding Supporting Actress in 1991.

Darlene's career has been highlighted by a series of artistic relationships with some of the seminal artists in the entertainment media. Born into an Irish-German family and raised on Chicago's South Side, Darlene was discovered at age fifteen by legendary Broadway impresario Jed Harris, who cast her as the Irish maid in a touring production of *The Heiress*, which starred Basil Rathbone. After graduating from high school, she toured the country with classical theater companies before appearing in Shakespearean roles on Broadway with the Helen Hayes Repertory Theater. She later appeared in a Broadway revival of *The Night of the Iguana* with Richard Chamberlain and in David Merrick's musical *The Baker's Wife*. In Los Angeles she has appeared in *Cyrano de Bergerac* and *The Night of the Iguana* (both with Chamberlain), *The Time of the Cuckoo* with Jean Stapleton, and *Ring Around the Moon* with Michael York.

Alfred Hitchcock cast Darlene in her first feature film, *The Birds*, and she worked with John Cassavetes in *Faces* and *Minnie & Moscowitz*. She was also seen in *Valley of the Dolls*, *Play It As It Lays*, and *Lady Sings the Blues*, as well as *Tough Guys* with Burt Lancaster and Kirk Douglas.

Darlene's television career has been split between prime time, where she has appeared in a host of television motion pictures, miniseries, and many vintage dramatic series, and daytime television, a medium where she has developed a range of memorable characters on continuing drama serials. She appeared in the miniseries *Robert Kennedy and His Times* and in the television motion pictures *The Fighter*, *The Choice*, *Return Engagement*, and *The President's Plane Is Missing*, among others. She has made dozens of guest-starring appearances on such episodic dramas as *The Cosby Show*, *Murder, She Wrote*, *Cagney & Lacey*, *Little House on the Prairie*, *The Mary Tyler Moore Show*, and *Highway to Heaven*.

Daytime audiences remember Darlene for her portrayal of the nefarious Rose DeVille on *The Young and the Restless*, Edith Baker on *Days of Our Lives*, Louie on *Capitol*, and Trixie Monahan on *General Hospital*.

Darlene is presently enjoying success as a recording artist. She recently released a single in Europe and just performed in a series of concerts throughout the Netherlands and Finland.

Currently single, Darlene has raised one son and two stepsons.

Macy Alexander Forrester

Sally Spectra's proudest success is her daughter, Macy, a kind, poised, and generous woman. Macy is the proverbial "girl next door," but she's had her share of hard knocks. Macy is a recovering alcoholic. She was in love with Mick Savage but lost him to Kristen Forrester. Macy fell in love with Thorne Forrester and they married, despite their warring families. Her strained relationship with Thorne caused her to turn a romantic eye toward Anthony Armando for a period of time. She has since mended her relationship with Thorne and has taken a much more active role in Spectra Fashions. Macy is a talented singer, who appeared with her husband, Thorne, in a successful European concert tour.

Bobbie Eakes

Bobbie Eakes is the youngest of five daughters born to an air force family in Warner Robins, Georgia. Bobbie began her entertainment career as a young girl performing in a singing group with her sisters. She joined her first professional band at the age of sixteen as the lead singer in a traditional country and bluegrass group near Macon, Georgia.

Later, following in her sisters' footsteps, Bobbie competed in the Miss Georgia Pageant. She was the second sister in the family to win the title of Miss Georgia and emerged from the Miss America Pageant as a top ten finalist.

She then moved to Los Angeles to pursue her musical career. She sang with various Los Angeles–based bands and backup on albums and in concert with Eddie Money before signing up with Epic Records to record her first album, *Big Trouble*, produced by Grammy and Oscar winner Giorgio Moroder.

While promoting the album, Bobbie appeared on *American Bandstand*, was a guest veejay on MTV, and performed in venues across the United States and in Europe, including the Montreux Pop Festival in Switzerland.

It was during this time that Bobbie began building her television credits with guest roles on *Cheers*, *Jake and the Fatman*, *Matlock*, *Full House*, and *21 Jump Street*.

While portraying Macy on *The Bold and the Beautiful*, Bobbie has added theater to her credits with the title role in the Los Angeles Civic Light Opera production of Rodgers and Hammerstein's *Cinderella* at Hollywood's Pantages Theater with Steve Allen, Jayne Meadows, Rose Marie, and Jeff Trachta, and the lead role in *Love Letters* at the Canon Theater in Los Angeles.

Bobbie, who recently guest-starred in an episode of *Land's End*, currently can be seen in a few national commercials and is also enjoying the European double-platinum success of her CD, *Bold and Beautiful Duets*, recorded with co-star Jeff Trachta. Bobbie and Jeff recorded a followup CD that was released in Europe in the fall of 1995.

As a solo artist, Bobbie performed at the 1996 Starfest, alongside such country singers as Billy Ray Cyrus, Tammy Wynette, and Martina McBride.

Bobbie is married to writer David Steen.

C. J. Garrison

C.J. is Sally's son with Clarke Garrison. He is a precocious youngster who is trying to build a relationship with his dad, Clarke, who was absent from his life for several years. C.J. can be brash and a bully, but underneath his rough exterior lies a frightened boy who envies Rick Forrester's relatively stable upbringing.

Kyle Sabihy

While C.J. is Kyle's first role on television, the youngster has already been exposed to film, stage, and commercials. He recently appeared in director Danny DeVito's hit film *Get Shorty* and was featured in the stage play *Six Characters in Search of an Author*. Most recently, Kyle completed a Doritos commercial.

Kyle enjoys swimming, football, basketball, skateboarding, and playing with his two dogs.

Clarke Garrison

Fashion designer Clarke Garrison has come back to Spectra Fashions to help return the company to its glory, but it remains to be seen if he'll really be the company's undoing. Clarke was married to Sally Spectra, but that didn't stop him from playing the field. Clarke had an affair with Julie Delorean, had a son with Margo Lynley Spencer, and was then married to Kristen Forrester for a short time. Clarke is capable of being capricious, but he also has admirable qualities, such as trying to build a relationship with his son, C.J.

Dan McVicar

Born in Independence, Missouri, Dan McVicar grew up in Colorado in a family of twelve children. Dan became interested in acting while still in high school and at the age of nineteen he decided to try his luck in California, where he enrolled at the California Institute of Arts. To further expand his repertoire, Dan began working with the Comedy Store Improvisation Troupe. He continued studying with Stella Adler and spent a year at the Royal Academy of Dramatic Arts in London. During this time, Dan worked at odd jobs and had recurring roles in a variety of television series.

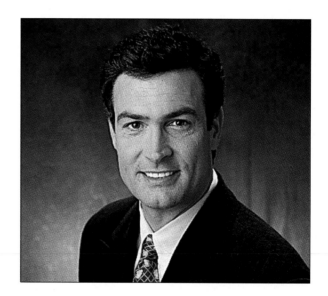

Dan made his professional debut on *The Young and the Restless*. He auditioned with a monologue from a Eugene O'Neill play and was immediately cast as "one of the boys in the shower." Later his audition and performance were remembered by the casting director of *The Bold and the Beautiful* and Dan was called in to read. Dan is a big enthusiast of daytime television, comparing the medium to the old Hollywood studio system.

During his hiatus from *The Bold and the Beautiful*, Dan played Rock Hudson in the TV movie *Liz—The Elizabeth Taylor Story* and starred in the films *Guardian Angel*, *Alone in the Woods*, *A Woman Scorned*, and *Night Eyes III* and in the comedy *The Silence of the Hams*. For European television, Dan appeared in the miniseries *Woman on the Run*, co-starring Gina Lollabrigida. Most recently, Dan spent six weeks on location in St. Petersburg, speaking only Russian, to star as American astronaut Sam Straiton in Russian filmmaker Dimitrij Astrakhan's *The Fourth Planet*.

Darla Einstein

Sally's sweet but ditzy secretary, Darla is faithful to Sally and regards her almost like a mother. Darla will do, and often does, anything for Sally. She has been involved with Bill Spencer. In the past, Darla has entertained thoughts of becoming romantically involved with Eric Forrester and Clarke Garrison.

Schae Harrison

Schae Harrison enrolled in her first dance class at age four. For many years she studied all aspects of dance, from ancient theories through modern movement. For three years Schae was a member of the NFL Seattle Seahawks' cheerleading-dance squad, performing for over 60,000 fans each game.

A California native, Schae has worked in the fiercely competitive L.A. market as a fashion model, hosted her own cable aerobics workout program, and is an active supporter of the National Special Olympics Organization.

Schae, who studied theater in college as well as

with private acting coaches, has appeared in the feature film *Twice in a Lifetime*, with Gene Hackman and Ann-Margret. In addition, Schae has made appearances on *Night Court*, *General Hospital*, *Freddy's Nightmares*, and *Throb* to her credit.

Saul Feinberg

Saul was the right-hand man to Sally Spectra for thirty years. He cared for Sally more than she realized and always put the interest of Spectra before his own. Sally was devastated when Saul passed away.

Michael Fox

Michael Fox, a veteran stage, screen, and television actor, often played against many outstanding leading ladies, including Mae West, Joan Crawford, Zsa Zsa Gabor, and Bette Davis. Developing a career that grew with the medium, from vaudeville to video, Michael also wrote, directed, and produced various projects for the industry.

Michael appeared in several feature films, including *The Longest Yard*, *Young Frankenstein*, *Quicksilver*, and *What Ever Happened to Baby Jane?*

Michael also guest-starred on *The Hogan Family*, *Cagney & Lacey*, *MacGyver*, *Quincy*, *St. Elsewhere*, *Simon and Simon*, *Knight Rider*, and *ER*, and most recently played an orthodox rabbi in an episode of *NYPD Blue*. Michael had recurring roles on *Perry Mason*, *Dallas*, *Falcon Crest*, and *General Hospital*.

Onstage, where his career began to take shape in the late forties, Michael appeared on Broadway in *The Story of Mary Stuart*, starring with yet another famous leading lady, Dorothy Gish. From his New York beginnings, Michael took his talents west and during the fifties was under contract with two leading studios, Columbia Pictures and Warner Brothers.

Continuing to cross mediums through his career, Michael toured with Dana Andrews in *Gaslight* and *Sextet* with Mae West and appeared on the first television daytime drama, *Clear Horizons*, for CBS.

KNBC-TV in Los Angeles commissioned Michael, a director and producer as well, to produce several documentaries on emotional and social issues of the seventies, including women's rights, prison overcrowding, and welfare recipients. He was also a founder of the elite actors organization Theater East.

Michael Fox passed away on June 1, 1996.

FRIENDS AND FOES

Dr. Taylor Hayes Forrester

When Taylor, a beautiful psychiatrist who was married to Ridge, was presumed dead in a Moroccan plane crash, Ridge resumed his relationship with Brooke. After Taylor's recovery and return to L.A., she still harbored feelings for Ridge but decided to stand aside so that he could pursue Brooke. Like Ridge, Taylor has a wry sense of humor and a playful nature.

Hunter Tylo

Hunter Tylo, widely considered the most beautiful woman on daytime television, was named one of the "50 Most Beautiful People in the World" by *People* magazine in 1993.

Hunter has acted on all three of the major networks in top daytime dramas. Her appearance as Robin McCall on ABC's *All My Children* gave her an introduction to the daytime medium. She is also known to daytime audiences as Marina Toscano on *Days of Our Lives* (NBC).

With several feature films to her credit, including *Zorro* for New World Productions, Hunter also has appeared onstage across the country in such productions as *The Star-Spangled Girl*, *Last of the Red Hot Lovers*, and *I Ought to Be in Pictures*. She recently completed the miniseries *The Maharaja's Daughter*, which was shot in India and Canada. During this project she met her former *Bold and the Beautiful* co-star, Kabir Bedi. Hunter also recently guest-starred on the CBS prime-time series *Diagnosis Murder* and *Burke's Law*, produced by Aaron Spelling.

Sheila Carter

Sheila fled to Los Angeles, escaping her criminal past in Genoa City, Wisconsin (on The Young and the Restless*). She accepted a position as nurse at Forrester Creations, where she fell in love with, and eventually married, Eric Forrester. Their marriage ended after*

Eric discovered the truth about Sheila's past, particularly her misdeeds toward his close friend, Lauren Fenmore. After holding the Forresters at gunpoint, Sheila was convicted and committed to an institution for the criminally insane. But with Dr. Brian Carey's help, she was declared mentally fit and released. Since her release she has had romantic interests toward Grant Chambers and James Warwick. She also has tried to be a good friend to Brooke Logan Forrester. Sheila laced Stephanie's calcium tablets with mercury to punish Stephanie for "stealing" Brooke's children. Sheila's logic is often twisted, causing people to think she's psychotic. But Sheila believes she's just misunderstood.

Kimberlin Brown

Kimberlin began her role as Sheila Carter on *The Young and the Restless* in 1990. Kimberlin was Outstanding Villainess at the 1992 and 1994 Soap Opera Digest Awards and was nominated in the same category in 1993 and 1995. She also received a 1992 Emmy Award nomination for Outstanding Supporting

Actress. Kimberlin began her acting-modeling career at nineteen after being discovered by modeling agent Nina Blanchard. She has modeled in the United States, Europe, and the Orient. She has guest-starred on numerous television series, including *Matt Houston*, *T. J. Hooker*, *Hawaiian Heat*, *Santa Barbara*, and *Capitol*. Kimberlin has also had roles in such feature films as *Who's That Girl*, *Eye of the Tiger*, and *Eighteen Again*. Kimberlin is married to Gary Pelzer, who owns a thriving boating business. They have a daughter, Alexis, age two.

Lauren Fenmore

Originally from Genoa City, Lauren moved to L.A. for a business venture with Eric Forrester. Previously (on The Young and the Restless*), Sheila stole Lauren's baby and tried to seduce her husband and kill her. Romantically, Lauren had her eye on Dr. James Warwick, even while she was flirting with Ridge Forrester. Once Lauren sets her sights on a man, she stops at nothing to win him over.*

Tracey E. Bregman

Tracey was raised in London until age ten. At eleven, she moved to Los Angeles with her family. She studied acting with Francis Lederer at A.N.T.A. and at the Lee Strasberg Theatre while continuing her regular college preparatory education at the Westlake School for Girls. Previously, Tracey has starred on *The Young and the Restless* and *Days of Our Lives*. During her daytime soap career, Tracey has earned a number of awards, including two for Best Actress in Daytime TV, Most Popular Newcomer (Daytime TV), Most Exciting New Actress in Daytime TV (Daytime TV), and Favorite New Actress (Canadian People's

Poll), and received a Best Actress award from *Soap Opera Digest*. In 1985, Tracey also won the Emmy Award for Best Supporting Actress for her work on *The Young and the Restless*. Tracey's other television credits include *The Girl with E.S.P.*, *Three on a Date*, *The Fall Guy*, *The Love Boat*, *Gavilan*, and

Fame. Her television film roles include *Fair Weather Friend* and *The Littlest Hobo*. Her feature film roles include *Happy Birthday to Me* and *The Funny Farm*. Tracey is also a singer and songwriter. She wrote the themes for *The Funny Farm* and *The Concrete Jungle*. She also appeared in a Muppets' music video with her son, Austin. Tracey is married to real estate developer Ron Recht.

Dr. James Warwick

Acclaimed psychiatrist who was Taylor Hayes's mentor during her college years, Dr. James Warwick resurfaced from her past to seek her professional help and clearly had romantic intentions as well. Also involved with Brooke Logan Forrester, James has more recently been linked with Maggie Forrester, a relationship with complications because Sheila has set her sights on James as well. James is considered a good listener. His desire to help his friends often places him in jeopardy.

Ian Buchanan

Emmy-nominated television, film, and stage actor Ian Buchanan was born in Hamilton, Scotland. Ian ventured to New York, where he worked both onstage and in various television shows such as *Quantum Leap*, *Room for Romance*, *The Flash*, *Columbo*, and *The Equalizer*.

After moving to New York, Ian quickly landed a role on the daytime drama *General Hospital*, where he portrayed Duke Lavery for three years before leaving the show to join the cast of *The Gary Shandling Show*. For two years he played Gary's next-door neighbor, Ian.

After meeting director David Lynch while taping a Calvin Klein commercial opposite Lara Flynn Boyle, Ian was asked to join the cast of *Twin Peaks*, as the pompous Richard Tremayne. When *Twin Peaks* came to an end, Lynch called upon Ian again to portray Lester Guy on the ABC series *On the Air*, which is currently airing in Europe.

Ian portrayed Peter Lawford in USA Network's *Bobby & Marilyn* and guest-starred on the hit CBS television series *The Nanny*. Ian's other film credits

include *Double Exposure*, *The Cool Surface*, and *The Seventh Sign*.

Before joining *The Bold and the Beautiful*, Ian starred as psychiatrist Martin Dysart in a performance of *Equus*, a role for which he received a Drama-Logue Award. Ian also starred in stage performances of *The Maids*, *Losing Venice*, and *The Heiress*. Ian has received Outstanding Supporting Actor nominations for the 1993, 1994, and 1995 Emmy Awards.

Before he became an actor, Ian did extensive modeling work throughout the world. At one point, Ian was the fitting model for Giorgio Armani's designs.

When not acting, Ian enjoys relaxing at home with a good book, a brisk walk (part of his daily routine), or hitting the courts for a few sets of tennis.

Dylan Shaw

A young go-getter who received a summer internship at Forrester Creations, Dylan had a relationship with Ivana, a fashion model at Forrester, despite the standing rule against dating models. He then developed an interest in Eric's niece, Jessica, which culminated in a statutory rape trial. After a brief romantic interest with Jessica's mother, Maggie, Dylan had a relationship with his roommate, Michael Lai. More recently, he has been involved with Jessica again. Dylan is a complicated young man who occasionally makes impulsive choices, such as becoming

a male stripper to finance his education. But ultimately, he always manages to do the right thing.

Dylan Neal

Though Dylan Neal has appeared in films and made television appearances, this is his first daytime role.

Dylan, who describes himself as a "simple, small-town kind of kid," grew up in Oakville, Ontario, Canada. He attended a private boys' school until the eleventh grade. He was interested in becoming an actor but was not sure how to do so. He switched to public school for his final two years of high school and began appearing in stage productions. After graduation, Dylan traveled between Toronto and Los Angeles, making numerous commercial, television (including *Kung Fu: The Legend Continues* and *The War of the Worlds*), and film appearances (including *Prom Night III* and *Police Academy 4*).

Most recently, Dylan portrayed Canadian Olympic rowing champion John Wallace in the Canadian TV Movie of the Week, *Golden Girl— The Silken Laumann Story*.

Dylan enjoys a host of activities, including squash, drawing, and woodworking.

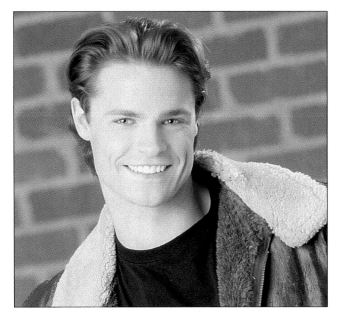

Michael Lai

Michael is an international studies major at UCLA. Her boyish name caused her to accidentally end up with Dylan as a roommate. Her girlish charm led Dylan to become interested in her. Michael was wooed by Clarke Garrison, but she is currently putting the moves on Grant Chambers. Michael can be an enigma. She's often demonstrated the ability to be a good friend.

Lindsay Price

Lindsay Price was born on December 6 in Arcadia, California. Her acting talent was first discovered by her teachers in charm school when she was three and a half years old. They encouraged her mother to get her an agent, which immediately led to her appearance in a Vivitar commercial.

In 1991, Lindsay relocated to New York at the age of fourteen, where she played An Li Chen on *All My Children* for three years while attending high school. After that, she moved back to Los Angeles and completed her last year of high school. She is currently in her first year of college.

Lindsay has appeared on numerous television series, including *Life Goes On*, *Parker Lewis Can't Lose*, *The Wonder Years*, *Newhart*, and *My Two Dads*. She also appeared in the theatrical release *Angus Bethune*.

Lindsay has a unique family tree. Her grandfather's adopted daughter ended up marrying her grandfather's son, which means that Lindsay's mother is her aunt and Lindsay's father is her uncle.

Sly Donovan

Sly is the bartender at the Bikini Bar. Sly had a short-lived relationship with Macy Alexander. More recently, he has pursued Jessica Forrester because of his interest in the Forrester fortune. Sly puts on a false front of being an affable guy, but lurking beneath the surface is a violent streak.

Brent Jasmer

Brent Jasmer, who made his soap opera debut in the role of Sly, has his roots firmly planted in the American musical theater. He has starred in such diverse musicals as *West Side Story, My Fair Lady,* and *A Chorus Line.* Brent has also appeared in *Fiddler on the Roof, Baby,* and *Once Upon a Mattress.*

Brent was schooled at the American Academy of Dramatic Arts (West). Upon graduating in 1988, Brent was asked to stay on with the Academy Production Company for the 1988–89 season. Brent went on to appear in many plays, including *The Taming of the Shrew, Bury the Dead,* and *Geniuses.* He recently produced and starred in an original play, *669 Mockingbird Lane,* in Hollywood. Brent also recently appeared on the

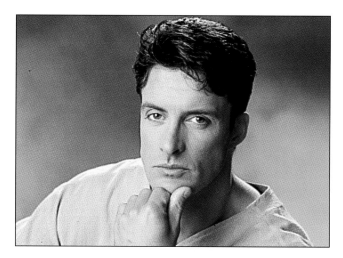

cover of the steamy publication *Playgirl.*

Brent recently juggled his schedule on *The Bold and the Beautiful* so that he could star in the movie *Leprechaun Four,* which will be released late this year.

In his spare time, Brent works out with weights and plays basketball (with his celebrity/charity team) and volleyball. He is also an accomplished singer and drummer and is currently at work on a record album.

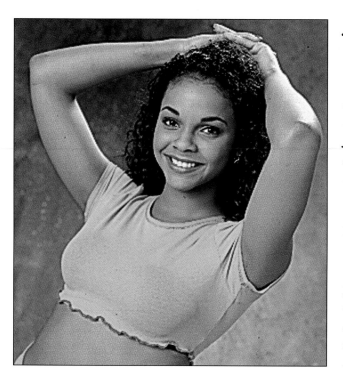

Jasmine Malone

A friend to Michael Lai, and now a roommate of Michael and Dylan, Jasmine made a splash by replacing Anthony Armando as Spectra's head designer. After she discovered that she was merely a pawn in Sally Spectra's scheme to knock-off Forrester designs, she quit. Jasmine was attracted to Sly, but has tried to fight it since she witnessed him taking advantage of Jessica Forrester.

Lark Voorhies

Lark Voorhies began her acting career by appearing in national television commercials at the age of twelve. Lark quickly became a familiar television personality through guest-starring roles on such series as *Small Wonder* and *The Robert Guillaume Show.* Her biggest break came in 1988 when she starred in the successful hit teen series *Saved by the Bell* as the popular Lisa Turtle.

Lark made the move to daytime dramas in 1993 when she joined *Days of Our Lives* as Wendy Reardon. She continued to make guest-star appearances on such prime-time shows as *Star Trek: Deep Space Nine*, *The Fresh Prince of Bel-Air*, and *Martin*.

She also recently starred in the CBS Schoolbreak Special *What About Your Friends*.

She is currently on a leave of absence from the honors medical program at a Los Angeles–area college.

Grant Chambers

Grant is the new designer at Forrester Creations. He and Dr. Taylor Hayes were good friends in their college days. Grant is being pursued by Sheila Carter and Michael Lai. A loyal friend, Grant has no problem placing his job at risk to defend someone he cares about, like Taylor. Grant won Ridge's respect when he insisted that Ridge stop taking Taylor for granted. Nevertheless, when it comes to women, Ridge and Grant often find themselves competing in the same arena.

Charles Grant

Charles Grant is a familiar face to daytime audiences, having starred in *Santa Barbara* as Connor McCabe. Other daytime roles include Evan on *Another World* and Preacher on *The Edge of Night*, which was his first professional acting job.

Since departing *Santa Barbara*, Charles has appeared in the feature films *Poisoned Well* and *Lady in Waiting*, and the made-for-television movies *Co-ed Call Girl*, starring Tori Spelling, and *Never Give Up the Search for Sarah*, with Patty Duke and Richard Crenna.

Charles has guest-starred on the television series *In the Heat of the Night*, *Kung Fu*, *Phenom*,

Saved by the Bell, *Renegade*, and *Silk Stalkings*.

Charles also butted heads with J. R. Ewing when he played the recurring role of blackmailer David Sheldon on the CBS hit *Dallas*.

Most recently, Charles entered the computer age when he starred as an Indiana Jones–style hero in a CD-ROM called *D.C.2*.

Charles, who is single, shares a hillside home with his four dogs.

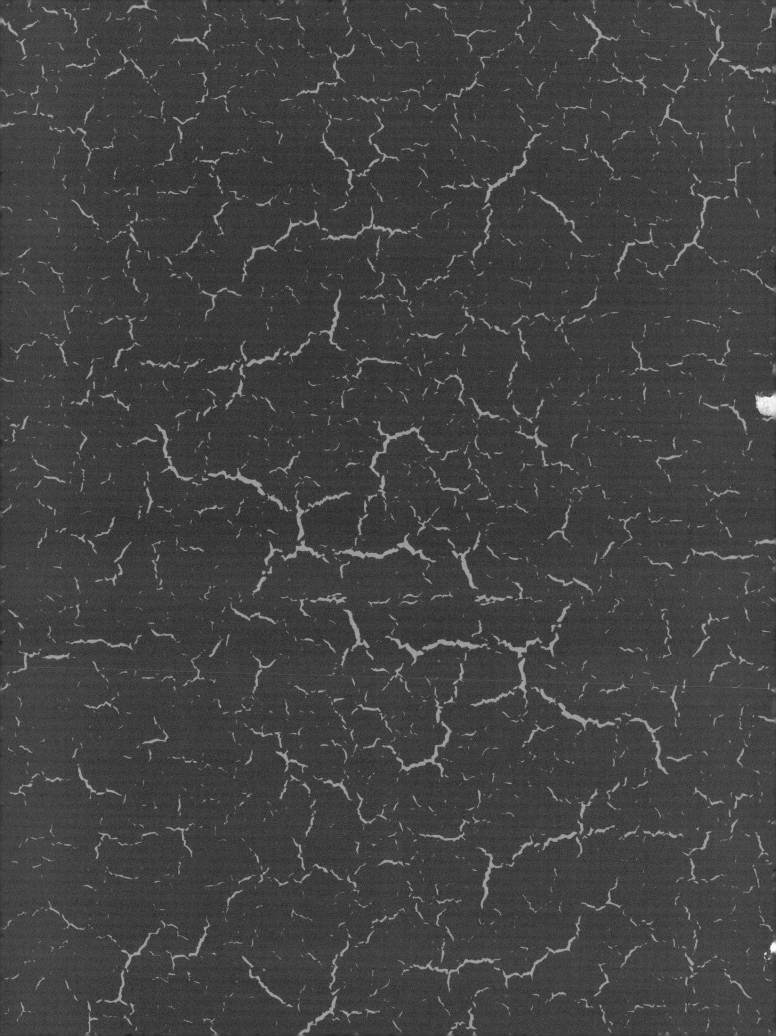

Q & A for B & B Stars

B&B Stars Reveal How They Dress Off the Set

Barbara Crampton

I go to work in my running clothes. I exercise at the studio or I go to the gym in the morning and then directly to the studio. During the day I'm always in exercise clothes. Generally, I do love fashion and I like to keep up with the styles and when I go out at night I like to dress up. Before joining *The Bold and the Beautiful,* I've always played characters who had good fashion sense. Mindy was a fashion designer. Leanna used to wear bizarre, bright outfits. This is a big change for me because I feel like I'm wearing Kmart reject clothes. In a way, it's fun because I don't have to worry so much about my clothes and I like the comfortability that the character has. But I find myself looking at other people on the show and seeing what they're wearing and thinking, That's nice. I'd like to have that. It's probably how Maggie would feel. I'm working on a show that completely deals with fashion and Maggie is the antihero of fashion.

Schae Harrison

The wardrobe Darla wears is a perk because it keeps me aware of the new trends in fashion, which really helps when I do dress up and go out. But for the most part, I'd say my favorite designer is Levi Strauss.

Brent Jasmer

I wear more clothes than Sly does. That's the most important thing. For some reason, Sly pretty much likes to be naked a lot and, well, Brent just likes to be a little more clothed than that.

Dylan Neal

My wardrobe mainly consists of a pair of jeans, my beaten-up brown Doc Martens boots, and a revolving array of flannel shirts. I don't know if it comes from my Canadian heritage or just from my general lack of ability to iron, but I'm very casual. I don't get dressed up too often. I don't go out to events that require being dressed up that often. The character I play on the show also dresses casually, but he changes his pants more often than I do! Like Dylan Shaw, I also enjoy wearing sports jackets. However, that usually requires an ironed shirt underneath and that's where we run into a problem. I send away most of my stuff to the dry cleaners to get ironed, so I usually have to do that before I wear a sports jacket. Appearing on a fashion-show-format soap opera hasn't affected the way I dress, other than to make me more aware of how casually I do dress in my everyday life!

Lindsay Price

I usually wear jeans away from the studio. When I go to a formal event, I don't have a particular designer that I prefer over anyone else. I just know what I like specifically. It's usually romantic-type clothing. On the show I'm dressed sexier or more seductive than I would be in my own life, with exposed midriffs and short skirts. I don't know that I'd have the guts to wear stuff like that all the

Schae Harrison

time outside of work. But it's certainly helped me with knowing that I can pull that off if I have to or want to!

Lark Voorhies

My style of dress away from the studio is usually more conventional, a kind of a classic that doesn't go in and out with the trends. At formal events I usually wear gowns designed by Alaïa. His clothes have simple lines. They're soft, pretty, and elegant. I really enjoyed it when Jasmine was a designer because I got to wear experimental-type clothes. She started on the show as a designer and I hope she goes full circle, back to designing again sometime in the future.

B&B STARS SHARE REAL-LIFE TALENTS THEY'VE USED ON THE SHOW

Bobbie Eakes

I had already recorded an album that was released by Epic Records called *Big Trouble* and had probably been on the show for five or six months when I thought to myself, I wonder if they know that I can sing. I had seen other soaps where people sang, such as Patty Weaver on *The Young and the Restless* and *Days of Our Lives.* Since I didn't think that the show's writers and producers knew that I could sing, I wasn't sure how they'd feel about it because they didn't write Macy as a singer. It wasn't part of my audition. So I brought them a copy of a music video I had performed in with Big Trouble. Brad and Billy passed it around upstairs in the production office. Soon after, they called me and said, "We'd love for you to sing on the show. What about bringing all of the girls in your band on the show?" I told them that the band had broken up, but that I'd love to do it. A couple of months later, Jeff was cast on *The Bold and the Beautiful.* I guess the writers thought, Here are two people who both sing. It may also have been what prompted them to think about bringing the two characters together.

Katherine Kelly Lang

At Brooke's wedding to Eric, and her later marriage to Ridge, I rode horses, which is something I've done all my life. At the wedding to Eric in Palm Springs, the producers asked if I wanted to use one of my horses. But I have Arabians, which are kind of wild. They might've been frightened by the cameras, the cars, the different people, and vague things dropping in and out, things that could really spook the horses. At Brooke's wedding to Ridge in Malibu, the producers asked me again if I wanted to use one of my horses and I actually used a horse that belonged to one of my girlfriends. It was a dark brown, almost black horse, which contrasted with the white wedding dress flowing behind as the horse trotted.

Jeff Trachta

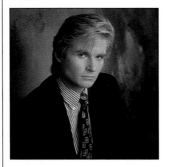

The day I was cast on *The Bold and the Beautiful,* I told Bill Bell that I'd like to sing on his show. He smiled and said, "You and probably every other actor I've ever hired for both of my shows!" He then added that Thorne was having a nervous breakdown and that he didn't have anything to sing about. He said to wait a few months and then we'd talk about my singing on the show again. After a few months had passed, I hired a pianist and told everyone that I would be singing on the third floor at three o'clock in one of the rehearsal rooms. Some of the producers, and Brad, came to watch. The next day Bill asked if I would sing for him. A week later they wrote the episode where Thorne and Macy sing for the first time.

Maitland Ward

When I was cast on the show I wrote on my résumé that I played the violin. So Brad [Bell] thought it was true. But all I could play was scales. I was told at the place that helped me with my résumé to put everything on it that I could vaguely do. Shortly after I was cast, I picked up a script and it said that Jessica would play the violin! Since I could play scales that's what they had me play. But actually playing the violin adds to Jessica's character. It

seems like the instrument that she would play. It's more Jessica's talent than mine. Ever since Brad found out that I don't really play he sometimes jokingly says, "Maitland, we're going to have you play the violin on the show today!"

MEMORABLE MOMENTS ON LOCATION

Katherine Kelly Lang

When we were shooting the scenes after Brooke and Ridge's wedding, on a boat, people were throwing up, because of the constant rocking of the boat. John Zak, who was producing the sequence, had to take over for the director, who had become seasick. It seemed like everybody was hunched over the side of the boat! Meanwhile, Ronn and I were sitting on the boat at a small table, performing a scene with whipped cream. I put whipped cream on Ronn's nose and then licked it off. It looked romantic on-camera, but I remember telling Ronn, "Please, just don't throw up!" We both felt sick, but we never threw up.

Dan McVicar

We were shooting a very realistic fight scene in an alley near the studio. Sally had hired two thugs to beat Clarke up because he was blackmailing her with a tape. Two stunt doubles were hired. We rehearsed the fight a couple of times and then we started to shoot it. All of a sudden, a police helicopter started hovering over the alley and two squad cars quickly pulled up. One of the police officers said there was a report of a fight in the alley. The funniest thing is that we already had policemen with us! They explained to the other officers that it was a staged fight for television and to ignore any further 911 calls they might get about this particular scuffle.

When we taped the fashion show on the *Queen Mary,* I caught an upper respiratory infection. This was a long, complicated shoot that eventually stretched into three or four days. It started to feel like we were really out to sea, even though the *Queen Mary* is docked, because nobody ever left the ship! Finally, during a break, I jumped ship and saw a doctor to get some antibiotics. I wanted to knock the infection out right away because I didn't want it to get worse when I was needed to work. In John McCook's dressing room there's a Polaroid picture of the people who were on that shoot making funny faces. In the photo, I almost look seasick!

Ronn Moss

When we were in Barbados, where Ridge was trying to find Brooke, he got horrendously smashed at a dinner with Lauren. Later, he goes to the beach, drunk as a skunk, praying to find Brooke. Emotionally, he's a wreck and at his wits' end. He looks up at the stars, asks for help, collapses into the sand, and passes out. I had to stay in the sand until the next setup, which was Brooke coming up and ripping the necklace off Ridge. It was the first time that Ridge actually saw Brooke in Barbados. I'm lying in the sand and the tides are coming in. They kept coming closer and closer, until they actually swept over me. I was wearing a suit. I expected the cameraman, or someone, to give me a clue before it happened. But everybody was distracted for a couple of seconds, and just as the tides were coming in, they yelled, "Ronn, look out!" I was soaked and I thought to myself, Well, that's the way the scene is going to play; there's no turning back. It's nine o'clock at night; nobody's going to blow dry me! So I just lay there soaked. Actually, I wished we had gotten it on-camera!

When Ridge married Caroline I remember a silly little thing that happened with Susan Flannery during one of the breaks. Susan had borrowed a cellular phone and it was tiny. She had never used one before, and instead of holding it up, the way you would a phone, Susan would talk into it like it was a walkie-talkie and then hold it to her ear. I watched her go back and forth doing this, and I thought to myself, She's got to be kidding. So I went up to her and said, "Susan, what are you doing?" and she answered, "Well, this thing is so tiny, it's the only way I can talk!" I told her, "Susan, you just hold the phone up to your ear and the person at the other end of the line can hear you." When I showed her the tiny hole that was the microphone, she looked up at me and laughed, and then we both almost fell on the ground laughing.

Dylan Neal

Dylan Neal

When we shot at Universal Studios, Scott, my then-roommate, who is also an actor, had a couple of part-time jobs. One of them was being a tour guide for Universal Studios. So it was rather appropriate that we got Scott to be the tour guide for Jessica and Dylan while they were spending the day at Universal Studios.

Maitland Ward

When Dylan and I taped the scenes at Universal Studios, we had one scene where we rode on the tram. Whenever the shark from *Jaws* popped up, we had to look surprised. It was toward the end of a long day, and everybody was getting really tired and hot, because we were shooting in the summer. Finally, an extra who was in the back of the tram yelled out, "Let's just eat the dumb fish!" After we finished the first day's taping, some of us stayed at Universal Studios and went on the rides until one in the morning. We were really tired the next day because we had to be back by six A.M. for another full day of taping!

MEMORABLE MISHAPS AND UNEXPECTED OCCURRENCES

Ian Buchanan

When we shot the scenes in the dungeon, Sheila chained James to a wall. During one of the five-minute breaks, no one could find the keys to unchain me! The person who had the keys from the prop department was in a different area of the building and couldn't be located. So after that Kimberlin kept a set of the keys on her at all times, so that if I ever needed to be unchained, I could. Actually, it fit quite nicely with Sheila's character that she would be the one with the keys!

Lauren Koslow

The first time I was pregnant, I was ready to move on and leave the show, which I communicated to the producers. But a decision was made to write my pregnancy into the script. A few weeks after I announced that I was pregnant, there was a scene in the script where Margo is sitting in Clarke's apartment sketching. Viewers suddenly discovered that there was a connection between Margo and Clarke, who had been having a secret affair. Margo became pregnant with Clarke's baby. I thought it was wonderful. During my second pregnancy the show didn't write it into the script. So we had to hide the pregnancy. During my first pregnancy, when Margo was also pregnant, viewers wrote to the show saying, "You're not padding her very well because she doesn't look pregnant." But during my second pregnancy, when we were trying to hide it, the audience didn't even notice it. I thought it would be obvious because Margo always wore fantastic, form-fitting designer outfits. But we didn't get one letter commenting on my second pregnancy.

Katherine Kelly Lang

A few months after the show started, I woke up one morning and my entire face was swollen. I couldn't even open my eyes. It was an allergic reaction to an antibiotic I was taking. I was supposed to work that day, but I had to call in sick. Catherine Hickland, who I used to love watching on *Capitol,* stepped in and played Brooke for a few episodes. Whenever we see each other we joke about the time she had to play Brooke because my face was too swollen to work!

I remember a scene where Brooke and Stephanie were fighting. I'm not sure what the fight was about, but it had become very emotional and intense. Susan had to hit me and then I had to hit her. After Susan hit me, I hit her back so hard that she staggered and fell off her feet. The cameras kept going. Everybody loved it because it was really dramatic. But once the scene was over, Susan said, "She will never hit me again—ever!" Brooke and Stephanie have never had a fight like that again.

John McCook

On my fiftieth birthday the writers had added a scene that wasn't originally in the script. It was a scene with Susan Flannery at the beginning of the day. Stephanie rings the doorbell at Eric's home and I'm supposed to answer it. We rehearsed the scene and blocked it. When it came time to tape the scene, I get up to answer the door. But instead of seeing Susan when I open the door, my entire family is standing there! Everybody started singing "Happy Birthday." It was a wonderful surprise.

Jeff Trachta

During Thorne and Macy's first wedding ceremony, I fell on the floor at two o'clock in the morning. Bobbie and I were singing "Here and Now," Thorne and Macy's wedding song. I couldn't remember the words, even though we had performed the song several times before. We were laughing and I started jumping up and down. I ended up falling on my butt. So when we were singing, I was in terrible pain. You can see the tears in my eyes singing to Bobbie because my back was hurting!

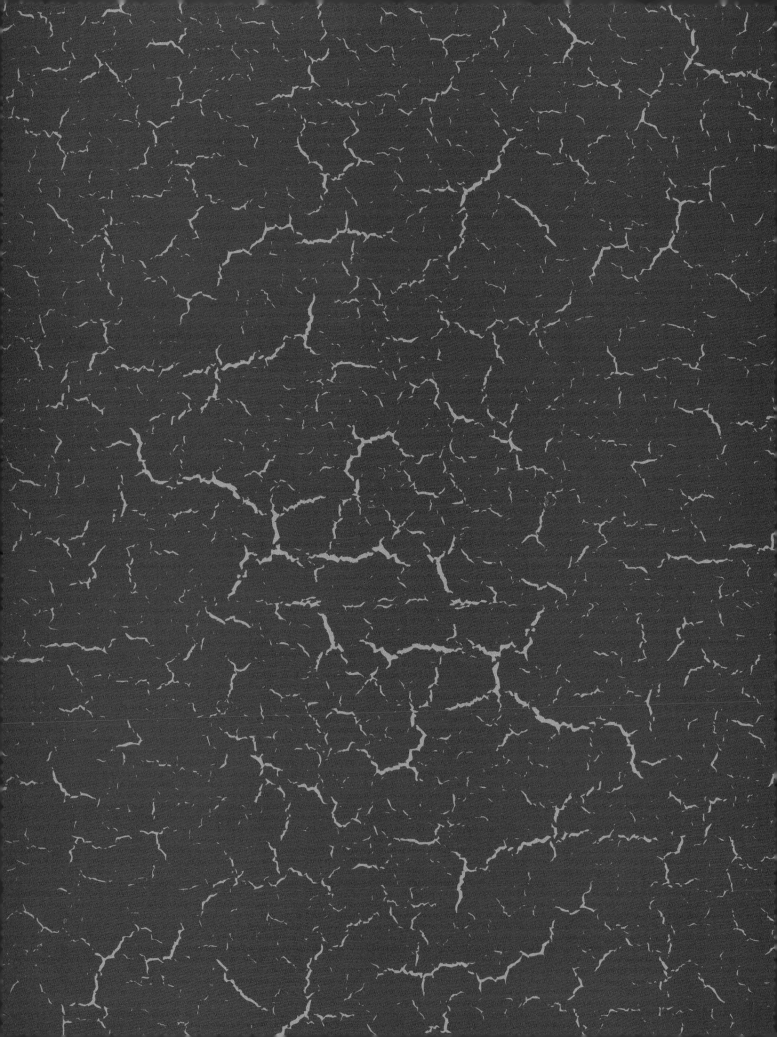

Celebrity Guests

When *The Bold and the Beautiful* stages its spectacular fashion shows, Hollywood celebrities can usually be spotted in the audience, watching with eager anticipation as the models sashay down the runway, unveiling the newest collection of exquisite fashions from Forrester Creations and Spectra Fashions. "We try to include celebrities so that they're an organic part of the story, rather than bringing them on just for the sake of stunning the audience," says producer-director John Zak. "We're able to intermesh reality with our fictitious story because it's believable that the Forresters and Sally Spectra, who are in the fashion industry, would function within the cadre of Los Angeles, and know people in film and television." At other times, *The Bold and the Beautiful* casts well-known performers, such as comedienne Phyllis Diller and veteran actor Joseph Campanella, in short-term roles. Included in this section are highlights of celebrity appearances on *The Bold and the Beautiful* over the years.

Carol Channing

Carol Channing and John McCook

Carol Channing was delighted to guest-star on *The Bold and the Beautiful* as herself during the "Salute to Hollywood" fashion show in 1993. Carol, who knew Bill and Lee from Chicago, where she frequently guested on Lee's TV talk show, has been a faithful follower of *The Bold and the Beautiful* since its first season and took great delight in sharing her knowledge of the show's intricate storylines and characters with *B&B* cast members, producers, and crew. Carol even knew the types of dishes that Stephanie's longtime housekeeper Maria prepared for the Forrester family! Producer-director John Zak told *Soap Opera Digest*'s Michael Maloney, "Carol added a couple of lines when Stephanie told her to come to the party after the show. Carol said, 'Only if Maria makes her famous enchiladas.'"

Steve Allen and Jayne Meadows

Steve Allen and Jayne Meadows guest-starred as themselves, viewing the "Salute to Hollywood" fashion show in 1993. Previously, they worked with Bobbie Eakes and Jeff Trachta in a stage production of the musical *Cinderella*. "It was a reunion for me," says Jeff, "because Steve Allen and Jayne Meadows had played my parents."

Joseph Campanella

Joseph Campanella appeared in the spring of 1996 as Jonathan Young, a lawyer who represented Eric in his bid to win custody of his young children, Rick and Bridget, when Brooke was missing. He also appeared on *The Guiding Light* as Joe Turino in the late fifties, when *The Bold and the Beautiful*'s creator William J. Bell was the long-running serial's associate writer.

Phyllis Diller

Phyllis Diller and Hunter Tylo

Phyllis Diller, who paved the way for female comics in the fifties, has made several appearances, beginning in 1995, on *The Bold and the Beautiful* as Gladys Pope, a makeup artist. In Phyllis Diller's first appearance, Gladys helped Taylor, who was presumed dead, disguise herself when she returned to Los Angeles to see her father, Jack Hamilton, who had suffered a heart attack. Several months later she made a return appearance when Gladys applied for a job at Spectra Fashions and boasted that Taylor Forrester was among her prestigious clients. When Dylan Shaw debuted as a male stripper, Gladys, with dollar bills in hand, had a ringside seat at the Beverly Hills Hideaway. "Lark Voorhies and I had a scene with Phyllis Diller," recounts Lindsay Price. "Phyllis waved a dollar bill over my head and got a stripper to kiss me. The scenes were shot toward the end of the day, so there was a lot of waiting. And then when we performed the scenes, we spent most of our time watching the strippers perform. Phyllis was completely professional and very funny. We had a great time working with her."

James Doohan

James Doohan, who's most famous for his role as Scotty on the television series *Star Trek,* guest-starred for several appearances as James Warwick's dad, Damon, in 1994. Ian Buchanan felt there was an irony to James Doohan being cast as his dad on *The Bold and the Beautiful.* Ian explains, "When I first came to the United States as an actor, people who heard I was from Scotland would speak to me in a thick, put-on Scottish accent and say, 'Beam me up, Scotty!' I'd look at them blankly and answer, 'I don't know what you're talking about.' Finally someone told me about *Star Trek* and I watched a little of it. I wondered, 'Where do people think I come from that they believe this is a proper Scottish accent?' It was sort of an impression of a Scottish accent. Then, when friends of mine who watched *Star Trek* found out that James Doohan was going to play my father on the show, they were very impressed and told me, 'You've arrived! Scotty's playing your father!'"

James Doohan and Ian Buchanan

Debbie Dunning

Home Improvement's Debbie Dunning made an uncredited cameo appearance on *The Bold and the Beautiful* in 1995. Debbie Dunning, who's a close friend of Schae Harrison, was visiting the studio on a day when a swimwear fashion show was being shot at the Bikini Bar. "She was in the crowd during the fashion show," reveals Schae.

Jose Eber

Beverly Hills stylist Jose Eber guest-starred as himself on *The Bold and the Beautiful* in the fall of 1994. Ivana hired him to give a makeover to Jessica, who was depressed about Dylan's arrest for statutory rape. "It was neat having someone so famous come in and do my makeover," enthuses Maitland Ward. "Everybody on the show thought that he was going to cut my hair up to my chin. But Brad

[Bell] knew I was worried and told Jose just to do a minor cut. When I met Jose earlier in the day, in the rehearsal hall, he started talking about my hair, which made me nervous. So Jeff Trachta came over, gave me a hug, and said to Jose, 'Don't do anything to my cousin!' I thought that was really sweet."

Fabio

Darlene Conley with Fabio

Fabio made a guest-star appearance during Sally's bachelorette party, when she was engaged to marry Jack Hamilton in 1993. *The Bold and the Beautiful*'s producers got the idea to cast Fabio when they saw him paired with Darlene Conley as presenters on the Soap Opera Awards show. Fabio, who was on a heavy promotional campaign for an album of romantic songs, could only spend three hours at the studio, so three exotic dancers, Scott Layne, David Andrew Sojka, and Victor Brookes, were also cast by *The Bold and the Beautiful* to add to the festive feeling at Sally's party. One particular scene, in which Fabio kisses Sally's hand, had to be shot several times for various camera angles. During one camera setup, Darlene good-naturedly looked into the camera and quipped, "How am I supposed to work under these conditions? And couldn't you have found someone a little more attractive for me?"

George Hamilton

George Hamilton made a guest-star appearance in 1994 as Sonny Stone, a former flame of Sally's who resurfaced just as Sally was launching her Grand Diva collection. "Sonny was trying to get a peek at Sally's Grand Diva collection," says Darlene, "being very smooth and charming." Sally, however, was well aware of her ex-boyfriend's slick ways, and the possibility that he would lift ideas from her collection, so she kept him at bay. "The show really utilized George Hamilton's real-life persona, and the things that he's so good at doing," observes Darlene. "He was wonderful."

George Hamilton and Darlene Conley

Tippi Hedren

When Tippi Hedren appeared in a short-term role on *The Bold and the Beautiful* in 1990 as Margo and Jake's mother, she already had a friend in the cast, Darlene Conley. They had worked together in the feature film *The Birds,* directed by Alfred Hitchcock for Universal Studios, where Darlene was a starlet. "The first picture I ever did was for Hitchcock," says Darlene. "It was in the last years of the contract system. Tippi was Hitchcock's *star.* He was like Svengali with her because he enjoyed taking actresses who didn't have much experience and then putting his stamp on them. So Tippi could never go anywhere at the end of the day, after we finished filming. I used to come on the set in the morning at Universal and give her a devil of a time. I'd tell her how I went to some big Hollywood party the night before and sat next to Cary Grant. She'd look disappointed because she wasn't in on the fun, and I'd tease her and say, 'What are you complaining about? You had lunch with Jessica Tandy!'" With a fond laugh, Darlene adds, "Tippi and I had a great time. It was wonderful to see her again."

Tippi Hedren

Charlton Heston

Veteran film actor Charlton Heston appeared as himself during the "Salute to Hollywood" fashion show in 1993. He performed scenes with Susan Flannery and Darlene Conley. In the story, Sally Spectra discovers that Charlton will be participating in Forrester Creations' fashion show and she cons the film star into also including Spectra Fashions, much to Stephanie's chagrin. "This was a perfect idea," enthuses Darlene Conley, who relished the idea of playing Sally at her best, a woman who quickly checks out all the angles and then moves full speed ahead to make sure Spectra Fashions is at the front of the line, soaking up as much limelight as possible. "Sally will do anything to get what she wants," observes Darlene. "When she nailed Heston and got him to agree to let Spectra Fashions participate in the fashion show, it was great. It's one of the reasons people love Sally, because she thinks on her feet. Viewers don't know how she's going to jump, because Sally doesn't think first before doing it. She jumps and then she justifies it. That's how she came in contact with Charlton. Sally got wind that Charlton Heston was Stephanie's guest for the American Film Institute's fashion show fund-raiser and then conned her way onto a film set where he was working. She sold him on the idea of letting Spectra Fashions participate in the show by flattering him, telling him that she had seen everything he'd ever done, even down to one of his obscure films, *Major Dundee*! Charton was disarmed and fascinated by this creature and she eventually convinced him to combine two fashions shows in the American Film Institute's event."

Mike Piazza

Mike Piazza, catcher for the Los Angeles Dodgers, was Sally's escort at her successful Grand Diva fashion show in 1994.

Tommy Tune

Broadway legend Tommy Tune guest-starred on *The Bold and the Beautiful* in early 1996. Jeff Trachta was cast in a lead role of the long-running Broadway revival of *Grease* and *The Bold and the Beautiful*'s writers decided to overlap the show's fantasy life with reality, by having Thorne Forrester also land a lead role in *Grease*. Tommy Tune appeared as himself. "Before I came on *The Bold and the Beautiful,* I watched it to find out what was happening," says Tune. At the time,

Darlene Conley and Mike Piazza

Eric was on a mission to prevent Sally from stealing Forrester Creations' new collection of clothes for her own line. His efforts included romancing Sally and ultimately proposing marriage. "Of course, I got carried away with Eric's marriage proposal to Sally!" reveals Tommy.

Tommy Tune and Jeff Trachta

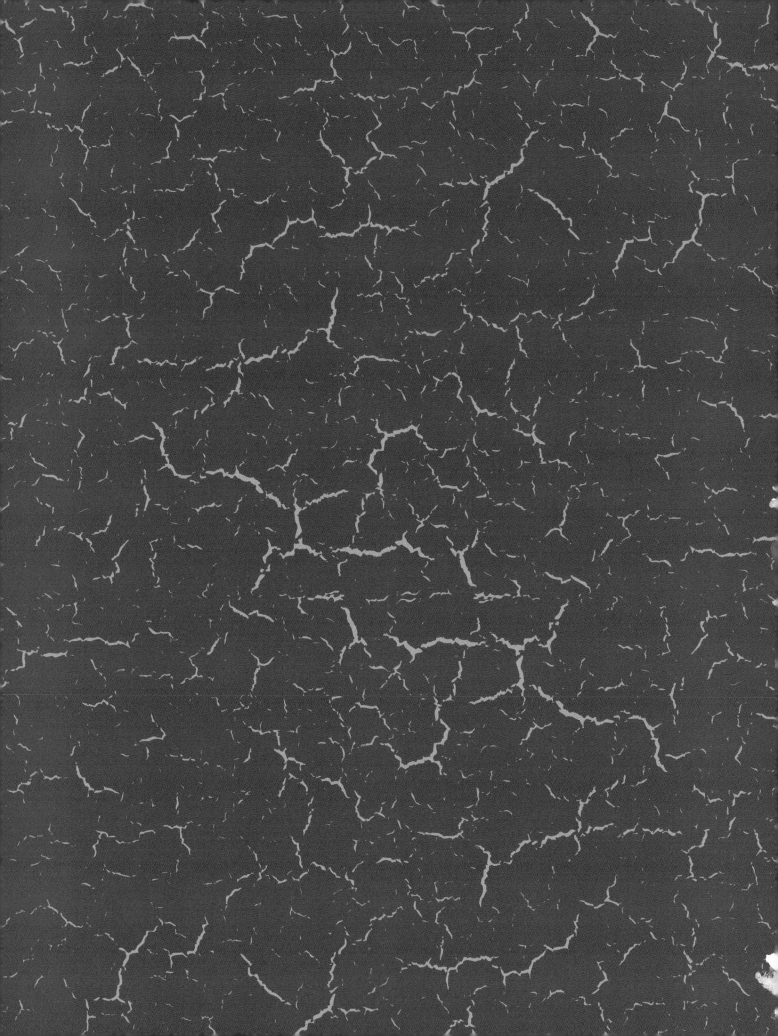

Stars Behind the Cameras: Creators, Producers, Writers

William J. Bell Sr.
CREATOR

If it hadn't been for a part-time job writing comedy sketches, William J. Bell would be practicing medicine today. He was a premed student at DePaul University when he accepted a gig penning scripts for a Chicago radio station to earn money. But Bill discovered he enjoyed writing so much that he set aside his plans to become a doctor.

Soon after, Bill's writing talent caught the attention of McCann-Erickson, a high-profile advertising agency, and he accepted a copywriter position. Three years later Cunningham and Walsh, a competing agency, lured him over with a lucrative offer. Bill's first assignment in his new job was creating a national ad campaign for Sara Lee.

While Bill was working in advertising, he met Lee Phillip, a prominent Chicago TV talk show host. Bill's clients appeared as guests on Lee's show and Bill often accompanied them to the studio. Bill and Lee went on a date, and afterward, Bill immediately knew he found the woman he wanted to marry.

At twenty-nine, Bill realized that working at an ad agency was not how he wanted to spend the rest of his life. Now married to Lee, he decided to return to the field that brought him the most satisfaction, writing. In 1957 he submitted a sample television script to Irna Phillips, a fellow Chicagoan who had practically created the form we know as television soap opera. Irna hired him to write dialogue for *The Guiding Light*. A year later Bill began writing for *As the*

Co-creators Lee Phillip and William J. Bell

World Turns, another Irna Phillips creation, and in 1964 he co-created *Another World* with Irna. A year later, Bill co-created with Irna Phillips the prime-time serial *Our Private World*. In 1966 he assumed head-writing chores for *Days of Our Lives*, which premiered on NBC to lackluster ratings. "It was a real challenge," says Bill. "All the numbers were at CBS, which carried *As the World Turns* and *Guiding Light*. NBC had no numbers at all." Thanks to Bill's efforts, however, *Days of Our Lives* soon skyrocketed to the number one position.

In 1973, he co-created *The Young and the Restless* with his wife, Lee, which premiered on CBS. *Variety* praised the new serial, which sought to present a broad base of wholesome, identifiable young characters in situations that reflected contemporary life, for its sophistication. In 1987 *The Bold and the Beautiful*, which Bill also co-created with Lee, premiered.

Bill has received seven Emmy Awards, two as a writer, one each for *The Young and the Restless* and for *Days of Our Lives*, and five as a producer of *The Young and the Restless*, most recently in 1993. Other awards for excellence in writing and subject matter include multiple Media Access Awards, The Nancy Susan Reynolds Award from the Center for Population Options, and numerous other awards and citations from Mothers Against Drunk Driving, the Hollywood Entertainment Council, and the Men's Fashion Association of America, to name a few.

Bill has also been the subject of retrospectives at the Museum of Broadcasting and the Museum of Broadcast Communications, and the recipient of the Governor's Award from the National Academy of Television Arts & Sciences and the Silver Circle from the Chicago chapter of NATAS. He has received the Editor's Award from *Soap Opera Digest* and is one of the inaugural inductees into *Soap Opera Weekly*'s Hall of Fame. He is the recipient of awards for Most Popular Drama Series from networks in Italy, Holland, and Switzerland.

More recently, Bill's two current daytime drama series have popularized the soap opera format with audiences in over ninety foreign countries, opening up a vast new and appreciative international audience to the phenomenon of American daytime drama.

For nearly four decades Bill has remained the medium's fiercest advocate and its most enthusiastic champion, preferring the daytime drama format to all other writing and producing venues and opportunities. His stories, plots, and characters epitomize the rich diversity and complex ingenuity that American daytime dramas represent.

In addition to being the creator of *The Bold and the Beautiful*, Bill is also the creator and senior executive producer of *The Young and the Restless*.

Lee Phillip Bell
CO-CREATOR

A native of Chicago, Lee attended Northwestern University, where she received a degree in microbiology while working part-time in her family's thriving flower business. Lee intended to pursue a career in social work but was detoured into broadcasting. She frequently accompanied her brother to a local television program, where he demonstrated flower arranging. WBKB asked Lee if she would be their resident florist. Several months later CBS purchased the station and renamed it WBBM, and Lee was offered a job as a vacation replacement, beginning with station breaks.

She eventually became director of special projects/programming and soon began hosting her own program, *The Lee Phillip Show*, which was a pioneer in the evolution of the afternoon talk-show format and a trailblazer in the exploration of timely social issues. The program featured TV's first on-air self-breast examination for women, a prototype for similar projects broadcast throughout the country. She was also a contributing editor to *Daybreak*, the early-morning program, and continued to produce and narrate numerous award-winning specials and documentaries on such social concerns as foster care, rape, children of divorced parents, and babies born to women in prison.

Today, Lee's involvement in social issues continues with such institutions as the National Committee for the Prevention of Child Abuse, the Mental Health Association, Children's Home & Aid Society, the Salvation Army, Family Focus, and Northwestern University.

While working at WBBM-TV, Lee met her future husband, William J. Bell, then a rising advertising executive with McCann-Erickson. "As soon as we started dating, I needed scripts, and I forced Bill into writing them," Lee told the *Los Angeles Daily News*. "He was the best writer I knew."

Lee and Bill have maintained a truly collegial relationship over the past three decades. While Bill was writing such series as *The Guiding Light* and *As the World Turns* and co-creating *Another World* with Irna Phillips, Lee continued her own career as a broadcast journalist, passing along to her husband her research on documentary topics from her talk show, which he later wove into his dramatic storylines. Bill, in turn, would assist Lee in the preparation of her own materials and in formulating her approach to her subject matter.

As a drama series producer, Lee has been honored by awards and nominations from the National Academy of Television Arts & Sciences, the NAACP Image Awards, and the Soap Opera Digest Awards. She recently received the 1993 Broadcaster of the Year Award from the American Women in Radio & Television and the 1993 Directors Choice Award from the National Women's Economic Alliance Foundation.

Lee was also the recipient of sixteen local Emmys, a National Emmy for Community Service, and the Alfred I. DuPont/Columbia University Award for the special *The Rape of Paulette*, the first program in Chicago to explore the issue. In 1977, she was the first woman to receive the coveted Governor's Award from the Chicago chapter of the National Academy of Television Arts & Sciences. In 1980 she was named Person of the Year by the Broadcast Advertising Club of Chicago and the Outstanding Woman in Communications by the Chicago YMCA. She recently received the Salvation Army's William Booth Award for her distinguished career in community and social service.

Long-time residents of Chicago, the Bell family moved to Los Angeles permanently shortly before *The Bold and the Beautiful* debuted in 1987. They reside in Beverly Hills in a former residence of Howard Hughes which they have extensively renovated.

Bradley Bell
EXECUTIVE PRODUCER AND HEAD WRITER

Bradley Bell began his career in daytime television as a man of few words. For three years he simply sat and observed story conferences between his father, William J. Bell, and the writing staff of *The Young and the Restless.* However, as he gained more knowledge of the medium, Bradley started sharing storyline ideas, first on *The Young and the Restless* and then on *The Bold and the Beautiful.* Presently, Brad is executive producer and head writer of *The Bold and the Beautiful,* and is responsible for creating hundreds of pages of story each week. Ironically, the man of few words now can't express his ideas fast enough in a medium with a voracious appetite that demands two hundred and fifty scripts a year.

Born in Chicago, Brad is the second son of William J. Bell and Lee Phillip Bell. As far back as Brad can remember, the soaps were a significant part of his family's life. "I can remember watching *Days of Our Lives* as a kid," says Brad. "I literally grew up with these shows." He also recalls the image of his father sitting in front of the typewriter writing during the day and at night, or hashing out story ideas on the telephone with his writers and producers. "Our apartment was Soap Central in the Midwest," observes Brad.

While Brad was a senior at the Chicago Latin School, he expressed an interest in writing for the soaps and arranged to sit in on his father's story conferences for *The Young and the Restless.* It wasn't an easy commitment for a high school student to make, but Brad was determined to learn as much as he could about how soaps were put together. "Sometimes those story conferences would go from eight in the morning until six at night with, really, no break," recalls Brad. "It would be a beautiful day in Chicago, my friends would be at Wrigley Field watching the Cubs play or out on the beach. And I would be at home with my dad and Kay Alden and Jack Smith of *The Young and the Restless,* who flew in at different times of the year." He smiles and adds, "At the time, they were really smoking heavily. So it was hot and stuffy, with all these people who were older than I was, and the room would be filled with smoke. I sat there for years, hour after hour, just listening to the conversation, writing notes, as though it was a class," says Brad. "I really wanted to absorb what everyone was doing and watch how the whole writing team worked."

Brad's senior year in high school proved to be pivotal for him, both personally and professionally. He met his future wife, Colleen Bradley, who lived next door to his family's home in Lake Geneva, Wisconsin. As he told *Soap Opera Digest,* "I mowed her family's lawn. They lived next to our summer home. I saw her doing cartwheels and thought, She's so cute."

In the fall Brad left home to attend the University of Colorado, and later he transferred to the University of Wisconsin at Madison, where he enrolled in

Executive producer and head writer Bradley Bell

a television production class and directed an action/adventure scene involving private eye Paul Williams, from a *Young and the Restless* script. Modestly downplaying his directorial debut, Brad said, "It was nothing major, but the excitement of directing that one scene really sent me on track."

Meanwhile, after observing *The Young and the Restless* story conferences for two years, Brad finally offered his first story idea. At the time Paul Williams was desperate to find singer Lauren Fenmore, who'd been kidnapped by an obsessed fan, Shawn Garrett, and buried alive. "Paul only had a certain amount of time before he could find Lauren and dig her out, because the oxygen would only last a couple of hours," recalls Brad, whose contribution to the story included the suggestion that they heighten the tension by putting a time clock on the screen to show the minutes ticking away as Lauren inched closer to death. "It was such a thrill when they used that idea," says Brad, "especially because I was still living in Chicago and it seemed like where the show was produced was a whole world away."

In his junior year of college, Brad transferred to UCLA, where he continued pursuing his interest in television writing and production, while he also continued sitting in on story meetings at the home of *The Young and the Restless* writer Sally Sussman, who lived in Santa Monica. Brad also used UCLA's relatively close proximity to CBS Television City, where *The Young and the Restless* was shot, to extend his knowledge of how the show was put together. For a while he spent time sitting in the control booth observing. "Wes Kenney, who was producing, and Frank Pacelli, who still directs, were wonderful in teaching me what goes on in the booth, how they related to the actors, and how they took the written word and turned it into actual drama and dialogue. So I really had a chance to learn what daytime drama was all about."

Occasionally, to supplement his income, Brad also appeared on *The Young and the Restless* as an extra. "I was in the background and never had any lines," Brad told *Soap Opera Digest*. "But seeing what the actors did with a script was a great learning experience." Brad also enjoyed hanging out in the greenroom with the other actors who appeared as extras. He says, "It was interesting to see things from yet another angle."

Brad grew anxious to write dialogue for *The Young and the Restless*. For the first two years with the show, he understood and accepted his role as an observer. "You have to be familiar with all the characters on the show. What would this one say? How would they react to this situation?" he explained to *Soap Opera* magazine. "It's tough to keep forty different personalities in your head, as well as stick to the emotions and mood the writers intended." Eventually Brad started writing scripts based on story outlines written by his dad. Each time Brad completed a script, he'd turn it over to his dad, hopeful that he'd react positively to his work and use it on the air. "I would feel that I'd arrived, that I could do it. Then my dad would take one of the scripts and really edit it," Brad told *Soap Opera Digest*. Although Brad felt disappointed, he also appreciated the personal attention his work received from a master in the field of soap writing. "It was great because he probably spent more time with me than he would with other people," Brad continued, "making sure I did everything the way he thought was right."

Remembering Brad's days as an aspiring writer, Bill Bell told *Soap Opera Digest*, "For about the first year, I frustrated the hell out of Bradley. I didn't use any of his stuff because I didn't feel he was quite ready for it."

Meanwhile, Brad's mom, Lee, served as the voice of reason, easing the tension that was building between father and son. "She was always great because I could talk to her and say, 'Look, he's driving me crazy,'" Brad said. "I think my dad would do the same thing with her, so she was the person in the middle saying, 'This is where your father's coming from, and I know you're working hard, but he feels you need another couple of months before he's ready to entrust you any further.' She's always functioned as the quiet voice who keeps everything running well."

"It wasn't that I didn't want him," Bill explained. "I knew that being my son was, in many respects, a disadvantage for Brad. His work was more closely scrutinized than it would have been if he were someone whose last name wasn't Bell. By the time everything connected, it was great, because there was minimal editing and rewriting."

Soon after Bill approved Brad's scripts, he joined *The Young and the Restless*'s writing staff. Although Bradley enjoyed writing dialogue for *The Young and the Restless*, eventually he entertained the idea of expanding beyond daytime and writing scripts for prime-time sitcoms. Putting his idea into action, Brad spent his evenings working on a sitcom script. "I wrote a spec script for *Family Ties* and I shopped it around," says Brad. "I actually had some interest in it. A producer from *Charles in Charge* called me into his office, said he liked it, and asked if I could write a couple of *Charles in Charge* scripts. I was so excited. It was a dream of mine."

Brad expected his dad to be thrilled that the producer of a prime-time sitcom was interested in his writing. Instead, Brad says, "My dad didn't react the way I thought he would. At that point, he had spent a lot of time training me. In the back of his mind, I guess he was really thinking that I would become a part of the shows. He said, 'This is really a time where you have to choose. Are you going to pursue your own career and try to break into television sitcoms, or are you going to stay with us and devote your time and attention to learning this system and way of doing *The Young and the Restless*? Ultimately, Brad decided to stick to daytime. When *The Bold and the Beautiful* premiered, he moved to the new show as a dialogue writer.

During *The Bold and the Beautiful*'s early years, Brad lived in a guest house on the estate his parents purchased when they moved to Los Angeles. "My dad and I were inseparable, which was great because it was a very good learning opportunity," Brad said to *Soap Opera Digest*. "But it was also very difficult, because there was a time I wasn't sure if he was my boss or my father. He is a workaholic, and was especially back then. At dinner, we'd talk about the show. At breakfast, we'd talk about the show. On the weekends, we'd be switching sides at the tennis court and he'd say, 'Hey, what about Sally Spectra?' That was something that took me a while to get used to. I was young; I wanted to have fun." Brad was also aware that there were people in the industry who felt he'd had an easy ride because of his father. "People talk about nepotism and how easy it is," acknowledges Brad, "but anyone who works with their family knows that there's another side to the coin. You're scrutinized even more."

By the early nineties, Brad became concerned about the sustained workload his dad was carrying. "He'd been running a tremendous course for years, especially with two shows," says Bradley. "He didn't let anything slip through the cracks. He worked seven days a week, and really worked. I could tell that he was having difficulty maintaining that pace." In 1992 Bill took a rare vacation from work with Lee to attend the Olympics. During Bill's vacation, Brad found himself at a crossroads in his career. Although his dad had written enough outlines to cover his absence, Brad came to a realization. "I said to myself, 'Sometimes you can wait for someone to give you the green light and pass the baton, and sometimes you just gotta grab it.' So while he was gone that week, I worked with Jack and we ended up doing four or five more episodes beyond what my dad had written. He came back and these shows were already finished. We moved the show forward without him. I knew he was either going to blow up at the idea or he was going to say, 'Okay, you've got the ball. Now run with it.'" To Brad's delight, Bill approved of the ideas he developed with Jack Smith and gave them leeway to continue their work.

"He watched very carefully, but from that point the show was ours. Jack and I took it over," says Brad, who was officially appointed *The Bold and the Beautiful*'s new head writer in 1993.

During Brad's tenure, the show has risen to second place in the Nielsen ratings. "I really haven't tried to reinvent *The Bold and the Beautiful*," Brad told *Soap Opera Digest*. "I've kept the style of the show consistent with the way my father did it. I've watched soaps over the years, and I think it's terribly jarring. It's not fair to the viewers."

Meanwhile, Brad's relationship with Colleen Bradley, who organized promotional and special events for corporations, continued to grow. They fell in love and married in 1991. Soon after, Colleen resigned from her job, because it kept her on the road for up to eighteen days a month. When a position as receptionist for *The Bold and the Beautiful* opened up, Colleen accepted it. She later became an assistant to the casting director. After Colleen gave birth to their first child, a boy, Bradley Chasen, in 1993, she continued to work part-time at *The Bold and the Beautiful* as a production assistant. In 1996 Colleen and Brad had their second child, a girl, Caroline Catherine.

As head writer of *The Bold and the Beautiful*, Brad developed a deeper appreciation of the pressures his dad has faced for nearly forty years as a head writer. "Each script is a new challenge," Brad told *Soap Opera Digest*. "You want to make it the best it can be, and you have only one day because they're eating up a show every day. So it never gets to the point where it's easy."

Bradley Bell and Colleen Bradley Bell with their children.

In 1996 Brad, in addition to his position as head writer, was appointed executive producer of *The Bold and the Beautiful*. Meanwhile, Brad says he has no regrets about not pursuing a career in sitcoms. "I'd be very happy if I could make a good living in daytime and never venture into sitcoms or films," he told *Soap Opera Digest*. "This is what I know how to do. I want to follow in the footsteps of my father—maybe take this show to an hour and create another show. But I'm in no hurry to do that."

John C. Zak
SUPERVISING PRODUCER

John Zak was born on June 6, 1954, in Washington, D.C. The son of TWA executive Ed Zak and his wife, Juanita, John spent the early years of his life traveling. By the time he was fifteen, he had visited more than thirty-five countries all over the globe. Those youthful adventures inspired a passion for travel that remains with John to this day. John earned his bachelor of arts degree in film and television from UCLA in 1976 and was hired immediately as a lighting director at ABC Television in Hollywood, where he was assigned to *General Hospital* as the show was in the process of expanding from a half-hour format. "I was not a regular soap watcher in my youth," states John. "Except for summers spent with my grandmother in Chicago, when we never missed *The Lee Phillip Show* and *As the World Turns*, which I later found was written by Bill Bell Sr. at the time. I never could have imagined that one day I would be working with him." John cut his teeth in daytime TV working for Gloria Monty, legendary producer of *General Hospital*. "Gloria had assembled a team of young, bright creative people on the show—directors, camera operators, designers—and I was right in the middle of the daily panic and excitement. That's when I became interested in directing for drama." John received six Emmy nominations and an Emmy Award there, and after seven years he felt it was time to move on. He left ABC and spent a year at Universal Studios, lighting *The Facts of Life* and *Silver Spoons*. Then a stream of directing assignments came his way, including stints on *Rituals*, *Santa Barbara*, *Capitol*, *General Hospital*, *Days of Our Lives*, *The Young and the Restless*, and finally *The Bold and the Beautiful*, where he has remained as producer-director for the past nine years. "I am so proud of the creative team we have in place on this series," says John. "The Emmys our people have won would fill a large room—and those awards are well deserved! As we enter our tenth year, I'm pleased that almost the entire cast and crew are still excited about their work. . . . Another opening, another show, as they say. And it's also pretty thrilling when you find yourself above the Arctic Circle, or on the Via Veneto, or on the Acropolis, or in the jungles of Malaysia, and someone comes up to you and says, 'We just love your show.'" John is very involved in industry activities, having served on the Board of Governors of the Academy of Television Arts & Sciences, and during a three-year period he was on the faculty of UCLA. He received a Directors Guild of America nomination in 1995. A lover of languages, John is fluent in French, Spanish, Italian, and Portuguese.

Supervising producer John C. Zak

Hope Harmel Smith
PRODUCER

Hope Harmel Smith has been producer of *The Bold and the Beautiful* since the fall of 1988. Hope is a charter member of the show's producing team, having been brought aboard as associate producer in January 1987.

Hope entered the daytime arena in 1982 at Saatchi & Saatchi/Compton Advertising in New York City. She worked in the programming department, servicing the business affairs needs of three Procter & Gamble dramas: *The Guiding Light*, *As The World Turns*, and *Search for Tomorrow*.

Producer Hope Harmel Smith

In 1983 Hope started as a production coordinator at *The Guiding Light*. Under the guidance of her mentor, Gail Kobe, she soon became a booth production assistant and at twenty-four was named associate producer, overseeing the show's budget as well as line producing.

Looking back on her ten-year association with *The Bold and the Beautiful*, one of Hope's most gratifying moments was when Michael Stich was awarded the Directors Guild of America Award for Ridge and Brooke's Malibu wedding episode, which Hope produced. She also takes great pride in the many Emmys the show has garnered in the production areas of costume and set design, lighting, camera, and audio work.

Ron Weaver
COORDINATING PRODUCER

Ron Weaver is a veteran of the conception, development, organization, and execution of numerous television series and programs spanning a thirty-year career.

For the last ten years he has been associate producer, then coordinating producer for *The Bold and the Beautiful*. He handles the production office management and the business and financial aspects of the series and its related international and marketing ventures.

Prior to that, he served as associate producer and writer for the half-hour, prime-time daily dramatic serial *Rituals*.

Since arriving on the West Coast in 1981, Ron has also been executive in charge of production for *The Scheme of Things*, a science series of sixty-five episodes produced in San Francisco for Disney Cable, as well as senior production manager of a daily syndicated magazine-format series, *Breakaway*.

Coordinating producer Ron Weaver

His previous thirteen years were spent as director of operations and production services for the Children's Television Workshop in New York, where he was part of the original production team that created the award-winning series *Sesame Street*, *The Electric Company*, *3–2–1 Contact*, *Feeling Good*, and *The Best of Families* for PBS.

Comparing his *Sesame Street* and *The Bold and the Beautiful* experiences, Ron says, "I feel blessed to have spent, so far, twenty-three years of my career on two world-class shows. Given the amazing domestic and international success of both of the series—who could ask for more? I've had two great jobs where it's wonderful to come to work every day with talented people who you respect and who you like to be with."

Early in Ron's career, he was a writer and producer for *Eye on New York*, the award-winning documentary series produced by WCBS-TV in New York.

Ron is a graduate of the Michigan State University Theatre Arts Department and studied acting and directing with Herbert Berghof at the HB Studio in New York City.

Rhonda Friedman
ASSOCIATE PRODUCER

As associate producer, Rhonda is involved in all areas of *The Bold and the Beautiful*'s production.

Her career path has been extremely circuitous. After earning a bachelor's degree in anthropology in 1975, she did graduate work in special education before moving on to public relations, where she was first exposed to the inner workings of the entertainment industry. Here, she realized, was where she belonged. Her first job in show business as a script reader quickly led to a position as assistant to the president of a TV production company. When the company's first project, a soap opera called *Rituals*, went into production, Rhonda was hired as production coordinator and later promoted to associate producer. Her interest in daytime television outlived *Rituals*, which was canceled in 1985.

Bill and Lee Bell hired Rhonda in October 1986 as part of the original team that brought *The Bold and the Beautiful* to life, and she's been with the show ever since.

Associate producer Rhonda Friedman

John F. Smith
SENIOR WRITER

Emmy Award–winning television writer John F. (Jack) Smith has been a senior writer for *The Bold and the Beautiful* since the show's premiere in 1987. Jack has also written for *The Young and the Restless* since 1979, receiving a 1992 Emmy Award as a member of the Oustanding Writing Team for a Drama Series.

Jack noted, "You can't have a more creative atmosphere than what the Bells have provided me. They've always been very supportive of me and my work, much like a family. I feel the freedom to create, knowing that I have their complete support, and that freedom fosters my creativity. Working for the Bells has been the perfect writing situation for me."

Born in Pittsburgh, Jack received his undergraduate degree from Marquette University and his master's in communication arts from the University of Wisconsin at Madison. While he was pursuing his doctorate in communication arts in Madison, he became acquainted with Kay Alden, who is now co–head writer of *The Young and the Restless*, and was subsequently invited to join the *Y&R* writing team.

Before becoming a screenwriter, Jack was a musician and restauranteur. Jack and his wife, Norma, who make their home in Hawaii, have a daughter, Asia.

Writer John F. Smith

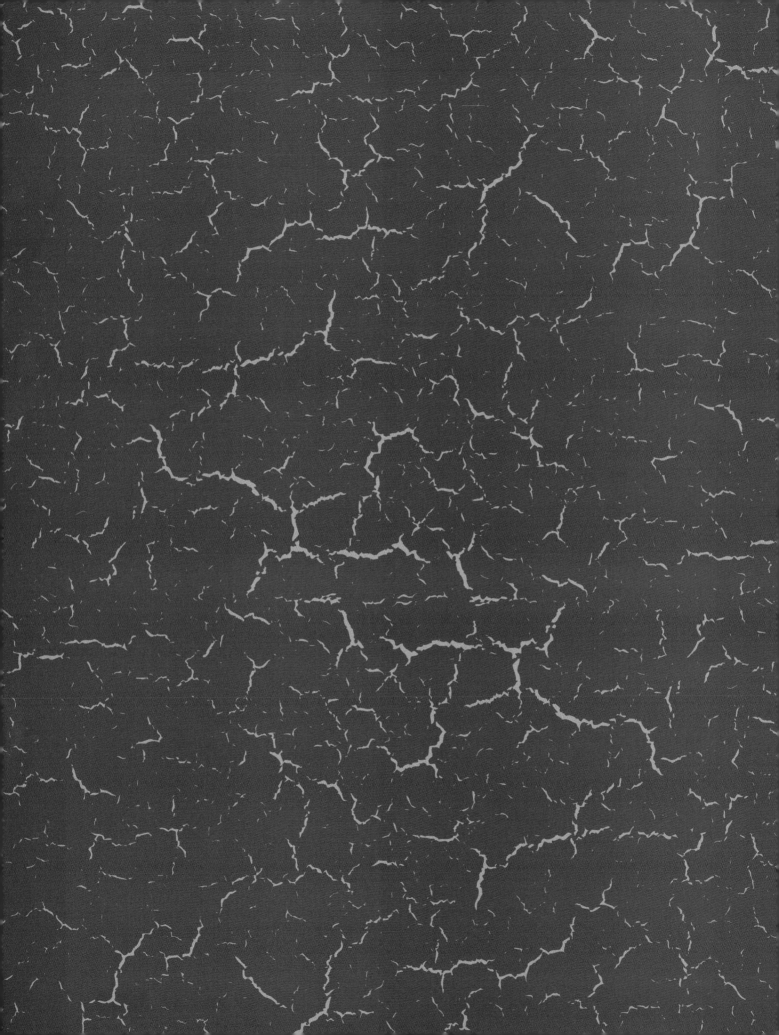

Part V

Behind the Scenes

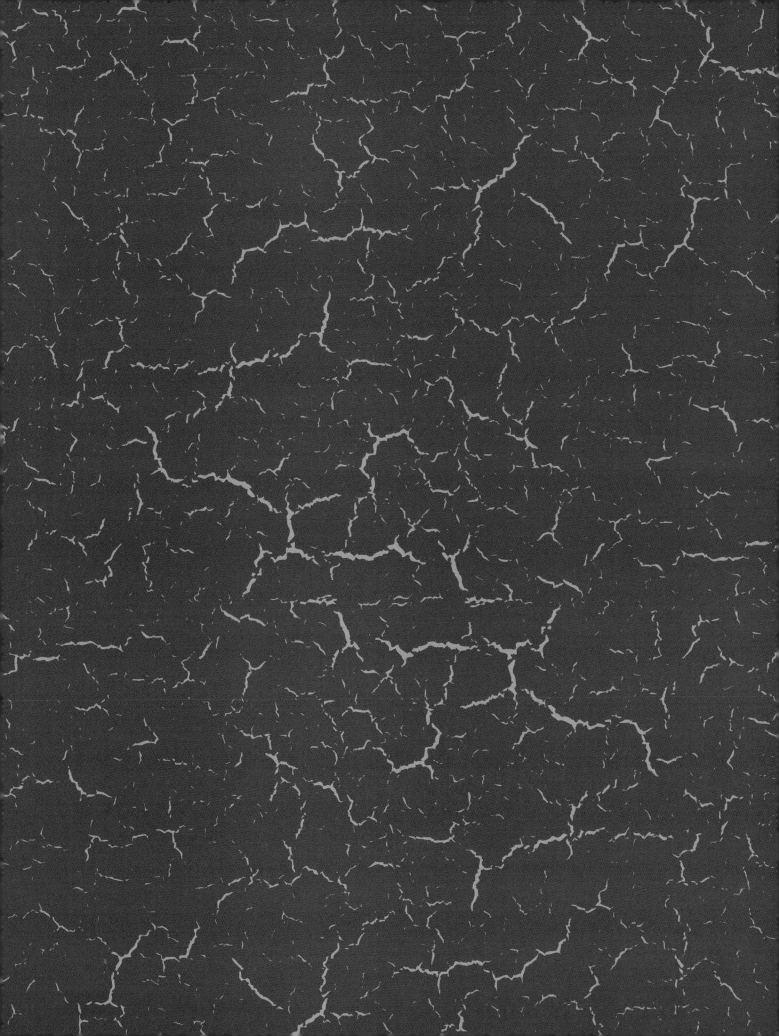

Building Bold and Beautiful Places

When you watch *The Bold and the Beautiful* five days a week, year in and year out, the homes and offices where the imaginary lives of such characters as Eric Forrester, Sally Spectra, and Brooke Logan Forrester unfold can become as familiar as the sights you see in your own neighborhood. After all, what long-time *B&B* viewer doesn't recall Ridge helping Brooke deliver her daughter, Bridget, in the Forresters' cabin in Big Bear, or the sinister dungeon, secretly located beneath Eric's second house, where Sheila held James captive for several weeks, or the Forrester swimming pool, which served as an appropriate backdrop for the simmering passion that passed between Brooke and Ridge the summer they met? A successfully designed set enhances the drama but doesn't distract from the primary focus, the carefully constructed characters and their complex, often emotionally charged, relationships.

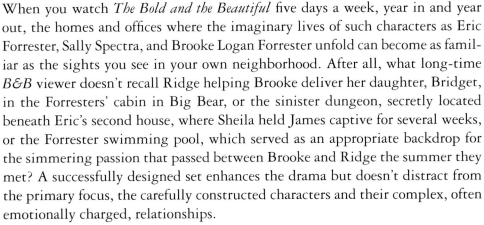

The most gratifying experience for production designers is to be involved in the creation and conception of a new show. Such was the case for Sy Tomashoff in November 1986, when he was asked to become the production designer for *The Bold and the Beautiful.* The immediate task at hand was to assemble a first-rate team. Jack Forrestel, an art director, was the first person hired. From the very start, Sy and Jack were soulmates when it came to creating and maintaining the look of *The Bold and the Beautiful.* The next two people hired were set decorators Jay Garvin and Randy Gunderson, both of whom worked with Sy on *Capitol,* which had earned each of them an Emmy the year before. This group was destined to be a winning team from the very beginning. Jay and Randy remained with the show for four years as the set decorators, and, with Sy and Jack, each won four Emmys for their work. After that Elsa Zamparelli, Richard Harvey, Lee J. Moore Jr., and Joseph Armetta carried on the tradition of their predecessors. Each of them has done the show proudly and Lee and Joe have remained to carry the standard with extraordinary grace. Sy and Jack have each won five Emmys for work on the show.

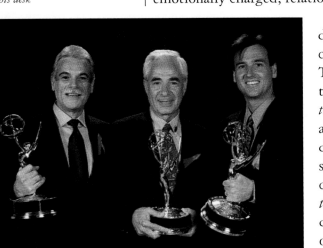

When the decision was made to move *The Bold and the Beautiful*'s setting from Chicago to Los Angeles shortly before the series' premiere, it was a production designer's dream. Los Angeles is practically the resort capital of the world. It is the home of Hollywood, the movies, and the fantasies that everyone dreams of. It's the land of beautiful people, beautiful places, and everlasting sunlight. For a production designer, the chance to portray the glorious, glittery city of Los Angeles is irresistible. It rivals any place in the world for vistas and panoramic views. Los Angeles boasts villas—Spanish and Italian—quaint houses, and grand estates. There are skytop restaurants and coffeehouses. The show has them all.

Most of the show's interiors would reflect L.A.'s sunlit, spacious feeling. Spaces would open onto other spaces so that there were endless plains, creating a sense of infinity. Light and shadow would be the main theme in the design. As for color, the palette would be a subtle one that would enhance the clothes, costumes, and fashions that were a central part of the show's theme. Everything had to be BEAUTIFUL.

More than patterns, the show boasts wonderful varied textures and materials that more than make up for the understated design coverings on the furniture and walls. The settings' drama comes from the architecture, the lush furnishings, and the lighting that creates patterns, highlights, and rich shadings of bright and dark (Sy and Jack swear that the lighting directors are their closest allies and they work very closely with them on the settings).

Sy Tomashoff and Jack Forrestel have been doing the show together since its inception and have never lost their enthusiasm and zest for the challenge of creating bold and beautiful sets. Sy Tomashoff offers a fascinating, and rare, behind-the-scenes glimpse at how several of *The Bold and the Beautiful*'s most notable sets were created.

THE FORRESTER LIVING ROOM AND FOYER

Visiting the set of your favorite soap can often be a letdown, at least when it comes to getting an up-close view of the spacious living rooms and expansive kitchens you've previously enjoyed seeing on your twenty-inch television set. A chic penthouse apartment that looks palatial on your home television screen suddenly seems dramatically diminished in stature, as if it's nothing more than a cramped collection of furniture and three chintzy plywood walls, struggling for space in an overcrowded furniture store. An in-person tour of the Forrester living room, however, would be far from disappointing. When Sy Tomashoff and Jack Forrestel were creating the sets for *The Bold and the Beautiful,* they designed them with an eye toward making the rooms as large as possible, even matching the actual size of a living room or a kitchen in a real house. "The Forrester living room is eighteen feet high," says Sy, "which is not humongous, but it's as big as you can get into the studio." When *The Bold and the Beautiful* took over the CBS studio space where the defunct soap *Capitol* was shot, Sy had hoped that several of the mainstay sets, such as the Forrester living room and Eric's office, would remain standing on a permanent basis. "But we were told that the network wanted to use the studio on the weekends for game shows," Sy reveals. "So we had to build the Forrester living room in such a way that it could easily be moved out of the studio. Now, the stairway unit in the foyer is eighteen feet high, so it had to be framed in steel and put on wheels, along with the walls in the back of the foyer, so they could be rolled out of the studio. We did, however, have to hoist pieces up onto the second floor of the stairway, where the landing is seen. On, and

The Forrester living room

The Forrester foyer

around, the stairwell was also tricky. But the carpenters and steelworkers created a masterful solution to our problem. It was built in large units, which could be easily moved." A distinct feature in the Forrester living room, which is fashioned after the actual house where Bill and Lee Phillip Bell live in L.A., is a very large window situated on the back wall. Initially, Sy says, he was worried about placing a window with a vista of the world in such an unusual location. "It hadn't been done before on soaps," he explains, "and I was a little timid about having upstage center such a huge backdrop behind a very dominant window. But everybody was very happy with it." Sy proudly notes that in the ten seasons that *The Bold and the Beautiful* has been running, the Forrester living room set has not changed. "Once in a while, someone will say, 'Don't you think you should bring it up to date with contemporary furnishings?' But the producers haven't asked for any changes. I think the Forrester living room still holds its style," he observes. "It's timeless. Whenever we create a set, we're always planning ahead." Sy also believes the room's subtle color and clean lines have also discouraged any misguided attempts to update the set. "I think the setting needs to be subtle," he says. "The interest should come from the architecture, the forms, the shapes, and the light." One of the most striking qualities of the Forrester living room is the way the intense Southern California sunshine seems to literally spill through the windows. "The light is such an important element," Sy stresses. "That's the other reason for the windows and the vistas: the lighting director can create a pattern of the window on the wall. That immediately gives life to a picture and makes it feel real. Even in the case of the Forrester swimming pool, which was a challenge. How do you give something situated inside a studio the feeling of outdoors?" Sy solved the problem by designing an open logroof and covering it with plants, such as sprawling vines. "The first thing I did was make a sketch for the lighting director," says Sy. "A single source of light needed to come through so that there would be strong shadows, which would simulate the shadows of the sun coming in from one direction. Somehow, that design really worked for us." When Sy was planning the Forrester living room, a cornerstone for the show, he recalls bringing photos of proposed interior styles to William J. Bell. "Bill told me he wanted it simpler, very simple," reveals Sy. "That gave me a good direction. There aren't any antiques in the Forrester living room, nor is there

The Forrester patio and pool area

a lot of *frou-frou*. It's all very strong. The set is interesting because the architecture works. Everything is subtle, which is the key to what I feel is good design. You don't need to have strong colors in your sets, or even in the furnishings. They need to be subdued so that what you're really watching is the story."

THE FORRESTER OFFICES

Sy's experience living in New York, and walking through Manhattan's fashion district, paid off when he was designing the fitting room and offices at Forrester Creations. "When we first started to tackle the Forrester showrooms, the image that came to me was of Ralph Lauren, particularly his shop on Madison Avenue, which is in a landmark building. It's a fabulous building, in the style of a French château built of stone." A highlight at Forrester Creations is the floor in the reception area. "There's a wonderful marble floor, which is actually painted on the back of linoleum," Sy reveals. "I just wanted to do something unusual in the reception area. I had seen a photograph in a book of a fabulous-looking floor and I simply adapted it. I asked the scenic artists to paint on linoleum and it's a winner. "

Stephanie and Eric in his office

Forrester Creations' reception area

ERIC AND SHEILA'S HOUSE

Eric and Sheila's living room

Although viewers were startled to discover that there was a secret dungeon lurking beneath Eric and Sheila's house, it had always been part of the house's design. "When we designed Eric and Sheila's house, Brad asked if we could make a secret door out of a bookcase or something in the living room," says Sy; whose previous job experience in daytime soaps taught him a thing or two about concealed doorways. "I told Brad, 'You know, you're talking to the guy who designed sets for *Dark Shadows* [a phenomenally popular, Gothic soap that aired in the late sixties]; sure we can do it. So we designed it, never knowing whether it was going to be used or not." Nearly two years later Sy discovered the reason for Brad's request. "Sheila captured James," says Sy, "and she and Mike, the security guard, imprisoned him in the basement."

SHEILA'S DUNGEON

Shortly before Bradley Bell wrote the storyline involving Sheila's kidnapping of James, "Brad told me that he wanted a dungeon," offers Sy. However, the dungeon Brad had in mind wasn't your typical, everyday, run-of-the mill house of horrors, because the dungeon had once belonged to legendary magician Harry Houdini, who had left behind several of his more intriguing props, including ominous chains, a Chinese water torture, and a guillotine. Sy relished the opportunity because it brought back memories of his days working on *Dark Shadows*. "We decided to make the dungeon really spooky," says Sy. "So we pulled out all the stops. We made it stone. The first thing I started with was the staircase. Remember the images you have in your mind, of being a kid and seeing the old *Frankenstein* and *Dracula* movies? That's the kind of ambiance I was going for. One of the images that always stayed with me from those old horror movies was a curved wall with a stairway running inside of it. So I designed the stairway first and then created the dungeon." Sy also wanted to include a window, so that the light coming through it would create shadows and heighten the dramatic effect. "Originally, it was to be a hidden room and nobody knew it was in there," he says. "So it couldn't have a window. But again, I'm always so conscious of source of light and the need for a window. So I went to Brad and I said, 'Can we have a window so we can create an ominous shaft of light?'" Sy showed Brad sketches of the proposed dungeon, pointing out where he'd like to place the window. Concerned that a window could potentially draw viewers away from the story, because they'd be wondering why no one ever noticed the window of the room before, Brad asked, "Would anyone be able to see it from the outside?" Sy responded, "No, because it's like a basement, there'd be too many weeds growing in front of it." A delighted Sy got his window and a twisted Sheila soon had her perverse playground!

Sheila's "Chamber of Horrors"

RIDGE AND BROOKE'S LIVING ROOM

"That was a wonderful set to design," enthuses Sy, "because it's kind of fashioned after Brad Bell's house." Just as William and Lee Phillip Bell's house was used as a model for the Forrester home, Sy designed the front door of Ridge and Brooke's home as an exact match to Brad's house. The stairway in the living room is also similar to the one in Brad's house. "I didn't copy the fireplace," Sy notes, "but I tried to give Ridge and Brooke's living room the same kind of scale." Sy designed a set of French doors near the fireplace, and just as he had done with William and Lee Phillip Bell's house for the Forrester house, he took photographs of the view from the back of Brad's house and had them made into chromotrans, a backlit photo backdrop, for the exterior view of the living room, where the patio is located. When you're standing on the set looking through the front door, Sy reveals, "the circular drive you see is what's actually in front of Brad's house." Sy deliberately created a duplicate view with future storylines in mind. "So that if at any time we needed to get exterior footage outside the house, we could do it at Brad's and it'd be an exact match," he explains. "I don't know whether that will ever be done, but it's an option."

SALLY'S WORKPLACE

"We designed Sally's office based on Bill's instructions," says Sy. "He described what kind of an office it was and the kind of lady Sally was." Since Sally is eager to create a profit, she isn't interested in spending money to make her offices look lavish. "Her offices are grungy and messy," says Sy. "But she has a big window. When Sally's designing she pins up on the walls all of the knockoff fashions that she's going to be making. She's a bigger-than-life character." Recalling an incident in an early Spectra storyline, when a member of the Forrester family was stopping by Sally's office for the first time, Sy wondered if Sally would make any improvements in her office to make it look more impressive. "I figured, she's gonna want to make an impression on them, maybe we should fix it up a little bit," relates Sy, who conferred with William J. Bell about possibly adding new pieces to the set or at least washing the windows. But Bill, who has an innate understanding of the characters he creates, nixed the modifications, sensing that she'd have other things on her mind, even with an impending visit from one of the Forresters.

SALLY'S APARTMENT

Sally's apartment is as grand as her office is grungy. Since viewers had an opportunity to watch Sally in action at work, before getting a glimpse of her home life, Sy says, "People probably thought, Okay, she's going to have a sloppy, rotten-looking place. But Sally's done well for herself and could afford a nice place. But the way it would differ from some of the other sets is that Sally's place would be a little more gussied. It's one of the few sets, certainly one of the few permanent sets that we have where we've used print fabrics. We don't usually use print fabrics on the sofas and chairs. But Sally has print fabrics, even on her throw pillows and things like that. Even her rug is an Oriental design. It helps to give it a sense that this is a home Sally had a personal hand in designing. Her windows have a fussy window treatment. Most of the windows on the show are very simple because we don't want anything to interfere with the view. But Sally has some swags around the window, jabots, and tie-back curtains." However, with a smile, Sy adds, "Even those are not sufficiently significant to encroach on the beautiful bay window and the view outside it."

DYLAN, MICHAEL, AND JASMINE'S APARTMENT

Sets on *The Bold and the Beautiful* are designed with the possibility that pieces from them may show up one day on another set, but with modifications. The apartment where Dylan lives with Michael and Jasmine is a prime example. Sections of it, such as the kitchen area, once belonged to Ivana's apartment (the famous model Dylan was briefly involved with before she was murdered by Anthony). The French doors leading to the balcony had also been used in the Mexican hotel where Thorne chased Anthony and Macy after he was accused of killing Ivana. Before that, they were part of a private club. "Originally, they were used in Angela's bedroom," reveals Sy. "We're proud that we are able to recycle. That's why when we build anything, even if it's only for one episode, we make it a good design, detailed architecture and strong construction. So that it's something that will last because we're probably going to recirculate it again in a different configuration."

THE BIKINI BAR

"The Bikini Bar is something that went up fairly fast, right after we came back from St. Thomas," says Sy. "The reason I mention that is we had a hotel room set that was supposed to be in St. Thomas. It seemed to be very adaptable to turning into the Bikini Bar. We had a deck with sliding glass doors, which we transformed into something that looks like garage doors. It made up the core of the set. It's nice when you can turn something you already have into a new set."

THE LOGAN HOUSE

Sy and Jack recall designing the Logan house, where Brooke grew up with her family, as one of their biggest challenges. Like the Forrester mansion, the Logan house set the tone for *The Bold and the Beautiful* in its early days. The Logan house, set in a working-class area of the San Fernando Valley, was supposed to be in marked contrast to the luxury of the Forrester mansion. Viewers needed to see why Brooke found her own family's home miserably lacking, in comparison to the magnificent setting where Ridge lived with his family. "Everything that I would design and bring to the meetings, Bill would say, 'It's too good; it's too nice.' Ultimately, Sy notes that Bill Bell's input was valuable in giving him a direction. Unlike the Forrester living room, which was spacious, the Logan living room was small, as were the other rooms in the house. "You walked into the Logan house through the front door directly into the living room, and the back wall of the set was a little stairway leading up to the second floor. The two bedrooms that were used in the house both had dormer windows, so that you knew they were almost like attic rooms. The Logan house is probably the only place where we ever used wallpaper," says Sy. The kitchen was also supposed to reflect a lower-middle-class family, because Beth Logan worked as a caterer. To enhance the drabness of the Logan house, the windows were also smaller and covered with old-fashioned window shades. Simple lace curtains covered the windows. The furniture was also mismatched, as if some of the pieces had been inherited. "The Logan house was a tough one to design because 'rich' is always more fun," he says, "but we pulled it off."

The Queen Mary *stateroom*

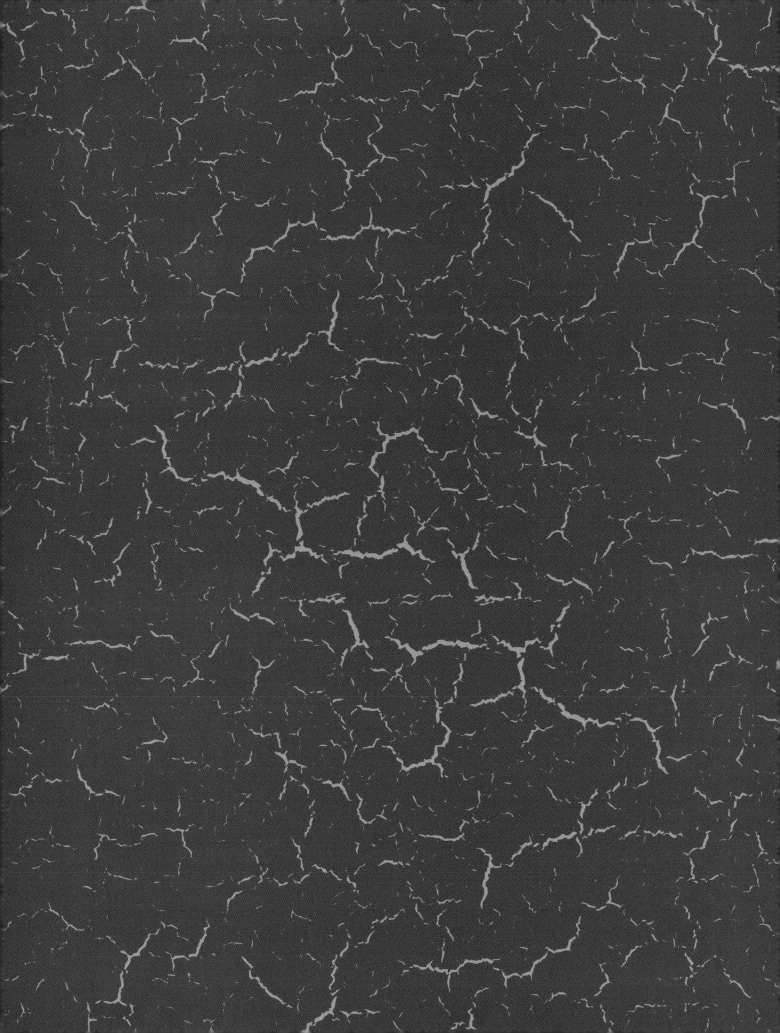

Dressing Bold and Beautiful People

The entire cast at a masquerade ball.

With the fashion industry as its backdrop, *The Bold and the Beautiful* takes great care to create a unique and dynamic look for its characters that you won't find on other shows. Besides purchasing clothes from several of the top designers in Hollywood, Lori Robinson, *The Bold and the Beautiful*'s costume designer, also designs clothes specifically for the characters.

Lori shares her secrets for dressing a wide-ranging variety of bold and beautiful characters.

Eric Forrester

Since Eric is the patriarch of the family, we try to keep him fairly elegant. His wardrobe leans toward upscale. He's always a well-groomed, well-dressed man. We usually dress him in Armani suits, but lately he's also been wearing several suits that were designed by Donna Karan. We purchase his shirts and sweaters from several different places and we try to punch them up with color. John McCook looks good in just about everything, no matter what I put on him.

Stephanie Forrester

I tend to design a lot of the clothes that Susan Flannery wears on the show, particularly the suits. Lately, Susan's been experimenting with different colors that she enjoys. She looks really good in jewel tones, such as sapphire, ruby red, emerald green: good, strong, vivid colors. The choice of colors is partly influenced by her blond hair. Pastels wash her out. Depending on the season and what's going on in the outside design world, sometimes it's hard to find jewel tones because they're not available, which is why I tend to design and make a lot of her suits. When she's not in suits, we try to do really pretty blouses over slacks for a semi-casual look.

ABOVE: *Stephanie's gown was inspired by the film* Dangerous Liaisons, *starring Glenn Close. Producer Hope Smith quipped,* "As many of our characters know, any liaison with Stephanie can be a dangerous one."

LEFT: *Hunter, Ronn, and Katherine in clothes that exemplify the style* The Bold and the Beautiful *strives for in its costumes.*

Ridge Forrester

Ronn Moss is great to dress. He's very tall and lean. So we can use some of the styles that are a little bit longer. Thanks to Ronn's height and build, he can carry off the more nontraditional cuts in sportcoats. We can also try a little more fashion-forward things on him because he has such a great body. He's really such a good size to dress. There isn't any color that looks particularly bad on him. We can do a variety of different clothes on him, but we tend to dress him mostly with Armani,  Donna Karan, and Hugo Boss. Ronn's personal style of dress is very different from *B&B*'s style for the character of Ridge. Ronn has a very strong sense of his own personal style that's very unique. He's very eclectic. We dress him a little more straightforwardly on the show, depending on what he's doing. If he's working with models, then, of course, we put him in a more "roll up your sleeves" type of outfit than if he's attending business meetings or something more serious, where he'll wear suits or sportcoats. We run the gamut with Ronn. He goes from very casual to very dressed up—and everything in between!

Brooke Logan Forrester

Katherine Kelly Lang is another great body on the show. She's a fabulous, fabulous girl to dress. There's very little that doesn't look good on Katherine. We tend to dress Brooke with body-conscious, body-revealing clothes because they look good on Katherine. Even with Brooke's executive position at Forrester, where you'd expect to see her in traditional business attire, we go a little bit out on a limb fantasy-wise and make the clothes more revealing. Katherine looks great in just about every color, but she doesn't like red in her personal wardrobe, so we don't dress her in red on the show, either. Depending on the clothes, sometimes I'll take something and totally redesign it and recut it to make it more body-conscious for Brooke.

Macy Forrester

Macy went through quite a transformation in the last year. When she started taking an interest in the business end of Spectra, we dressed her in what we call the "power suit" look. She's no longer in pretty, soft, flowing dresses. We kind of toughened her up a bit in her dressing. She's usually seen now in suits. We're also keeping her in the type of suitings that are currently really popular, such as shorter jackets that button up the front, sort of a sixties style. We alter Bobbie Eakes's clothes because she's a small person. Without alterations, the jackets tend to be too boxy on camera. Lately, we've dressed Macy in neutral colors because it's in keeping with the "power" look. It also plays in contrast to Macy's mom, Sally, who tends to wear brighter colors, which works with Darlene's character. Parallel is a good brand that we often use on Macy. The line runs the gamut. They offer dresses, suits, and a variety of different things.

Sally Spectra

BELOW: *Sally in a zebra-print outfit for Spectra's environmental fashion show.*

BELOW RIGHT: *When Thorne ended his romance with Macy, Sally disguised herself as a man to sneak into Forrester Creations. She was caught in Eric's office and arrested for trying to steal Forrester designs. Here, Darlene is surrounded by Bill Goodwin, Kathy Weltman, and Christine Lai from* The Bold and the Beautiful*'s hair and makeup department.*

With Darlene Conley we can go over the top. She's a very strong personality, so Sally's really fun to dress. For instance, she still wears big earrings. Sally's clothes have more sparkle and spangle, even in the daytime. One suit line I like to use on Darlene is Criscione. Their jackets fit her wonderfully. I get them right from the source in New York. Each season I'll go through their drawings, just to decide which ones I want for her. They also have evening wear, but most of the evening wear I'll either design

for her or rip something apart to work for her. So it's a combo effort. In the most recent cast photo I used a new caftan-type of sequin material that's really soft. Darlene's really good in the bright colors. In fact, I don't think I've come across a color that Darlene doesn't like. She looks good in just about everything, but I don't think I'd use orange or red because of her hair color.

Darla Einstein
Darla is another character that we dress in body-revealing clothing. You often see her bare midriff. Earlier in the year, Schae Harrison had her belly button pierced. Sometimes I wonder if I cross the line with the way Darla is dressed. But Schae's really fun to dress because I can take the trendiest of the trendy and put it on her. Schae also has a great figure. So really, Schae's game for just about anything. In the last year, though, we've tried to tone Darla's dress style down to make her a little bit more businesslike. We haven't dressed her in as much body-revealing clothing because Sally's been busy trying to get Spectra back on its feet again, and everyone's buckling down and working. But Darla's version of business dress is totally different from what the average working woman would wear. We used to accessorize her with very large earrings, but it started to get a little distracting. So we've toned it down. Schae's hair was longer and it balanced the look of the large earrings. But when Schae switched to a shorter hairstyle, the earrings became a little too distracting. On camera, the earrings really came breezing by and that's all you noticed. The majority of clothes for Darla are in bright colors and pastels. Darla's not a neutral person, so you won't usually see her in neutral tones, such as taupe, beige, and gray.

Sheila Carter Forrester
Since being released from prison, Sheila has also been going through a transition. When she first got out she spent a lot of time in her house and we dressed her in what we call "California casual." She wore jeans, shirts, T-shirts, blouses, leggings, and tops. But when it looked like a romantic interest was developing between Sheila and Grant, we started dressing her to look more sultry. We softened her wardrobe and made it more revealing.

Lauren Fenmore
Lauren came from *The Young and the Restless*, where she owned a chain of department stores. So Lauren is always dressed very fashion forward, very on the edge. Often we'll go into a department store, and see the kind of clothes where people would say, "Who would possibly wear that?" Well, that's what we put on Lauren. Tracey E. Bregman, incidentally, loves fashion and clothes. She's very small, so we alter absolutely everything that she wears. She's smaller than a size two, which provides quite a challenge. Finding really great, funky designer clothes that small is sometimes difficult. Depending on the situation that Lauren is in, she goes from suits to dresses to casual wear. But whatever she wears reflects her sophistication. Her clothes are on the cutting edge. We can actually go into a store, see a unique outfit, and say, "Yep, that's a Lauren!" She's very distinctive in the way she dresses. There was a scene shortly after Lauren first joined *The Bold and the Beautiful*. We dressed her in a great Italian silk suit. You don't put

a blouse on Lauren. That's just not done! So we decided to dress her in just a bra underneath the suit. We chose a gray velvet bra. Then we realized, she's going to prison to visit Sheila. Maybe that's a bit much. So we put a dyed mesh T-shirt, so that you still have that illusion and transparency to it. It was memorable and I'm proud to say that it was one of my better outfits. I enjoyed that one. Lauren's also worn some great fur jackets. Lauren's the one character that can wear that type of clothing. She looks good in any color, but we don't dress her in pink. Tracey personally doesn't like pink. She has strong color preferences. For instance, there are certain shades of green that she doesn't really like. She looks really great in earth tones. We use several different designers for Lauren, including Moschino, Betsey Johnson, Donna Karan, and Victor Alfaro. We've also purchased items from Banana Republic for her.

Jessica Forrester

There's a sweetness, innocence, and wholesomeness about Jessica that we try to reflect in her clothes. Usually we dress her in very subtle print dresses with soft fabrics. Maitland Ward is five-ten, so I do have trouble fitting her. We have to be careful because several of the dresses we get are not cut long enough for her. So when I'm shopping for clothes, I'm always with the measuring tape, to make sure the dresses will be long enough. For Jessica, I usually browse through the junior departments and we also use junior designers, mostly California junior designers.

Maitland, Dylan, and Barbara play three different characters with three different, and distinct, ways of dressing.

Dylan Shaw

Dylan started on the show as a college student and then he went to work for Spectra. Then he decided that he wanted to go back to school to study and become a fashion designer. So he's been through several transitions. When he was working as a stripper, there was a collaboration between the producers and myself to decide what the waiters at the Beverly Hills Hideaway, where Dylan stripped, would wear. We designed Dylan's dance costumes. There was a correlation between what he wore onstage and the song that he would strip to in his routine. But when Dylan was working at Spectra he was definitely a T-shirt, sportcoat, and jeans kind of guy. It was stuff that looked like it had been worn and washed. Brad Bell really likes a broken-in look on Dylan. Usually we'll dress Dylan in jeans, polo shirts, T-shirts, long-sleeved three-button shirts, what we call the "all-American guy" look. We've used several pieces on Dylan from a store called Replay. They tend to have clothes that are already faded out, so we don't have to wash them out. They already have that worn-in look.

Maggie Forrester

Barbara Crampton's character has gone through a transition since joining the show. Maggie started off as a real country girl. But gradually she became more sophisticated. Currently, we're trying a mix of the sophistication with the country girl again, which reflects the character's wholesomeness and Midwestern values. I usually buy those pieces at stores such as the Gap. With Maggie I tend to pick up pieces, instead of actual outfits. I'll see something that strikes me as a "Maggie" blouse or a "Maggie" skirt and then go from there. When Maggie is in her sophisticated mode we use several of Nark Wong's designs.

Three Forrester models show off the different ensembles that The Bold and the Beautiful's *costume designer has selected for one of the fashion shows.*

James Warwick

Ian Buchanan is so elegant and sophisticated, both as his character on the show and in real life. Ian's terrific to dress because he's a former model. He's another one that you know, no matter what you put on Ian, he's going to look great. We've used some very interesting Japanese designers, such as Yohji Yamamoto, for James's wardrobe. We also use several suits designed by Jean-Paul Gaultier. But we do have to be careful with what James wears because he's a psychiatrist. So we try to have his clothes reflect a sense of professionalism. We usually dress him in suits or sportcoats and shirts, often with no ties. We try a mixture, in terms of colors, for James. Sometimes we'll dress him very monochromatically, and then suddenly we'll throw a bright shirt on him. It depends on the situation. If it was up to Ian he'd wear black every day. He loves black. But black is so hard to use on camera because it's just turned into coal. You feel like you're looking into an abyss. He also prefers neutral tones, such as beige, taupe, gray, and brown.

Michael Lai

We try to keep Michael on the trendy side. This is the one character I'm putting most of the newer sixties shift dresses on. But I don't always use the neckline that the designer had originally intended. Usually, I cut it down so that it's a little more revealing because Lindsay Price also has a very good figure. When Michael's just casually spending time in her apartment sometimes she'll wear short shorts. But the character actually has quite a few different looks. We go from long, soft, floral dresses to short sixties dresses. She pretty much wears the current styles. Lindsay looks really good in red. With her skin tone she's great in hot colors.

The costume worn by this model at a Forrester fashion show is one of dozens that The Bold and the Beautiful's *costume designer coordinates.*

Grant Chambers

Grant Chambers is a Ralph Lauren kind of man. We also dress him in suits created by Italian designers. Grant is a rugged sort of fashion designer. We've tried to make him look the way designers really dress. They're very casual when they're working. So Grant usually wears jeans, a sportcoat, and faded-out vintage denim shirts, as well as fitted T-shirts. We've also tried a mix of cowboy boots and motorcycle boots to contrast him with Ridge, who has a more elegant, classic look. Ridge would never go to work in jeans and an old denim shirt. When Charles Grant joined the show he contributed several suggestions for the way his character would dress. Ultimately, with his input, we decided to give Grant an approachable appearance that would also reflect that he is a nonconformist.

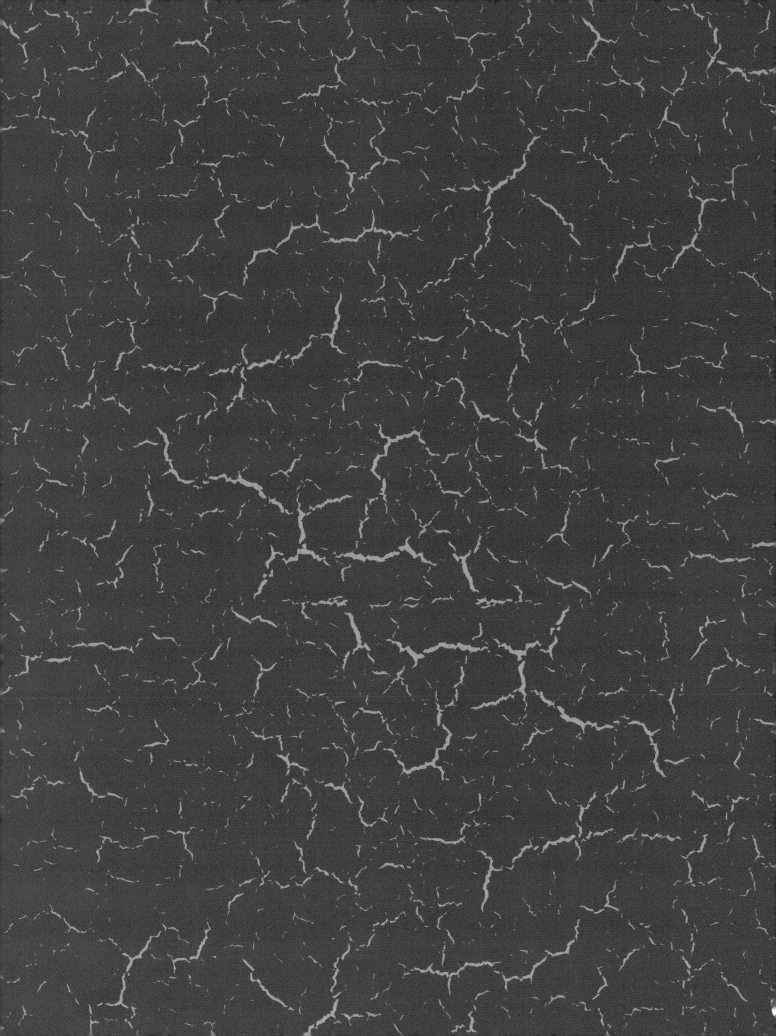

Appendices

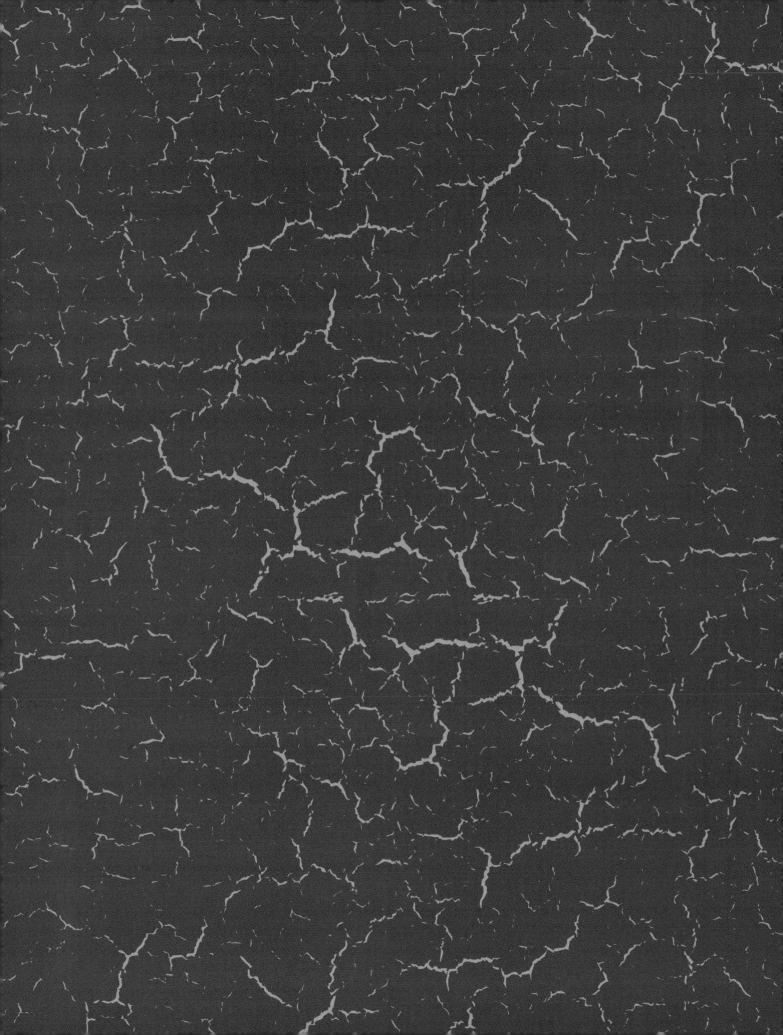

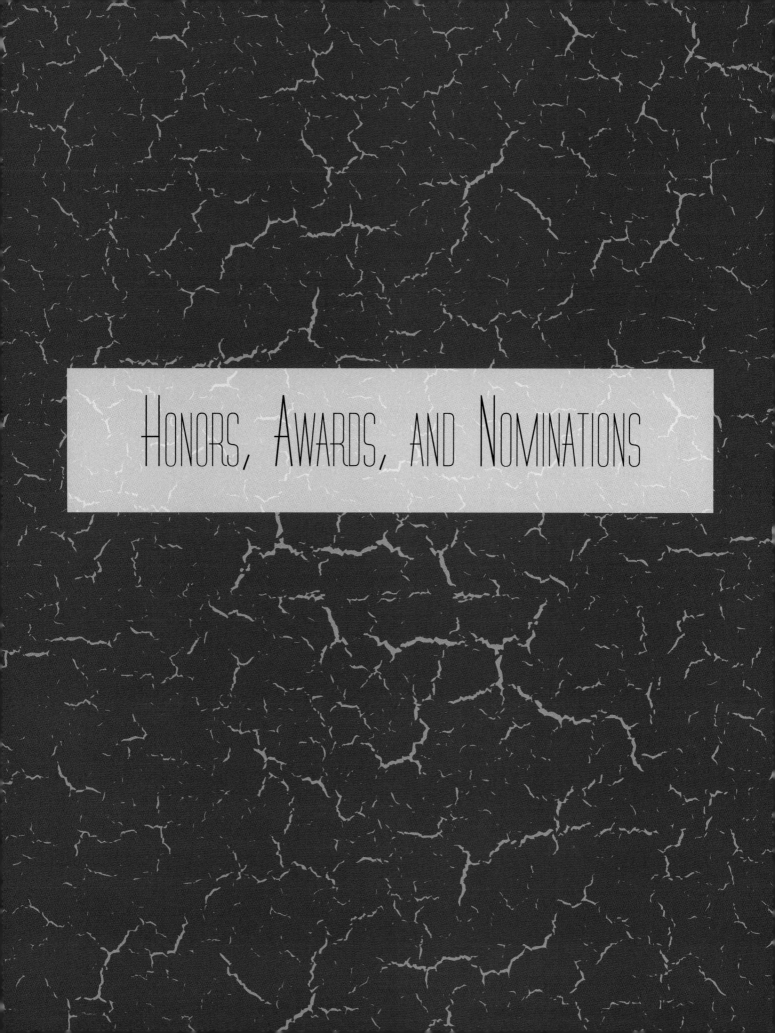

Honors, Awards, and Nominations

1996

1995–1996 23RD ANNUAL DAYTIME EMMY AWARDS

Outstanding Supporting Actor in a
Drama Series: Ian Buchanan
Outstanding Achievement in Costume Design:
Lori Robinson
Outstanding Achievement in Hair Styling*
Outstanding Achievement in Multiple
Camera Editing
Outstanding Achievement in Technical
Directing/Electronic Video Control*

12TH ANNUAL SOAP OPERA DIGEST AWARDS

Outstanding Villainess: Kimberlin Brown
Outstanding Female Scene Stealer:
Barbara Crampton
Outstanding Love Story: Ronn Moss,
Katherine Kelly Lang, Hunter Tylo
Outstanding Supporting Actress:
Susan Flannery

1995

1994–1995 22ND ANNUAL DAYTIME EMMY AWARDS

Outstanding Supporting Actor in a
Drama Series: Ian Buchanan
Outstanding Achievement in Art Direction/
Scenic Design for a Drama Series
Outstanding Achievement in Multiple Camera
Editing for a Drama Series*

1995 DIRECTORS GUILD OF AMERICA AWARDS

Outstanding Directing in a Daytime Television
Drama Series: Susan Flannery

SOAP OPERA UPDATE—MVP AWARD

Ronn Moss*
Katherine Kelly Lang*

*Indicates winner in category

11TH ANNUAL SOAP OPERA DIGEST AWARDS

Favorite Show: *The Bold and the Beautiful*
Outstanding Villainess: Kimberlin Brown*
Outstanding Female Newcomer:
Maitland Ward
Hottest Female Star: Hunter Tylo
Hottest Soap Couple: Ronn Moss and
Katherine Kelly Lang

1994

1993–1994 21ST ANNUAL DAYTIME EMMY AWARDS

Outstanding Supporting Actor in a
Drama Series: Ian Buchanan
Outstanding Achievement in Art Direction/
Scenic Design for a Drama Series*
Outstanding Achievement in Technical
Direction/Electronic Camera/Video Control
for a Drama Series*
Outstanding Achievement in Multiple Camera
Editing for a Drama Series*
Outstanding Achievement in Live and Tape
Sound Mixing and Sound Effects for a
Drama Series*
Outstanding Achievement in Lighting
Direction for a Drama Series*

1994 DIRECTORS GUILD OF AMERICA AWARDS

Outstanding Direction in a Daytime Drama:
Michael Stich*
Outstanding Direction in a Daytime Drama:
John Zak

CHANNEL 5 TELEGATTO AWARD—ITALY

Most Popular Drama Series*

10TH ANNUAL SOAP OPERA DIGEST AWARDS

Outstanding Villainess: Kimberlin Brown

SOAP OPERA UPDATE—MVP AWARD

Ronn Moss*
Kimberlin Brown*

1993

NATIONAL WOMEN'S ECONOMIC ALLIANCE FOUNDATION

Directors' Circle Award: Lee Phillip Bell*

AMERICAN WOMEN IN RADIO & TELEVISION

Broadcaster of the Year Award:
Lee Phillip Bell*
National Easter Seals—EDI Award
Keith Jones and *The Bold and the Beautiful*

1993 DIRECTORS GUILD OF AMERICA AWARDS

Outstanding Direction in a Daytime Drama:
Michael Stich

1992–1993 20TH ANNUAL DAYTIME EMMY AWARDS

Outstanding Direction in Art Direction/
Set Decoration/Scenic Design for a
Drama Series*
Outstanding Achievement in Costume Design
for a Drama Series*
Outstanding Achievement in Lighting for a
Drama Series*
Outstanding Achievement in Makeup for a
Drama Series*
Outstanding Achievement in Hairstyling for a
Drama Series
Outstanding Achievement in Multiple Camera
Editing for a Drama Series
Outstanding Achievement in Live and Tape
Sound Mixing and Sound Effects for a
Drama Series
Outstanding Achievement in Technical
Direction/Electronic Camera/Video Control
for a Drama Series

9TH ANNUAL SOAP OPERA DIGEST AWARDS

Outstanding Villainess: Kimberlin Brown*

SOAP OPERA UPDATE—MVP AWARD

Ronn Moss*
Hunter Tylo*

NAACP IMAGE AWARDS

Outstanding Daytime Drama Series

1992

2ND ANNUAL ENVIRONMENTAL MEDIA AWARDS

Outstanding Daytime Drama*

1991–1992 19TH ANNUAL DAYTIME EMMY AWARDS

Outstanding Supporting Actress in a
Drama Series: Darlene Conley
Outstanding Direction in Art Direction/
Set Direction/Scenic Design for a
Drama Series*
Outstanding Achievement in Costume Design
for a Drama Series*
Outstanding Achievement in Technical
Directing/Electronic Video Control for a
Drama Series*
Outstanding Achievement in Lighting for a
Drama Series*

1992 NATIONAL ACADEMY OF TELEVISION ARTS & SCIENCES GOVERNOR'S AWARD

William J. Bell*

8TH ANNUAL SOAP OPERA DIGEST AWARDS

Soap Opera Digest's Editor's Award:
William J. Bell*
Outstanding Villainess: Jane Rogers

*Indicates winner in category

Dutch Silver Televizer Tulip Award
1992
Most Popular New Television Series*

1991

1991 Directors Guild of America Awards
Outstanding Direction in a Daytime Drama: Michael Stich*

Soap Opera Update—MVP Award
Todd McKee*
Katherine Kelly Lang*

Chicago Museum of Broadcast Communications
Tribute to William J. Bell and Lee Phillip Bell, August 1991

1990–1991 18th Annual Daytime Emmy Awards
Outstanding Supporting Actress in a Drama Series: Darlene Conley
Outstanding Direction in Art Direction/ Set Decoration/Scenic Design for a Drama Series*
Outstanding Achievement in Costume Design for a Drama Series*

Italy's Refereum Popolare Olio (Award of the People)
Premio Video D'oro, Umbriafiction International Television Festival

Men's Fashion Association Aldo Award
For Distinguished Fashion Contributions in Daytime Television

1990

1989–1990 17th Annual Daytime Emmy Awards
Outstanding Original Song: "This Time Around"
Outstanding Achievement in Art Direction/ Set Decoration/Scenic Design for a Drama Series
Outstanding Achievement in Makeup for a Drama Series
Outstanding Achievement in Hairstyling for a Drama Series
Outstanding Achievement in Live and Tape Sound Mixing and Sound Effects for a Drama Series

Soap Opera Update—MVP Award
Susan Flannery*
Ronn Moss*

1988

1987–1988 15th Annual Daytime Emmy Awards
Outstanding Achievement in Graphics and Title Design*
Outstanding Achievement in Art Direction/ Set Decoration/Scenic Design for a Drama Series*
Outstanding Achievement for a Drama Series
Outstanding Achievement in Live and Tape Sound Mixing and Sound Effects for a Drama Series
Outstanding Lighting Direction for a Drama Series
Outstanding Achievement in Costume Design for a Drama Series

*Indicates winner in category

Cast List and Crawl

Bobbie Eakes and Jeff Trachta

Joanna Johnson and Jim Storm

Eric Forrester	John McCook	1987–
Stephanie Forrester	Susan Flannery	1987–
Ridge Forrester	Ronn Moss	1987–
Thorne Forrester	Clayton Norcross	1987–89
	Jeff Trachta	1989–
Kristen Forrester	Teri Ann Linn	1987–90; 1992; 1993; 1994
Beth Logan	Judith Baldwin	1987
	Nancy Burnett	1987–88; 1989; 1990; 1994; 1996
	Marla Adams	1991
Brooke Logan Forrester	Katherine Kelly Lang	1987–
Storm Logan	Ethan Wayne	1987–88; 1994
	Brian Patrick Clarke	1990–91
Donna Logan	Carrie Mitchum	1987–91; 1994; 1995–
Katie Logan	Nancy Sloan	1987–88; 1994; 1995–
Grandma Logan	Lesley Woods	1987–88; 1989
Clarke Garrison	Dan McVicar	1987–1992; 1996
Bill Spencer	Jim Storm	1987–94
Caroline Spencer Forrester	Joanna Johnson	1987–90
Margo Lynley Spencer	Lauren Koslow	1987–92
Rocco Carner	Bryan Genessee	1987–88
Dave Reed	Stephen Shortridge	1987
Mark Mallory	Michael Philip	1987
Conway Weston	Jerry Ayres	1987; 1991
Alex	Rosemarie Thomas	1987
Ron Deacon	Greg Wrangler	1987
Jeff Talon	John Castellanos	1987
Tommy Bayland	Tim Choate	1987–89; 1990
Maria	Irene Olga Lopez	1988–91
	Rita Gomez	1991–95
Stephen Logan	Robert Pine	1988; 1994; 1996
Lt. Burke	Jeff Allin	1989–1995
Nick Preston	Allan Hayes	1988–89
Angela Forrester/Deveney Dickson	Judith Borne	1988–89
Dr. Todd Powell	Cal Bartlett	1988–89
	Joseph Rainer	1989

Mark Lynley Garrison	Zachariah Koslow	1988–92
Sally Spectra	Darlene Conley	1989–
Saul Feinberg	Michael Fox	1989–96
Darla Einstein	Schae Harrison	1989–
Macy Alexander Forrester	Bobbie Eakes	1989–
Mick Savage	Jeff Conaway	1989–90
Michelle Brookner	Karen Moncrieff	1989
Jeanne Wolfe	Herself	1989
Dr. Joyce Brothers	Herself	1989
Felicia Forrester	Colleen Dion	1990–1992
Pierre Jourdan	Robert Clary	1990–92
Jake Maclaine	Todd McKee	1990–92
Taylor Hayes Forrester	Hunter Tylo	1990–96
Julie Delorean	Jane Rogers	1990–92
Rick Forrester	Jeremy Snider	1990–95
	Steven Hartman	1995–
Blake Hayes	Peter Brown	1991–93
Adam Briggs	Rod Loomis	1991–92
Ruthanne Owens	Michelle Davison	1991–93; 1995
Clarke Garrison Jr.	Michelle Heap	1991
	Tyler and Jacob DeHaven	1991–93
	Christopher Graves	1994–95
	Kyle Sabihy	1995–
Faith Roberts/Karen Spencer	Joanna Johnson	1991–94
Bonnie Roberts	Dorothy Lyman	1991–92; 1994
Helen Maclaine	Tippi Hedren	1991
Ben Maclaine	John Brandon	1991
Charlie Maclaine	Chuck Wallings	1991
Heather	Shari Shattuck	1992
Jack Hamilton	Chris Robinson	1992–94; 1995
Zach Hamilton	Michael Watson	1992
Sheila Carter	Kimberlin Brown	1992–95; 1995–
Irving "Sly" Donovan	Brent Jasmer	1992–
Lauren Fenmore	Tracey E. Bregman	1992; 1993; 1994; 1995–
Ganz	Alex Kubik	1992
Dr. Jay Garvin	Brett Stimely	1992–93
Molly Carter	Marilyn Alex	1992–94
Bridget Forrester	Morgan and Brittany Turner	1994–95
	Caitlin Wachs	1995
	Landry Allbright	1996–

Darlene Conley, Dan McVicar, and Jane Rogers

Robert Clary

Michele Davison

Todd McKee and Tippi Hedren

Monika Schnarre

Dr. Tracy Peters	Marnie Mosiman	1992–93
Mike Guthrie	Ken Hanes	1993–96
Keith Anderson	Ken LaRon	1993–95
Connor Davis	Scott Thompson Baker	1993–95
Kevin Anderson	Keith Jones	1993–95
Steve Crown	Perry Stephens	1993
Elliott Parker	Robert Gentry	1993; 1995
Brad Carlton	Don Diamont	1993
Fabio	Himself	1993
James Warwick	Ian Buchanan	1993–
Anthony Armando	Michael Sabatino	1993–95
Scott Grainger	Peter Barton	1993
Charlton Heston	Himself	1993
Damon Warwick	James Doohan	1993; 1996
Maggie, Scottish Innkeeper	Layla Bias Galloway	1993
Jean Firstenberg	Herself	1993
Steve Allen	Himself	1993
Jayne Meadows	Herself	1993
Carol Channing	Herself	1993
Jessica Forrester	Maitland Ward	1994–
Dylan Shaw	Dylan Neal	1994–
Ivana Vanderveld	Monika Schnarre	1994–95
Ceci	Brittany Powell	1994
Coco	Kathleen McClellan	1994
Michelle	Marjean Holden	1994
Rhonda	Bobbie Phillips	1994
Dr. Santana	Gina Gallego	1994
Don Navarone	Terrence Riggins	1994
Gordon	Marc Andrews Gones	1994–95
Prince Omar Rashid	Kabir Bedi	1994–95
Yasemin	Yasemin Baytock	1994
Imane	Roya Megnot	1994
Sonny Stone	George Hamilton	1994
Lt. Conran	Robert Craighead	1994; 1996
Teresa Emerson	Olivia Virgil White	1994–95
Jose Eber	Himself	1994
Megan	Maeve Quinlan	1995–96
Gladys	Phyllis Diller	1995; 1996
Maggie Forrester	Barbara Crampton	1995–
Michael Lai	Lindsay Price	1995–
Jasmine Malone	Lark Voorhies	1995–

Greg Danforth	Jeffrey Byron	1995
Samantha	Tamara Olson	1995–96
Jerry Birn	Russell Todd	1995
Dr. Benson	Richard Kline	1995; 1996
Betty	Carlease Burke	1995
Jill	Pamela Richarde	1995
Sarah	Ellen Wheeler	1995
Dr. Brian Carey	Kin Shriner	1995–96
Ramone	Joel Gretsch	1995–96
Tommy Tune	Himself	1995
Vince	Scott Layne	1996–
Christian Kramer	Jerry Penacoli	1996
Jonathan Young	Joseph Campanella	1996
Abigail	Rudee Lipscombe	1996
Grant Chambers	Charles Grant	1996–
Antonio Giovanni	Lorenzo Caccialanza	1996
Brenda	Barbara Niven	1996
Pamela	Lenore Kasdorf	1996

CRAWL

The following information is called the "crawl" because of the way it appears to crawl up the television screen at the end of the show. This is the 1996 crawl:

Created by
WILLIAM J. BELL
LEE PHILLIP BELL

Executive Producer
BRADLEY BELL

Head Writer
BRADLEY BELL

Supervising Producer
JOHN C. ZAK

Producer
HOPE HARMEL SMITH
DEVENEY MARKING KELLY

Coordinating Producer
RON WEAVER

Associate Producer
RHONDA FRIEDMAN

Writers
JOHN F. SMITH
TERESA ZIMMERMAN
MICHAEL MINNIS

Directors
MICHAEL STICH
DEVENEY MARKING KELLY
JOHN C. ZAK
NANCY ECKELS
SUSAN FLANNERY

Associate Directors
NANCY ECKELS
CATHERINE SEDWICK

CAST

Bridget Forrester
LANDRY ALLBRIGHT

Lauren Fenmore
TRACEY E. BREGMAN

Sheila Carter
KIMBERLIN BROWN

Dr. James Warwick
IAN BUCHANAN

Sally Spectra
DARLENE CONLEY

Maggie Forrester
BARBARA CRAMPTON

Macy Alexander Forrester
BOBBIE EAKES

Stephanie Forrester
SUSAN FLANNERY

Grant Chambers
CHARLES GRANT

Darla Einstein
SCHAE HARRISON

Rick Forrester
STEVEN HARTMAN

Sly Donovan
BRENT JASMER

Brooke Logan Forrester
KATHERINE KELLY LANG

Eric Forrester
JOHN McCOOK

Clarke Garrison
DAN McVICAR

Ridge Forrester
RONN MOSS

Dylan Shaw
DYLAN NEAL

Michael Lai
LINDSAY PRICE

C. J. Garrison
KYLE SABIHY

Thorne Forrester
JEFF TRACHTA

Dr. Taylor Hayes Forrester
HUNTER TYLO

Jasmine Malone
LARK VOORHIES

Jessica Forrester
MAITLAND WARD

Production Assistant
CYNTHIA J. POPP

Production Designer
SY TOMASHOFF

Art Director
JACK FORRESTEL

Set Directors
LEE MOORE JR.
JOSEPH A. ARMETTA

Costume Designer
LORI ANN ROBINSON

Assistant Costume Designer
CRAIG ASPDEN

Lighting Directors
LAURIE MOORMAN
PHIL CALLAN
RUDY HUNTER

Music Coordinator
LOTHER STRUFF

Production Supervisors
LYNNE BUSHYHEAD-RIPPLE
PAT STINE

Stage Manager
LAURA YALE

Production Coordinator
LISA CAMPBELL

Casting Director
CHRISTY DOOLEY

Controller
RICHARD GINGER

Production Personnel
JENNIFER HODILL
RITA D. RUSSELL
MIMI KERSEY
ERIN E. STEWART
SHANNON BRADLEY

Make-Up Artists
CHRISTINE LAI-JOHNSON
SALLEE WHITE SMITH
DONNA ANNE MOSS
CHRIS ESCOBOSA

Hair Stylists
CARLOS PELZ
KATHY WELTMAN

Publicists
FRANCIS X. TOBIN

Camera Operators
GORDON SWEENEY
TED MORALES
JOEL BINGER
DEAN LAMONT

Editors
JIM JEWELL
FRED RODEY

Technical Directors
CHARLES F. GUZZI
DONNA STOCK

Audio
CLYDE KAPLAN
JENNIFER SPANGLER

Postproduction Audio
JERRY MARTZ
STEVEN WACKER

Boom Operators
DAVID GOLBA
STAN SWEENEY
MIKE BRINES

Video Operators
ROBERTO BOSIO
SCHA JANI

PHOTOGRAPHY CREDITS

All photographs are copyright © CBS unless otherwise noted. Grateful acknowledgment is made to CBS photographers Tony Esparza, Geraldine Overton, Cliff Libson, and Monty Brinton.

(page)

43	*top*	John Paschal
51		John Paschal
63		Eddie Garcia
73		Lesley Bohm
81		Eddie Garcia
85		Jim Warren
108		John Paschal
110	*top*	John Paschal
110	*bottom*	John Paschal
112		John Paschal
113		John Paschal
114		John Paschal
115		Jim Warren
120		Jim Warren
151	*bottom*	Ron Weaver
152	*top*	Ron Weaver
152	*middle*	Ron Weaver
153		Rhonda Friedman
168		John Paschal
169	*top*	John Paschal
178		Ron Weaver
179		Ron Weaver
183		John Paschal
184		John Paschal
185		John Paschal
201	*bottom*	Eddie Garcia
203	*top*	Lesley Bohm
214		Jim Warren
218	*top*	John Paschal
219		John Paschal
220		John Paschal
223	*right*	John Paschal
223	*left*	John Paschal
226		Eddie Garcia
232		Cary Hazlegrove
240	*top*	Craig T. Matthew
243	*top*	Eddie Garcia
244		Eddie Garcia
245		Eddie Garcia

INDEX